DEDICATION

To my five children—Bill, Beverly, Becky, Brenda, and Barbi—who all served with my wife Donna and me together as a family musical ministry for 20 years—over 5,000 meetings in 50 states and 25 foreign countries. They are continuing faithful to the Lord with their own families, ministering for Him in many parts of this nation and of the world.

ACKNOWLEDGEMENTS

I want to thank the thousands of people who have read Book I—*Islam Rising: The Never Ending Jihad Against Christianity*. Their overwhelming appreciation and favorable comments have encouraged me in the writing of this second volume for which so many have been waiting. The most common appraisal that we have heard is that Book I is a definitive statement and the most complete coverage available on the critical subjects that Christians need to know about resurgent Islam.

I want to thank Marv Sanders and the American Family Association for featuring me in several national radio interviews. This thanks also extends to WWIB in Eau Claire, KTIS in St. Paul and KKMS in Eagan, MN, Jeff and Lee, and especially Jan Markel who has interviewed me several times on her radio commentary *Understanding the Times*. I also want to thank VCY's Crosstalk, Dick Bott and his radio network, and so many others locally and across the country who have featured me on radio and television publicizing the message of this book. I am grateful also for several positive reviews of Book I including those of Dr. Robert Sumner and Dr. Charles Thigpen.

I am indebted to so many friends and family who have read portions of Book II and given helpful comments and opinions. I want to thank my granddaughter Brittany for reading several chapters and making suggestions. Daughter Beverly, niece Julie Lauchner, son-in-law Terry Franklin, and friend Don Johnson also were a great help. Ruth Pontier read the whole manuscript and aided in making many corrections. Waldron

With extensive research coupled with keen insight Dr. Jim Murk has again hit a home-run in examining the true teaching of Muhammad and the Qur'an, this time as it relates to Israeland the Jews. Hard core ultra-orthodox Muslims today are unabashed in calling for the utter destruction of the Jewish nation and all the Jews in the world. If America and the Western world refuse to face this reality, they do so at their own peril, because "Death to America and the West" is the next goal on their agenda. Read Islam Rising, Book II, and share it with all your friends. It is a book for our time.

—James Combs, Author, Provost, Louisiana Baptist University

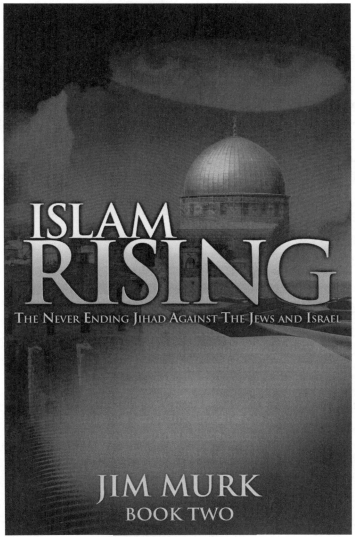

ISLAM
RISING

THE NEVER ENDING JIHAD AGAINST THE JEWS AND ISRAEL

JIM MURK

BOOK TWO

21ST CENTURY PRESS

PUBLISHING WITH PURPOSE

WWW.21STCENTURYPRESS.COM

ISLAM RISING: BOOK TWO
THE NEVER ENDING JIHAD AGAINST THE JEWS AND ISRAEL
By Dr. Jim Murk
Copyright © 2007

Published by 21st Century Press

Requests for permissions should be addressed to:
21st Century Press
2131 W. Republic Rd.
PMB 41
Springfield, MO 65807

ISBN 978-0-9779535-1-6

Cover: Lee Fredrickson
Book Design: Terry White

Visit our website at: www.21stcenturypress.com

21st Century Press
2131 W. Republic Rd., PMB 41
Springfield, MO 65807

21st CENTURY PRESS
PUBLISHING WITH PURPOSE
WWW.21STCENTURYPRESS.COM

Scott, who lived many years in Lebanon, and Dr. Kenton Beshore, who has had a ministry in Israel since 1973, made substantive suggestions and corrections, which were greatly appreciated.

I also want to thank those who helped make this undertaking possible with their substantial gifts and prayers. Major players have included Bob and Polly Reese, Julie Lauchner, Grace Elasky, Jerry Reding, the Orville and Ruth Merillat Foundation, and John W. Johnson who helped to make up all that was lacking in covering the expenses for this project.

For others besides the above who have promoted the book on their own time and at their own expense I will be eternally grateful. Some of these include Jack Van Impe, Jack Fleming, Andy Horner, Bob and Myrl Glockner, Bill and Jeanine Murk and family, Barbi and Terry Franklin, Becky and David Gardner, Bruce and Brenda Jackson, Elizabeth Buesing, Bert Niemann, Glenn Stairs, Joanne and Roger Adams, Jan Buck, Joe Farah, founder of WorldNetDaily.com, and Phil Brodsky and the Scripture Truth Book Company.

I want to thank the Palestine Academic Society of International Affairs (Passia) for permission to use the maps in this book. They greatly added to understanding the text.

Finally I am grateful for all our supporters through the years who have helped to underwrite the Murk Family Ministries, Inc. giving us time to produce these very important books.

TABLE OF CONTENTS

PREFACE

When we first wrote the book *Islam Rising*, the subject was so vast, and there was so much material, we soon discovered that the book was going to be too long. We decided to split it into two books. Book I looked at Islam particularly through the prism of Christian ideas and principles. Since Islam became an aggressive competitor with Christianity early in its history, we chose the subtitle *The Never Ending Jihad Against Christianity*. The purpose of the first volume was to cover as completely as we could within reason what Christians ought to know about Islam. This did not preclude instructing non-Christians, but we made it clear that our orientation was from a Christian and Biblical point of view.

Book I covers the subjects of the prophet Muhammad and the origin of Islam as a world religion. It examines Islam's sacred authoritative book the Qur'an, Islam's god Allah, and Islam's basic teachings. Because of its importance today an entire chapter is devoted to Holy Jihad and also to the major comparisons and contrasts with Christian faith and teaching. We tried to answer what Islam teaches about Jesus as related to Muhammad and how the Qur'an contrasts with the Bible. Finally we shared some personal critical thinking and evaluations concerning Islam and included in the Appendix two of eight letters written to an Islamic Imam as part of a correspondence carried on for almost a year.

Whereas Book I dealt largely with Islam's past history and the teachings of the religion, Book II deals primarily with Islam in the present. Two major areas of Muslim contact and activity in the present world relate to Israel and the western nations. This developed in the context of two World Wars and a revival of Jewish interest in their need for a nation of their own, a movement called Zionism, which Muslims have come to deplore with a vitriolic hatred. The ancient

Jewish home in Judea/Samaria/Galilee, now called Palestine, was a logical site for their renewed vision. Palestine, however, is in the heart of the Muslim Middle East. The relationship of Islam with the Jews and Israel therefore consumes much of Muslim consciousness and militant action in the contemporary world.

Book II begins by tracing the early relationships of Jews and Arabs through history and its impact on the present. It deals in detail with this relationship in the modern world from the time of WWI and the British Balfour Declaration, which established the beginnings of a Jewish homeland in Palestine. Supervised by a British Mandate over Palestine that favored Arabs over the Jews, it has led to an ongoing bitter conflict. Thus the title of Book II is *Islam Rising: The Never Ending Jihad Against the Jews and Israel.* WWII begins another chapter leading to the founding of the nation of Israel in 1948. From then on the collisions between Jews and Arab Muslims, and also with Iranian Muslims, become an interminable war, which brings us prophetically to the end of the age.

We learn in Book I that Islam is the third of three totalitarian systems that have tried to destroy Israel and America and rule the world. Marxist/Leninist/Communism and Nazism both tried and failed. Book II picks up the story as the Nazis provoke WWII and seek to destroy the Jews. The Nazis support the Muslim Arabs and the Islamic militants learn by the Nazi example and seek to emulate Hitler. The Communists led by the Soviet Union provoke the much longer and involved WWIII, which we called the Cold War. They also side with the Arab nations against Israel, and they meet the United States and western nations head on in the Middle East and elsewhere all over the world resulting in many separate wars in many places. Islamists provoke our War on Terror, which is really WWIV.

So Book II deals with the Muslims, in particular, the Arabs and the Jews and all of their conflicts through the years. Then there is the intervention of America and Europe in efforts to find a peaceful solution to the tangled web of the conflagration in the Middle East. This intervention and search for peace, which includes the Oslo Accords 1993-96, the Clinton/ Barak/Arafat meet at Camp David in 2000, and the current Roadmap For Peace. has been marked by a continuing abysmal failure. The effort to establish a Palestinian state is still the goal and negotiations with the Palestinian Al Fatah and Mahmoud Abbas are continuing based on the principle "land for peace."

Islam is the third major world movement that seeks to control the Earth. America has stood as a bulwark against each ambitious conqueror: (1) Red Communism representing secular materialism and atheism; (2) The black-shirted Nazis representing the Occult; and (3) Islam with its pale green flag representing false religion, the idolatry of a false god and an antichrist philosophy, which seeks to usurp the place and power of the Most High God of the universe, the God of the Bible. We ask the question what is going to happen? What do the Prophets of the Bible have to say about this time, these nations of Islam, and a restored nation of Israel? We examine Islam in Biblical prophecy and the predictions of a major attack on Israel by a large confederacy of Muslim nations in the last days, which the Prophets called "The Day of the Lord."

In the Appendices we begin by listing the Scriptures proving that God promised to restore the Jews to the "Promised Land" for His own sake and to select a final remnant who will represent the physical descendants of Isaac and Jacob. Finally we cover the major motivations and evil principles that are held in common by the "Quartet of Evil"— Commies, Nazis, Islamists, and Leftist/Liberals.

Addenda: I found that after writing Book II in which I had originally included "Islam in America" that it was still too long and involved two major subjects. So Book III, which is already written will be out early next year. It will deal with all the relationships of Islam with America, "the terrorists in our midst," our inept security apparatus in the past, which was handcuffed by liberal Democrats, and all the attacks upon this nation in a chapter called "Death to America." It will also investigate the past efforts of Islam to take over Europe and their success infiltrating the West today in what is being called "Eurabia." The title of Book III will be *Islam Rising: The Never Ending Jihad Against the West and America.*

Chapter 1

INTRODUCTORY CHAPTER

Why have our eyes been focused on and our feet been entangled with events in the Middle East for at least the last two generations? There are three closely linked reasons. (1) The discovery of oil that fuels the industries and facilitates the transportation of all nations; (2) The recovery of a homeland for world Jewry and the rebirth of the ancient nation of Israel; and (3) The resurgence of an orthodox Islam whose goals are to destroy Israel and rule the world. Over 60% of the world's oil is owned by Middle Eastern Muslims, which leaves a large part of the rest of the world dependent and vulnerable. What happens in the Middle East is of critical importance to all of us.

In greater detail, the plan of these militant Muslims is to (1) Destroy the nation of Israel and murder all the Jews on Earth; (2) Bring "death to America" the world's remaining superpower, which stands in the way of Islam's expansion and power; (3) Reestablish the Caliphate by uniting Muslim nations that have been purged of pagan, secular, and western influences; and (4) Conquer the rest of the world and bring all nations into submission to Allah, ruled by shari'ah law. Then at their leisure they can pressure all the people of the world to become Muslims. Contrary to a prominent idea that Islam is trying to convert everybody to their religion, today's resurgent Islam is principally a political movement seeking to impose the rule of Islamic law—their moral, social, and economic system—on all the nations. Both the Nazis and the Communists in their own way had very similar goals for the world.

In one brief statement in 1972, an Islamist leader Dr.

George Habash summarized the long-range vision behind everything that we see happening today.

> *Our revolution is a part of the world revolution. It is not confined to the reconquest of Palestine. Palestinians are part of the Arab nation; therefore, the entire Arab nation must go to war against Europe and America. It must unleash a war against the West. And it will. America and Europe don't know that we Arabs are just at the beginning of the beginning. That the best is yet to come. That from now on there will be no peace for the West . . . To advance step by step, decade after decade, determined, stubborn, patient. This is our strategy. A strategy that we shall expand throughout the whole Planet.*
>
> —Quoted by Orriana Fallaci in **The Force of Reason**

(Dr. George Habash, an Arab of Greek Orthodox background born in Lydda, Palestine, combined in himself and the organization he founded this common purpose. He became an avowed enemy of the Jews and Israel and fled from Palestine after the establishment of the State of Israel in 1948. He became the Secretary General of the Popular Front for the Liberation of Palestine, the PFLP. This was a radicalized Marxist-Leninist branch of al-Fatah, the military arm of the Palestine Liberation Organization led by Yasser Arafat. Dr. Habash was a hard-liner. He took a stand similar in severity to Hamas and Islamic Jihad in his uncompromising opposition to the Oslo Accords or any other attempts to solve the Palestine problem that were being negotiated by the PLO or the Palestinian National Authority with the western nations and Israel.)

Arabs, who make up most of the radical Islamists, number a little over 15% of all Muslims in the world. They consider themselves the custodians of Islamic orthodoxy because they are the Muslims most closely related to the Prophet Muhammad. There is a huge population of more moderate

Muslims especially in Turkey, in India and in parts of Pakistan, Central and Southeast Asia, Indonesia, and Africa. Most of these so-called moderates are really traditional literalists who would claim they believe firmly in the Qur'an and the teachings of Muhammad but have not exercised the implications of all of these teachings. The militants, called Fundamentalists, Islamists, or Islamofascists, who not only believe but also are putting into practice Muhammad's teachings, classify the moderates as less than dedicated to Islam, to the Qur'an, or to Allah. Secularized or less aggressive Muslims, on the other hand, have voiced the opinion that the militant Islamists are "ruining" the Islamic religion.

At the very heart of the Muslim world is Saudi Arabia, the original home of the Prophet, the sacred cities of Mecca and Medina, and the ultra orthodox Islamic teaching called Wahhabism. These are the literalists of the literalists. They identify with every word in the Qur'an as the very words of Allah, and in the Sunnah and the Hadith, the living example of the life and teachings of the Prophet. The teachings in Sura (Chapter) 9 in the Qur'an are very clear concerning the responsibility of all Muslims to participate in Holy Jihad, subduing or killing infidels, until the entire world is in subjection to Allah. This is considered by official Qur'an scholars as the final revelation of Allah to Muhammad when he was in Medina and supercedes all others. This strict interpretation of Islam called Wahhabism is right now being aggressively spread throughout the Muslim world financed by the billions of petrodollars the Saudis receive from the largest oil reserves on Earth. The Ayatollah Khomeini of Iran would approve. He said in 1979, *"The oil is Allah's treasure, which will enable us to achieve our destiny to rule the world."*

Orthodox Arab Islamists believe that they are the "chosen people." In their eyes they are the true children of Abraham by his oldest son Ishmael, who are elected by Allah, the Creator God, to impose Allah's will, including true peace and justice, on all peoples and nations. As such they have replaced the Jews, descendants of Abraham's younger son Isaac, and his grandson Jacob, who, though once anointed, have been rejected by Allah for their perversion of the truth revealed to them. Muhammad believed that he had restored in its purity the ancient monotheism, which is revealed through the Qur'an, the final authoritative revelation of Allah's will.

The new nation of Israel, or Jacob, is therefore a usurper, desecrating the land that belongs to Ishmael and his Arab descendants. All Jews and their supporters therefore must be eliminated. The United States, which stands in the way of this accomplishment, must be destroyed as well. "Death to America" and "Death to Israel" have become the universal cry among orthodox Islamists. They say that there is no possibility at all of compromise or reconciliation even if it should take the lives of multi-millions of the Muslim faithful to achieve these goals.

Contemporary Islamists

I am convinced that we have entered into the most dangerous time in world history. Few people realize that Islam has massacred more human beings in its 1400 year-old history than any other human juggernaut—well over 100 million people. This is as much or more than the Nazis and the Communists combined. Most Muslims will vigorously deny this assertion, but they either don't know their own history or are seeking to cover it up.

The statistics of history do not cover up the truth. Four million were murdered in Egypt alone. From the Middle East across North Africa to Spain millions more were massacred. It was the massacres of Christians in Muslim lands and pilgrims on their way to Jerusalem in the 11th century that motivated Urban II to call for the First Crusade. The blood bath throughout India, because of its saturation in idolatry, was worse than anything that has happened on Earth either before or since. Some of the massacres by Mongols and

Turks took place after they were converted to Islam. Almost 15 million people have also been massacred by Muslims in just the last 25 years. Muhammad commanded the killing of infidels and permitted the enslavement of prisoners. Over 14 million slaves were therefore taken to Muslim nations and 15 million more were sold to the rest of the world. In many cases slavery was a fate worse than death. Muslims were the slavers of the world. Both the murder and enslavement of infidels was part of their religion. Saudi Arabia did not abolish slavery in the Kingdom until 1962.

The teaching of Muhammad, which prevails to this day, is that any pagan infidels, which would include today's secularists and atheists, either must submit to Allah and his law or be killed on the spot. Jews, Christians, and Zoroastrians were given a pass if they would submit to Islamic law and pay a heavy poll tax to support Muslim regimes, but in these "last days" it is more often the case that all must submit or perish. Not only should all Jews be obliterated from the Earth, but also Christians are being killed throughout the Muslim world in great numbers. Of all the nations persecuting Christians severely, 7 of 10 are Islamic, according to the records compiled by *The Voice of the Martyrs*. Islam was restrained in most areas for scores of years, but gradually awakened following WWI in all its infamous glory and menacing rigidity. This has intensified to a fever pitch since 1979.

How can a religion that is supposed to be noble, peaceful, and tolerant be responsible for so much mayhem and bloodshed? There are two faces to Islam because there are two faces to the Qur'an. In his Meccan days, when Muhammad was in the minority and without any authority or power, he was tolerant and conciliatory. This benign teaching was recorded in the Qur'an. Soon after arriving in Medina, however, where he became the political leader, he gradually exerted what became totalitarian authority. He embodied every part of society. He was "prophet, priest, and king." His word became absolute law. To this very day

Muslims regard him as the "Perfect Model." His name is always linked with Allah, such as "Allah and his Prophet." He is Allah's alter ego. He is so revered that his name is never mentioned without adding the phrase "Praise be unto him" almost giving him the status of a god. In writings about him the abbreviation "PBUH" must always follow his name.

Today Muhammad's words, actions, appearance, dress, and manners literally command the words, thoughts, and actions of every faithful Muslim. His name is the most often used moniker given to male babies in the Islamic world. He is not considered to be divine, nor a god, or the son of god. Muhammad is a sinner, but he speaks with the voice of Allah, the word and authority of Allah himself. And his command is *"Kill the infidel!"* and *"Fighting in the name of Allah—Holy Jihad—is more important than two months of prayer."* Read the last commands from Allah in Suras 5 and 9 of the Qur'an, which replace and change any commands that had been given earlier. Then you will realize that Islam's militancy is because of Muhammad. He embodies the essence of the religion and the state.

A Biblical Worldview

It may surprise some readers that one cannot completely understand Islam or what is going on in the Middle East without some knowledge of the Bible. Orthodox Christianity, Judaism, and Islam share a similar worldview; namely, that there is a spiritual as well as a material world. We dealt with this at length in the Introduction to Book I. It is the Biblical worldview, a belief that there is an unseen world in other dimensions of which we cannot be aware empirically because our senses are limited to ascertaining matters in only our dimension of space and time. This spiritual world includes God and Satan, demons and angels, and probably unknown beings, places and things, which can only be understood by what theologians call "special revelation," i.e., what we are shown or taught that we cannot discover for ourselves with our senses or our own tools.

We cannot enter these other dimensions, but they can impinge on ours. It is on the basis of this special revelation given to us by holy men of God, Prophets and Apostles, and by Jesus Christ Himself that we can have some understanding of the cosmic battle of good and evil, the conflict of God and Satan, and the influence on Earth of God's Spirit and the spirits of disobedience called "familiar spirits" or "demons." This worldview is basic to our interpretation of history and to our understanding of what is going on today in the world experiences of Judaism, Islam, and Christianity.

The record of the past contained in the Bible also helps us understand the heritage of Israel, the claims of Islam and the conflict between them. We learn in detail about Abraham and his descendants who include both the Arabs and the Jews. We learn the significance of what is now called Palestine as "the Promised Land," and the place of Jerusalem in history. The Bible also has much to say about the destiny of the nations who are the Arab Muslims. It also predicts the rebirth of the State of Israel in the "last days" and the conflict with the surrounding Muslim nations. It predicts this hatred and competition of the descendants of Ishmael and Isaac and reveals a resolution and a conclusion, which will involve a direct intervention by the Most High God.

The Bible and the Qur'an both claim to reveal the words and the will of God. Originally Muhammad, not having much accurate knowledge of the content of the Hebrew Scriptures, said that the Bible was an earlier revelation of Allah and should be respected, but that the Qur'an updated the earlier revelation and was Allah's final word. He did not realize how much the two "revelations" were in direct contradiction and dispute. The Qur'an not only presents many divergent, even fanciful or fictional, versions of Biblical history, but also contains totally different doctrines and teachings.

Some moderate Muslims may try to find a common ground for acceptance sake, but there are very many more differences than similarities. Both systems cannot be true, and there is absolutely no possibility of any reconciliation. Their orthodox beliefs are mutually exclusive in all the areas that are critical, especially with regard to the concepts of God and salvation. There are those like Pope Benedict XVI who would seek a dialogue between Christianity and Islam, but when you get down to the "nitty-gritty," the beliefs about Muhammad and Jesus by evangelical Christians are blasphemy to orthodox Islamists; and orthodox Muslim beliefs concerning Jesus and Muhammad are blasphemy to conservative Christians.

Later Islamic teachers were faced with this dilemma. They were forced to the explanation that when the Bible contradicted the Qur'an it must be that it had been corrupted by Jews and Christians. This is easily proved to be an unreasonable, untenable conclusion. The New Testament predates the Qur'an by over 500 years, and the Old Testament predates it by about 1000 to 2000 years. That there have been any changes in the Scriptures through the centuries is impossible to prove, and all the evidence points the other way. There would have been no purpose to make changes that would contradict Islam. The Qur'an did not exist.

Without any doubt, however, there have been absolutely no changes of any kind in these Judeo/Christian Scriptures since the advent of Islam. So we are left with two different religious traditions in Judeo/Christianity and Islam. Which is authentic and which is the counterfeit? Jesus gave a measure for testing the authenticity of the true prophets of God. He said, *"By their fruit you will know them."* In an overall evaluation, what kind of fruit have orthodox Judeo/Christianity and orthodox Islam produced through the years? What are they producing today?

Two Miraculous Discoveries,
60 Years Apart, Each Speak to Their Times

I. The Dead Sea Scroll of Isaiah

It is too amazing to be a coincidence. Just a year before the rebirth of the State of Israel, a complete ancient text of the Prophet Isaiah was discovered in a cave on the northwest shore of the Dead Sea near the Wadi Qumran in the West Bank. Nearby are the ruins of an ancient settlement Khirbet Qumran, which is thought to have been the residence of a strict Hebrew sect called the Essenes. During a period of about 13 years from 1947 to 1960, over 900 documents or parts of documents were found in 11 caves in the area. They had probably been hidden there from the Romans when their Legions came to conquer Jerusalem in A.D. 66-70. The scrolls were almost all dated during or before the first century B.C. The Isaiah scroll dates from at least 100 B.C. and is perhaps the most highly prized of all the documents found. It is on display at the Shrine of the Book Museum in Jerusalem.

Isaiah is called the Prince of Prophets, well known for his Messianic prophecies, but he also predicted a future regathering of God's Hebrew children from all the nations of the world where they had been scattered. In one of these passages he writes:

> *He will raise a banner for the nations and gather the exiles of Israel; He will assemble the scattered people of Judah from the four quarters of the earth* (Isaiah 11:12).

Later on He declares:

> *Do not be afraid for I am with you; I will bring your children from the east and gather you from the west. I will say to the north, 'Give them up!' and to the south, 'Do not hold them back.' Bring my sons from afar and my daughters from the ends of the earth— everyone who is called by my name, whom I created for my glory, whom I formed and made* (Isaiah 43:5-7).

This scroll detailing these prophecies was called to the world's attention less than one year before Israel's

Declaration of Independence as a new nation on May 14, 1948. Was this only a coincidence? Or was God declaring publicly to the world what He was doing so that there would be no mistake as to who was responsible for the return of these people to their "Promised Land" and the revival of the nation of Israel?

Is this hard to believe? Do you suppose that if a similar event took place again the world could be awakened to the fact that God was trying to get our attention? Almost 60 years later God sent the world another message.

II. A 1000-year-old Irish Psalter from a Bog in Ireland Speaks to the World from Psalm 83

An even more miraculous discovery was made in a bog in the Irish Midlands in July 2006. It was a 1000- to 1200-year-old, 20 page Irish Psalter, an ancient song and prayer book, dating from A.D. 800 It was turned up accidentally by a bulldozer. That it had survived at all in the bog was one miracle, but that it was open to Psalms 82-83-84 is almost beyond belief. Psalm 83 was legible. It is a lament to God over 10 neighboring peoples attempting to destroy Israel as a nation *"that the name of Israel be remembered no more"* (v. 4). These enemies of Israel say that they want to *"take possession of the pasturelands of God"* (v. 12). The prayer asks God to destroy these ten nations who conspire against God's people and plot against those whom He cherishes (v. 3). A comment was made, "It's as if God thrust these words into the light of day as a reminder." Most of these nations listed can be identified as ancestral to those that exist today. So the Psalm reads like a contemporary description of what is going on in the Middle East right now.

So we have two miraculous discoveries from the past, bringing us two well-timed messages from the Almighty. There is a principle in Scripture that applies to these two discoveries. At least two witnesses are required to establish the truth of a matter (Deuteronomy 17:6 and 19:15; Matthew

18:16 and 2 Corinthians 13:1). These two amazing finds are two witnesses that it is God, who is sending a special message to us that we are surely living in the last days.

The Phenomenon of Abraham and His Descendants

All of Abraham's children and extended family have come to the center of the world's stage at the end of the age. Two main people groups have emerged. (1) The descendants of Abraham's son Isaac and his son Jacob or Israel whom we call Jews today. (2) The descendants of all the rest of Abraham's progeny and their relations—Ishmael, Esau (Edom), Midian and other sons of Abraham's second wife Keturah, and Ammon and Moab, sons of Abraham's nephew Lot. All of these are the ancestors of the 250 million Arabs in today's world.

The Biblical account in Genesis 25 set the stage for all that was to come in the future down to our own time:

Abraham took another wife, whose name was Keturah. She bore him Zimran, Jokshan, Medan, Midian, Ishbak and Shuah. Jokshan was the father of Sheba and Dedan; the descendants of Dedan were the Asshurites, the Letushites and the Leummites. The sons of Midian were Ephah, Epher, Hanoch, Abida and Eldaah. All these were descendants of Keturah.

Abraham left everything he owned to Isaac. But while he was still living, he gave gifts to the sons of his concubines and sent them away from his son Isaac to the land of the east. (Arabia was to the east.)

Altogether Abraham lived a hundred and seventy-five years . . . His sons Isaac and Ishmael buried him in the cave of Machpelah near Mamre, in the field of Ephron, son of Zohar the Hittite, the field Abraham had bought from the Hittites. There Abraham was buried with his wife Sarah. After

Abraham's death, God blessed his son Isaac, who then lived near Beer Lahai Roi.

This is the account of Abraham's son Ishmael, whom Sarah's maidservant, Hagar the Egyptian, bore to Abraham. These are the names of the sons of Ishmael, listed in the order of their birth: Nebaioth . . . Kedar, Adbeel, Mibsam, Mishma, Dumah, Massa, Hadad, Tema, Jetur, Naphish and Kedemah. . . . These are the names of the twelve tribal rulers according to their settlements and camps. Altogether, Ishmael lived a hundred and thirty-seven years. . . . His descendants settled in the area from Havilah to Shur, near the border of Egypt, as you go toward Asshur. And they lived in hostility toward all their brothers (Genesis 25:1-18).

Chapter 2

ISLAM AND THE JEWS IN THE ANCIENT AND MEDIEVAL WORLDS

Early History of Arab/Jewish Contact

The beginning of the contacts between Arabs and Jews pre-dates Muhammad by many centuries. The history of the Israelites in the Bible mentions many contacts with Ishmaelites, Midianites, Edomites, Moabites, Ammonites, and others who were the original tribal groups that eventually made up the Arab peoples. After the children of Israel were settled in the land of Canaan promised to them by God, some of these early Jews migrated to other lands. A common destination must have been the neighboring desert area, which became known as Arabia. Part of this territory includes Yemen in the extreme southwest, which may have been the kingdom of the Queen of Sheba 3,000 years ago. The Yemeni Jews, who were airlifted to Israel following the War of Independence in 1948 as a part of the program called "Operation Magic Carpet," had a tradition and roots in Arabia that they claimed went back 3,000 years. These Yemeni Jews believed their deliverance was an example of God's promise to carry them "on wings of eagles." Historical records do show that Jews had trading interests in Yemen several generations before Christ.

This was certainly true in the Hijaz or western Arabia. Babylonian inscriptions describe a Jewish presence in the Hijaz in the 6th century B.C. Jewish tomb inscriptions there date from the 1st century B.C. Arab tradition says that Jews lived in Medina, which was known as Yathrib, from the time of King David, and some suggest that it was even from the time of Moses.

25

The Apostle Paul himself tells of going to Arabia after his initial flight from Damascus. (Galatians 1:17) Then during the disasters of the Jewish Wars with the Romans from 68 to A.D. 135, hundreds of Jews fled from the Holy Land into the western province of Arabia possibly to join Jewish communities already present there. As artisans and merchants they were the leading citizens in Medina, where they greatly enriched Arab life. Arab sources record that there were as many as 20 Jewish tribal or extended family groups living in Arabia.

At the time of Muhammad the Jews also lived among the Quraysh tribe in Mecca. It was their uncompromising belief in one God, which most certainly influenced Muhammad in his thinking about religion. Many Arabs had already come to believe that their chief deity or Al-Ilah, "the god," was to be identified with Jehovah or Yahweh, the God of the Jews and Christians.

Islam, Muhammad, and the Jews

In the early years of his revelations, Muhammad had looked with favor upon both Jews and Christians because of their belief that there was only one God. Those parts of the Qur'an revealed during these years (610 to 623) speak of them with some admiration. In fact, it was the presence of three Jewish tribal groups in Yathrib, 200 miles north of Mecca that led Muhammad to flee from Mecca to that city in A.D. 622. He expected a friendly reception as one who preached the ancient monotheism. As a religious man Muhammad was asked to mediate disputes among the people there. He thus became a political leader in Yathrib and is said to have had a constitution written for the city, which renamed Al Medina an-Nabi, the city of the prophet.

It seems that Jews and Arabs should have been natural allies. Muhammad's religion was even regarded by some as an Arab version of Judaism. Certainly he sought to establish continuity with Jewish history especially with Abraham,

Moses, and the prophets, and he adopted many of the teachings of the Old Testament, including laws, rituals, and dietary rules. Muhammad even identified with Jerusalem. He originally commanded all Muslims to say their prayers in the direction of the Holy City. Even though Jerusalem is never mentioned in the Qur'an, it is the third most sacred city for Muslims next to Mecca and Medina.

Conflicts soon developed, however, when the Jews discovered that this alleged prophet's revelations were in conflict with their Torah—the first five books of the Old Testament ascribed to Moses. They did not recognize Al-Ilah as the same as their God who is revealed in their historical experiences and in their Scriptures. Also Muhammad, although he knew much about the stories of the Old Testament, tended to get them all mixed up.

Muhammad was deeply offended by the Jews' challenges, their ridicule, and their rejection. It was the Jews' opposition to Islam, to Allah, to the Qur'an, and especially to Muhammad's foreign teachings, which turned the prophet in an aggressive direction. This militancy eventually developed into the doctrine of *holy jihad* or fighting in the name of Allah. A most helpful, brief summary of the development of this conflict, which "wrecked the life of Jews in Arabia," is found in the book *Islam and the Jews* (pp. 79-117) by Dr. Mark Gabriel (his new English name), former Egyptian professor at Al Azhar University in Cairo.

The tone and teaching of Muhammad changed concerning the Jews in his recitations in Medina that became the Qur'an. His personal teachings called the Hadith also began to reflect this conflict. Muhammad had regarded the Jews favorably and had copied many of their practices, but about a year into Muhammad's residence in Medina (A.D. 623), the honeymoon was over. Muhammad accused the Jews of perverting the revelations, which God had given them. He said, *"You have concealed what you were ordered to make plain."* Muhammad concluded that Jews were cursed by Allah, who had even turned some of them into monkeys and pigs. (Suras 5:60 and 7:166) He claimed that the Jews were among the worst enemies of Islam and were to be classed with idolators, polytheists, and pagans. *"You shall surely find the most violent of all men in enmity against the Umma to be the Jews"* (Sura 5:82).

Muhammad attributed most of the evil and the conflicts in his world to the Jews. Note a few relevant references from the Qur'an and one from the Hadith.

"O, true believers, take not the Jews and Christians for your friends. They cannot be trusted. They are defiled . . . filth." Sura 5:51 ("Filth" includes human excrement, dead bodies, and pigs, which is how the American soldier is viewed by religious Shiites in Iraq.)

> *The Jews are smitten with vileness and misery and drew on themselves indignation from Allah* (Sura 2:61).

> *Wherever they are found, the Jews reek of destruction— which is their just reward* (Sura 3:112).

> *The Hour* (day of resurrection) *will not arrive until the Muslims make war against the Jews and kill them, and until a Jew will hide behind a rock or tree, and the rock and the tree will say: 'Oh Muslim, servant of Allah, there is a Jew behind me, come and kill him* Muhammad's words in the Hadith (Sahih al-Bukhari or Muslim's Sahih, number 2922).

Muhammad began to teach that no Muslim could be resurrected until all the Jews had been eliminated from the Earth in the last days. This cornerstone belief precludes any possible permanent accommodation or peace in Palestine today between Arabs and Jews. Those who are still seeking such a "peace," though hopeful and well meaning, do not have a clear or complete understanding of the teachings and beliefs of orthodox Islam. Much of the Arab world, in fact, subscribes to the "three no's" of the Arab Khartoum conference of 1967—"no peace, no negotiations, and no recognition." Today the Jews are considered a permanent enemy that must be destroyed. There is no middle ground, no compromise.

The Jewish Tribes in Medina

At the time of Muhammad there were three clans or tribes of Jews in Medina—the Nadir, the Qaynukah, and the Qurayzah. Originally Muhammad had a contract or *dhimmi* with the Jews. They could continue to exist in the area and would not be threatened if they paid a heavy tax or jizya to the Muslims. This was the Muslims' chief source of income to run their city and their wars. From another Jewish tribe in Arabia called the Janbah, Muhammad demanded 25% of their date crop, 25% of the game taken from the river, and 25% of all the product of their women's spinning. If they paid this "tax" they would not be killed and could stay in their village. This is not unlike the extortion of mobsters like Al Capone in Chicago and other American urban jungles in what was called "the protection racket." Store owners would not be bothered if they paid the mob a certain amount of money every week or month. This is called "protection by extortion." In like manner Muhammad's practice could be termed "theocracy by extortion."

All three of these Jewish tribes in Medina came to oppose the Prophet. It was unfortunate that they went further and supported the Quraysh of Mecca, Muhammad's tribal enemies, during his wars with them. This made the Prophet determined to eliminate the Jewish tribes of Medina one by one.

He first sent two of the tribes into exile, where they had to establish villages outside the city of Medina. The village of the Nadir was later besieged for six days and their date palms, a source of wealth and food, were destroyed. This was a tragedy in a desert land where this crop was a highly prized source of nutrition. The Nadir surrendered and were allowed to leave with their families, their cattle, and their camels; but their other property was confiscated. Most of this booty was given to Muhammad's original supporters who had come from Mecca and had no income (Sura 59). The Muslim justification given for this thievery has been that the Jews' wealth was confiscated for the sake of the poor. Hitler gave the same excuse for his appropriation of Jewish possessions in Germany. The hypocrisy in this claim was evident when Muhammad allocated 20% of the Jews' possessions to himself.

The Muslims then besieged the community of the last tribe, the Qurayzah, for 25 days. When this Jewish tribe surrendered, the men numbering 700 or more were taken to the city square about five at a time. There they all were executed by having their throats cut or their heads cut off. Their maimed bodies were thrown together into a mass grave, which today is under the marketplace in Medina. Muhammad then took all their property and material goods and wives and divided them among his followers, selling their children into slavery. Muhammad took one Jewish wife and again kept 20% of the property for himself. Muhammad's share of all the Jews' possessions confiscated in Medina made him a wealthy man. Muhammad's followers rejoiced in that it was the largest and richest amount of booty they had ever enjoyed. Looking back on that example, Arabs in Palestine today have expressed their eagerness to share in the large amount of "booty" that will be available when all the Jews have been killed.

The Jews of Nadir had fled to the village of Khaybar, which had been founded earlier by the other exiled Jewish tribe, the Qaynukah, at an oasis about 90 miles north of Medina. After things had settled down with the Quraysh of Mecca, the ten-year truce of Hudaybiyyah having been signed in the year 628, Muhammad with an army of about 1600 men traveled north and attacked this Jewish village of Khaybar. The prophet's purpose, according to Ibn Ishaq,

Muhammad's biographer, was to confiscate whatever treasure the Jews possessed in order to pay for the needs of his army, in particular their war against Mecca. It was like an old fashioned "highwayman's raid." In spite of assurances of protection, Muhammad came to Khaybar to demand that the Jews give up all their gold and silver.

A keeper of the treasure, a tribal leader by the name of Kinana Ibnal Rabi was tortured to make him reveal the treasure's whereabouts. When he refused, the Muslims built a fire on his chest, but he still remained silent. So Muhammad ordered that his head be cut off because he refused to acknowledge the authority and command of Allah's Prophet.

Most of the Jews surrendered, gave up their goods, and were exiled again with only what they could carry with them. Over 90 of the Jews begged Muhammad to allow them to stay and harvest their crop, but when some treasure they had withheld was found, the Prophet had all these Jews killed. All their goods were confiscated, and their wives were distributed. It was considered another great victory provided to them by Allah.

Finally an unprecedented celebration was commanded by Muhammad. He had killed the chief of the Nadir tribe and had taken his wife Safiyya bint Huyayy for himself. She had no choice then but to become a Muslim. Soon after killing her husband and exiting the village of Khaybar, Muhammad decided to consummate his marriage to Safiyya in a tent he had erected for this purpose. Such ruthless, heartless arrogance is hard for civilized people to comprehend. What is almost worse is that this historic example motivates Muslims today. In the summer of 2006 when Hizballah was opposing the Israeli Defense Force successfully in Lebanon, Arabs in the streets of Kuwait City and elsewhere were chanting "Khaybar! Khaybar! Khaybar!" recalling this ruthless Arab victory over the Jews.

All of this wealth stolen from Khaybar helped to supply Muhammad's followers with the goods and finances to fight and win the final war with Mecca and subdue all the other tribes in Arabia. The Qur'an actually encouraged the taking of booty as a reward for conflict in the name of Allah. Sura 8:67 says, *"Enjoy therefore the good and lawful things which you have gained in war, and fear Allah."* This command provides a great motivation to steal from the infidel, which is sanctioned by Allah. To steal from an infidel is therefore not a sin, and it is also permissible to cheat, lie, and even kill the *kafir*, a disrespectful name identifying the unbeliever as only a "cow," without committing sin or incurring any guilt (Hadith 4:26 and 9:27). Also women taken as slaves according to Muhammad's rules could be raped as part of the spoils of war without any sin or guilt being ascribed to such nefarious, cruel behavior.

After this dramatic break with Judaism, Muhammad changed the Muslim Sabbath from Saturday to Friday. He changed the dates of principal feasts and rejected the Jewish dietary laws, which he had adopted except the prohibitions against pork, dead animals, blood, and some kosher slaughtering rules. He finally changed the direction, or *qibla*, in which prayers were said from Jerusalem to Mecca. Although they both were monotheistic religions, Islam and Judaism were forever irreconcilable. They have forever remained two separate religions at odds with each other. Today, in spite of many intervening years of passive or even friendly associations in many Muslim nations, the Islamists are now mortal enemies of all Jews.

Muhammad was determined that no other religion should compete with Islam in the sacred land of Arabia. In fact, it was one of his three deathbed wishes. His words as recorded in the traditions were *"The Lord destroy the Jews and Christians . . . Let there not remain any faith but that of Islam throughout the whole of Arabia."* To this day no Jewish synagogue or Christian church exists in the Saudi kingdom in Arabia. It is even forbidden to bring a Bible into the land on pain of imprisonment or even death. Anyone caught by the

Saudi religious police just having a private Bible study in his own home has been imprisoned and even executed by beheading.

Catholic Spain has often been condemned for exiling Jews and Arabs from their nation in the 15th and 16th centuries. Muhammad eight centuries earlier, however, had paved the way for this kind of practice in his resolution concerning Arabia.

Some Consequences for Today
The presence of military forces of the infidel Americans on Arabian soil during and after the first Gulf War was the last straw for Osama bin Laden. Being strictly committed to Muhammad's teachings, he was very vocal in his condemnation of this violation of Muhammad's deathbed request, and he broke fellowship with the Saudi princes. Osama had offered the services of the Holy Warriors, or *mujaheddin*, trained in the Afghanistan war to protect Saudi Arabia from a possible attack by Saddam Hussein on the kingdom. The Saudis, however, did not believe that these Arab fighters were any match for Saddam's army and felt more secure under America's protection.

This presence of America's infidel army on the sacred soil of Arabia was probably the greatest offense, which caused Osama to declare war on America. Actually he was just following the lead of the Iranians who had committed many acts of war against the United States without paying any significant price.

One of the Islamist terrorists' ultimate goals is the annihilation of Israel, which they realize can only be accomplished if the United States is neutralized. America must be rendered incapable of defending its ally. Attempts will be made therefore to cripple America, at least economically, by the use of some kinds of weapons of mass destruction. Some recent intelligence analysis suggest that they may try to use small nuclear weapons, smuggled into this country, against some of our major cities. Osama is known to have called this "The American Hiroshima" and wants to kill at least 4 to 10 million or more Americans in retaliation for America's invasions of Afghanistan and Iraq.

Because of our surveillance of telephone and other communications, conversations between Islamists have been overheard that suggest that al-Qaeda already had a suitcase bomb in New York City during the Republican convention in 2004, but it failed to function. The critical mass to produce an atomic explosion does deteriorate over time. Old bombs must be rebuilt. It is probably only a matter of time before we do suffer some weapon of mass destruction in America. The terrorists have the money, they have the opportunity, and given our open borders and lax security in the past, bombs and maybe chemical weapons are already in this country, and it is only a matter of time before they succeed against us. Washington is expecting it some day and has made contingency plans for the government's survival in such an event. Such a tragedy would shake our nation to its foundations. (Interview with Gregory Copley author of *The Art of Victory* on Fox News, July 5, 2007.)

With the destruction of New Orleans by the hurricane Katrina, Osama bin Laden is said to believe that Allah has given the Muslim militants a good example and a head start on this project to cripple America. Abu Musab al Zarqawi, Osama's first lieutenant in Iraq, before his death called for al-Qaeda cells to attack America's sources of oil throughout the world in order to disrupt our economy. Osama had also commissioned Zarqawi to extend his jihad beyond the borders of Iraq and make some kinds of plans to attack America itself.

The British authorities discovered a team of terrorists in August 2006, who were preparing to destroy ten passenger planes over the Atlantic with explosives carried in small bottles in their luggage. It is very likely that other terrorist efforts have been intercepted that haven't been revealed to the media, or there are those that we don't even know about. So far none of these proposed attacks have taken place since 9/11, but they are still a potentially lethal threat—a sword of Damocles hanging over the head of the world's last super power. The most dangerous of these proposed attacks, which was discovered in America, was a plan of four Muslim terrorists of the group Jamaat Al Muslimeen from Guyana and Trinidad to blow up the jet fuel supply tanks at JFK airport in New York, which would have totally shut down that facility which handles 1,000 flights per day. It would have been a disaster to rival the Twin Towers destruction on 9/11.

The Final Jewish Dispersion or Diaspora

Six hundred years before Muhammad, the Jews and Romans had been natural enemies because of the paganism and idolatry of ancient Rome. We see a small part of this conflict portrayed in the New Testament, which later led to all out war. No people were more difficult for the Romans to defeat than the Zealots of the Jewish nation. It took them almost four years alone (A.D. 66 to 70) to conquer the city of Jerusalem. At one time the Romans breached the walls of the city, and for two weeks the Jews fought the Roman legions hand-to-hand to a standstill inside the city walls, finally driving them out through the hole in the wall where they had invaded.

When Jerusalem finally fell in A.D. 70, the Romans in their frustration and anger are said to have slaughtered between 600,000 and 1.3 million Jews who had been weakened by starvation and incredible suffering, They also took 100,000 prisoners to be paraded through the streets of Rome and sold as slaves. Over 200,000 were crucified outside Jerusalem's walls. These victims were the children and grandchildren of the generation of the Jerusalem Jews who had said to Pilate concerning Jesus, *"We have a law and by this law he should die"* (John 19:7) and *"Let his blood be upon us and upon our children"* (Matthew 27:25). The Roman conqueror Titus, son of the emperor Vespasian, erected a colossal monument arch to commemorate his very difficult victory. The Arch of Titus stands in Rome to this day. Its immensity symbolizes the gigantic effort it took to subdue these children of Israel, who proved to be the most intrepid warriors the Romans had ever faced in their long history of conquests.

This did not end the Jewish rebellion. A small group of Zealots held out until A.D. 73 at the Herodian fortress at Masada south of Jerusalem, where over 900 of them finally committed suicide robbing the Romans of their victory. They rebelled again in A.D. 113 in the time of the emperor Trajan and had to be put down in the Kitos War 115-117. Then Hadrian, the next emperor, tried to make peace, promising the Jews that they could rebuild their Temple. He then changed his mind, and instead turned Jerusalem into a Roman city, erected a Temple to Jupiter on the Temple Mount, and renamed the city Aelia Capitolina.

The Jews reacted bitterly. In A.D. 132 Bar Kokhba, a self-styled Messiah, who was supported in his claim by the illustrious Rabbi Akiba, once again called the Jews of the world to arms. For two years Bar Kokhba ruled a revived Jewish state even creating a currency. Hadrian then sent his ablest general Julius Severus from Britain with an army of 35,000, which was literally decimated by the Jews. So serious was this defeat that Severus resorted to a scorched earth policy—the total desolation of the land and all the people in it. Rome was ruthless because they feared for its reputation as a fighting force in other areas where they were facing hostile foes.

In A.D. 135 the rebellion was finally quelled. About 580,000 more Jews were killed making at total of as many as 2,000,000 Jewish casualties in the two major Jewish/Roman wars. Jerusalem and Judea were then made off-limits to Jews, and the Romans changed the name to Syro-Palestina, probably referring to the Syrians and ancient Philistines. The Jews had caused the Romans so much trouble, that the empire wanted to eliminate all trace of them, including the names of Judea, Samaria and Israel from memory. For the last two thousand years, therefore, "The Promised Land" has been known as Palestine.

Jesus had told His disciples that all the mammoth stones of the Herodian Temple (some of them as large as 12' x 4' x 6') would be "thrown down." The disciples hardly believed this was possible, but when the Temple was burned, the gold, which covered the roof, walls and columns, melted from the intense heat and ran down between the cracks. So the stones had to be torn apart to recover the gold. Not one stone remained upon another, just as Jesus had predicted (Matthew 24:1-3).

The dispersion of the Jews throughout the world had begun in 722 B.C. with the defeat of Samaria and the ten northern tribes of Israel by the Assyrians. Just over 100 years later Judah was defeated and many Jews were captured, exiled and enslaved in 606 and 597 B.C. by Nebuchadnezzar and the Babylonians. Then in 587 to 585 B.C. the Babylonians destroyed the city of Jerusalem and the Temple of Solomon exiling all the rest of the most prominent Jewish citizens. Some Jews returned to their land under the leadership of Zerubabbel, Ezra, and Nehemiah (538 to 433 B.C.) and Jews lived there until their dispersion by the Romans. As a result of their wars with Rome from A.D. 66 to 135, the total dispersion of the Jews was finally completed. God in His mercy had taken over 850 years to complete the Diaspora, which He had warned would be the punishment for His people's continuing disobedience.

In spite of at least four separate returns of Jews to the Promised Land during these years, many Jews remained in Babylon where they had become leading citizens as artisans, merchants, and teachers embracing many different occupations. They were doubtless also joined by Jews who fled from the Romans. When the Arabs conquered Mesopotamia, which is now modern Iraq, in the 7th century A.D., we shall see that Jews became a very important part of the Muslim civilization.

After the Roman conquest in A.D. 135, Jerusalem and Palestine were all Roman, or Gentile. In the fourth century when the Emperor Constantine embraced Christianity, Christians began to erect churches and monasteries in Bethlehem, Nazareth, and Jerusalem commemorating Jesus' birth, life and death, and resurrection. Jerusalem became a Christian city and was the center for one of the five Patriarchates of the Church. The other four were Antioch in Syria, Alexandria in Egypt, Constantinople in what is now Turkey, and the city of Rome. Three of these major Christian cities were eventually absorbed into the Islamic empire by Muslim Arabs in the 7th century. The Patriarchate of Constantinople was finally conquered by the Muslim Ottoman Turks in A.D. 1453. Rome remained as the only Patriarchate. Its leading prelate was the Pope. Because he was the only Patriarch left, the Pope of Rome gained unrivaled recognition, leadership, and power in the Western or Roman Catholic Church throughout the world.

The Expansion of Islam and the Jewish Golden Age
Very soon after Muhammad's death in 632, Muslims began to expand their control outside of Arabia. In a mere 75 years they had conquered an area larger than the Roman Empire—almost all the Christian lands of the Middle East and North Africa. The Arab Muslims conquered Damascus in 635, Palestine and Jerusalem in 638, Egypt in 641, the Sassanids, successors to the Persians in 636, and Middle Eastern lands of the eastern Byzantine Empire including Babylon by 700. They completed the conquest of North Africa, the lands of St. Augustine and St. Cyprian, in 707. Then they crossed the Mediterranean and invaded Spain conquering the Western Goths in 711.

With a goal of conquering Europe and stabling their horses at St. Peter's in Rome, the invading Muslim army of Abd-er Rahman crossed the Pyrenees into France. If the Muslims had not been defeated at the battle of Poitiers near

Tours by Charlemagne's grandfather Charles Martel in 732, all of Europe might have fallen to the Muslims. The Arabs also tried to take Constantinople twice in 668 and again in 717, but were repulsed by the new invention of Greek fire and the natural disaster of a long, severely cold winter.

The Muslims destroyed hundreds of churches, especially in the three major Christian centers or patriarchates of Jerusalem, Antioch, and Alexandria, and also turned some church buildings into mosques. They imposed the acceptance of Islam or death on all pagans and idolaters but showed some tolerance for the "people of the earlier revelation," or "people of the book." This was suggested by Muhammad, who ordered that Jews and Christians could live as *dhimmis* under Islamic law and support the Islamic governments with a heavy tax (the *jizya*). This has been described only as being "second class citizens" but in practice it was much, much worse. (Note the work of Bat Yeor, *Islam and Dhimmitude: Where Civilizations Collide.*)

Where these Muslim armies conquered, they brought with them the Arabic language. Because of the influence of the Qur'an, it became the established tongue of these nations except for most of Iran, which is the modern name for Persia. Iranians are not Arabs. Their language is Farsi, an Indo-European language that developed out of Sanskrit. Arabic is a Semitic language. There are also a number of tribal languages scattered throughout these nations, such as Peshtun and Tadjik in Afghanistan. The principal spoken language of Jews and Christians in the Middle East became Arabic, although the Jews retained Hebrew for religious study and liturgy, and to this day some small Christian groups still speak Aramaic, the language of Jesus and his disciples.

Despite Muhammad's problems with the Jews, they were initially better treated than the Christians in Muslim society. Muhammad thought that Christians believed in "three gods." They also taught that God had a Son, an abominable notion to Muhammad. We have noted that when Jerusalem was conquered by the Muslim armies in 638, it had become one of the five most important Christian cities in the world.

In 691 the Arabs built the gold-domed mosque called the Dome of the Rock on the site where the Jewish Temple had been. Because of the internecine conflicts within the Muslim world at the time, some historians have believed that its original purpose was to replace the Ka'aba in Mecca as a religious symbol and center. As a monument, however, it was a public proclamation against Christianity's central tenet—the deity of Jesus Christ—the teaching that God was incarnate in Jesus who was Immanuel, or "God with us" (Isaiah 7:14). The Dome of the Rock declared in words from the Qur'an in fancy Arabic script, inscribed over the door and throughout its interior, "God has no son." This was a blatant denial of the deity or Sonship of Jesus erected boldly on the Temple Mount for all Christians in Jerusalem and Palestine to ponder. It remains there to this day, a beautiful edifice but an abomination to Christian faith—a slap in the face of Jehovah—the Judeo-Christian God of creation and redemption.

About the time that the Christians were defeated in Palestine and Syria by Muslim armies, the Pact of Omar was enacted restricting Christian and, to a lesser extent, Jewish behavior and practices.

1. The infidels were not allowed to display religious images or crosses in public including churches.

2. They were forbidden to build houses taller than their Muslim neighbors.

3. They were forbidden to conduct noisy processions, including funerals.

4. They were forbidden to wear religious dress or shave part of their heads except the very front, which would identify

them as unbelievers.

5. They were never to strike a Muslim and had to show deference by rising when a Muslim came into the room.

6. They were absolutely forbidden to try to convert a Muslim or, on the contrary, to prevent a Christian or Jew from converting to Islam.

7. They were not eligible for public office, could not serve in the military, and were not permitted to carry weapons.

8. They had to pay a head tax (*jizya*) for the privilege of living in the Islamic community.

Jews were supposed to be subject to similar restrictions including the color of their clothing to distinguish them from Muslims. Green was reserved for Muslims. Jews had to wear yellow. This may be where Hitler got his idea for the required yellow identification badges in the shape of the Star of David. The color may even have been suggested to him by his Arab confidante, the mufti of Jerusalem Hajj Amin al Husseini, who for a time lived under Hitler's protection in Berlin.

The color green was reserved only for Muslims. It was Muhammad's favorite color perhaps because it symbolized fertility and God's original creation—green grass, trees, and foliage, which were in short supply in a desert environment. Today the Muslim flag is pale green as are the armbands and headbands seen on militants today. The pale green neon lighting on the Temple Mount with its Al Aqsa mosque and the Dome of the Rock, which are ruled by the Muslim Waqf, reflects throughout Jerusalem at night. President Ahmadinejad of Iran claimed to have been surrounded by an aura of pale green light when he prayed to Allah at the end of his address to the United Nations General Assembly in October 2006. Some have identified this color with the Pale

Horse of Revelation 6:7-8. The Greek reads *hippos chloros*, or pale green horse, which is the Muslim color. The text says that the Rider of the Pale (Green) Horse is Death and Hades "follows close behind." Islam is taught and practiced by its radical, orthodox leaders it is "a cult of death." Osama said, "We will win because you want to live and we want to die." Finally as a result of the activities and events connected with this Rider, the prophecy says that 1/4th of the world's population is destroyed. We shall discuss in Book IV the implications of this prophecy for Islam.

Muhammad did not immediately destroy all the Jews in Arabia but made this contract with many of them called the *dhimma*, an agreement that allowed Jews to live under Islamic rule, practice their religion, and make their living as long as they provided a very healthy tax to their Muslim overlords. Although they were eventually expelled from the Arabian Peninsula, this contract continued in all other Muslim lands.

Although *dhimmis* were at the bottom of the social ladder, they provided much of the financial support of Muslim governments. You could say that Jews and Christians partially financed the Islamic Empire. Some were also relied upon to help administer the non-Muslim populations, which at first greatly outnumbered their Muslim overlords in the Middle East, North Africa, and Spain. Little effort was made to convert Jews and Christians because they were the "cash cows" of the Muslim regimes. Having to pay the jizya, however, was an incentive powerful enough for large numbers of nominal Christians to embrace Islam and escape this financial burden and other onerous restrictions. It is one reason why so many Muslim countries are over 90% Islamic.

Muhammad, the Jews, and Jerusalem
From the time of Muhammad, Islam has had a close connection with the Jews. Their common ancestor Abraham according to the Old Testament had given tithes to Melchizedek, a former high priest and king of the ancient

city of Salem—the early name for Jerusalem.

Muhammad believed that the Arab followers of Islam are the offspring of Abraham's oldest son Ishmael. They are to replace the Jews, who are the descendants of Abraham's other son Isaac. He said that this was because, as recorded in the Old Testament, Jews had been incorrigibly disobedient to God for centuries, and God had rejected them.

As a part of their military expansion, the Arabs took over the city of Jerusalem in A.D. 638. From this time on, Muslims considered the Holy City as their possession forever both because of Abraham and also because Allah had given it to them by conquest. An early Muslim name for Jerusalem was Iliya derived from the Roman name Aelia. Today the name for Jerusalem in Arabic is *al Quds*, which means "Noble, Sacred Place." Here Abd al-Malik built the beautiful ancient mosque on the top of the altar rock on Mt. Moriah, the heart of the Temple Mount. Its dome stands out today as the dominating feature in any contemporary photo of the old walled city of Jerusalem.

Mt. Moriah was considered the sacred site of the altar where Abraham's loyalty to God was tested in the command to sacrifice his son. The Bible says that this son was Isaac. Muslims teach it was Ishmael. (There seems to be a conflict in Muslim tradition here because many believe that the mountain where Abraham brought Ishmael for the sacrifice was near Mecca.)

The Temple Mount became known in Islam as "The Noble Sanctuary" or Haram al-Sharif. The entire top of the Mount was declared to be a mosque or a place of prayer. Besides the Dome of the Rock, another larger house of prayer was erected and called "the Farthest Mosque" or al-Masjid al Aqsa. It is considered the third holiest place on earth next to Mecca and Medina. The building with the name al-Aqsa was completed in A.D. 705 by Caliph al-Walid, but "al-Aqsa" or "the Farthest Mosque" also refers to the entire area.

When Muslims claim that Jerusalem is their third holiest place, they are not referring to the city of Jerusalem, which is not mentioned even once in the Qur'an. The city was never an Arab capital of anything and was nothing but a backwater throughout Islam's history. The city is only important for the Temple Mount, the holy place Muslims call the "Noble Sanctuary." When Muslims claim Jerusalem as a sacred city, they are referring only the Temple Mount. Along with the Grand Mosque in Mecca and the mosque and tomb of the Prophet in Medina, it is the Temple Mount with the Dome of the Rock and the Al Aqsa Mosque that are sacred to Muslims, nothing else.

We have noted that the basis for this belief is the legend of Muhammad's famous Night Journey, when he was supposed to have been translated to Jerusalem either literally or in a vision. He was said to have ascended to Paradise from the Temple Mount in Jerusalem where he led all previous prophets in prayer. This is based on Sura 17:1 which briefly states:

> *Glory be to him who made his servant go by night from the Sacred Mosque to the Farther Mosque, whose surroundings we have blessed that we may show him some of our signs.*

Although Jerusalem is never mentioned by name in the Qur'an, it was the only other place sacred enough to have a mosque comparable to the mosques in Mecca and Medina. The Caliph Omar's original idea was that this was David's place of worship, the site of Solomon's temple, and later of Herod's Second Temple, which were also "mosques" or earlier places of prayer to God. When the Muslims erected the mosques for worship on the Temple Mount in Jerusalem, therefore, they were simply replacing the previous temples whose purpose had been the worship of God, which in Arabic is Al-Ilah. The assumption was that Jews and Arabs worshiped the same God. All the early Muslim historians support this idea. The "farthest mosque" or place of prayer could therefore only mean the site of the Temple Mount in Jerusalem. There was no other possibility.

It is ironic that today Islamists deny that any Jewish temples ever existed on the site. They do not realize that this undermines the very reason that the Temple Mount was identified as "the farthest mosque" in the first place and called "the Noble Sanctuary."

The shrine of the Al Aqsa mosque draws as many as 350,000 Muslim pilgrims from all over the world during the sacred month of Ramadan. It is said to be able to serve 10,000 people for Muslim prayers. Although Israel has controlled Jerusalem since 1967, and annexed all of East Jerusalem as part of the city proper in 1980, the Muslims have been allowed by the Zionists or secular Jews to have jurisdiction over the Temple Mount in the name of keeping the peace. Nevertheless, the Jews have been regarded as usurpers and illegitimate occupiers of what Muslims claim is exclusively theirs. Muslims believe that the Qur'an, Islam's holy book, infers that the Jews' present claim to Jerusalem is not valid. Now Muslims are God's chosen people and Jerusalem as well as the Temple Mount belongs to them. This is a Muslim "replacement theology" not too unlike the theology of the Roman Catholic Church and many Reformed theologians who believe that the Jews have been replaced by the Church and Jerusalem belongs to them. (See Appendix 1.)

The present Mufti, or Islamic leader and judge of Jerusalem, recently issued an edict that all Jewish claims to the Temple Mount are a fraud. In spite of all Biblical history, it has now become an Islamic doctrine that the Jews never ever had a Temple there. Even the existence of David and Solomon are now regarded as myths. Muslims are also bent on making sure that no archeological evidence ever surfaces to support a Jewish claim to the area.

The entire top of the Mount is considered a mosque or

place of prayer because pilgrims who will not fit inside spill out of the buildings for daily prayers. Muslims are therefore building a new building for prayer on the top of the Mount to accommodate the crowds. On the site of the new mosque, after the Arab excavations of the area with construction machinery during the day, all the debris is carried away at night and hidden in unidentified landfills and garbage dumps. This is to get rid of any possible evidence of an ancient Jewish presence. If an inscription is found, workers have been instructed to destroy it and use the stones for paving blocks.

Archeologists are appalled. One is astounded at how Israel can stand by and permit this vandalism of their precious heritage. It may be that secular Zionists just don't care enough. They are more concerned for the political consequences of arousing more Arab hatred and aggression. Recent investigations at these dumps and the sifting of the debris has, nevertheless, turned up some items which can be dated from the early Temple period. Much more of this evidence of an early Jewish habitation is likely to come to light no matter what Muslims do to discredit Israel's claims.

At the Camp David meetings in July 2000 sponsored by President Bill Clinton, Ehud Barak was willing to concede to Yasser Arafat 97% of what Israel had captured in the 1967 war. The Palestinians were to be given official control and complete jurisdiction over the Temple Mount. Barak, however, insisted that what was under the top of the Mount must be regarded as the property and heritage of the Jews, because all of their ancient religious history was entombed there. Arafat could not accept this because it would admit that there had once been a Jewish presence on that spot. In spite of what their own historians say, this is heresy to Muslims today, who, strange as it may seem, have been deceived by a gross revisionist history that denies that Jews were ever there at all. Arafat surely knew that his life "wouldn't have been worth a plug nickel" if he had made such a concession.

Muslims believe that if Jerusalem is not restored to Islamic rule, the divine inspiration of the Qur'an, which teaches that the Jews have lost all favor with God, could be questioned. For devout Muslims therefore the idea of Jerusalem remaining in Jewish hands is unthinkable. It would jeopardize their Muslim faith and belief in the reliability and omnipotence of Allah.

Reasons Jews Were Favored in the Early History of Islam
In the early centuries of Islam, in spite of their historic differences with Muhammad, Jews were favored by Muslims. They had no offensive dogmas. Their habits of life and beliefs were similar. They were never a political or military threat, and their industriousness and intelligence were an asset to the Islamic *ummah*.

Jews prospered especially in Baghdad, which was near the old city of Babylon, where some were doctors and scholars and influential at the court of the Caliph. They had two major centers of scholarship, which produced the Babylonian Talmud. Their leader, the Exilarch or "Head of the Captivity," was honored with the title "Our Lord, the Son of David." We know from reliable reports of the time that Jews numbered as many as 40,000 in Babylon and lived in the wealthiest part of the city. They were the basis of Islamic trade throughout the empire establishing a network of financial and trading centers as far away as India and China.

Arabic became the basis of some Jewish scholarship. The most famous of the medieval Jewish scholars and teachers Moses Maimonides (1135-1204) known as Rambam, who had fled from southern Spain to Egypt during the persecution of the Jews in Andalus, wrote his most famous treatise *A Guide For the Perplexed* in Arabic. The Jews, however, were also conversant in other languages of the ancient world, especially Syriac and Greek.

Jews prospered as never before under Muslim rule, and many of the restrictions of the Pact of Omar were not enforced on them under the rule of certain Caliphs. What is called a Jewish Golden Age, in fact, took place simultaneously with the Muslim empire. When the Muslim empire declined and disappeared, so did the Jewish Golden Age.

But this Golden Age was not exactly Jewish; it was Greek. When the Arabs discovered the wealth of knowledge in the Greek culture, they enlisted the help of educated Jews and Christians in translating the Greek and Syriac manuscripts into Arabic. Much of what has been preserved for us today of Greek literature, philosophy, and even science is because of these translations by the Jews and Christians, who among themselves knew all the languages.

As the Jews immersed themselves in Greek thought they became "Hellenized." They became rationalists, philosophers, logicians, mathematicians, even astronomers, scientists, architects, and builders. They especially excelled in banking and continued their development of business enterprises. These were internationalized with major offices in Cairo, Bagdad, and Cordoba, Spain. They became financial barons and finance ministers. In a word, Jews became cosmopolitan secularists, men of the world.

The Jewish Golden Age coincided with the flowering of Islamic civilization. This was the most enlightened and prosperous culture of its day in the entire world. Without the Jews, however, the famed Islamic civilization would doubtless never have flowered as it did. They helped make it happen and may take a percentage of the credit for the celebrated civilized world of the Islamic empire. This was certainly true in Spain, called Al-Andalus by the Moors. Here the remnants of the Ummayad dynasty ruled in Cordoba at the same time as the Abbasids, who had conquered the Ummayad's in the East, ruled in Baghdad. In Spain Jews were doctors, scholars, poets, scientists and philosophers. In fact, in the 10th century Cordoba, Spain became the leading center of Jewish culture in the world.

One should not conclude, however, that all was rosy for

the Jews in the Islamic culture sphere. There were many places where Jews were severely persecuted and even killed. These included Yemen, Egypt, and Morocco. Under the Fatimid Caliph al-Hakim in 11th century Egypt, the Jews of Alexandria and Christians were severely persecuted and killed. Hakim also had the Church of the Holy Sepulcher in Jerusalem destroyed. These depredations of this Muslim leader were one of the motivations for the First Crusade of Urban II in 1095. Al-Andalus or Spain alone remained a haven for Jews until Castilian Christians forced the Muslims and Jews out of the Iberian Peninsula in the 14th and 15th centuries. At this time the Jews also were subjected to either forced conversion to Christianity or the tortures of the Inquisition. (For a more detailed summary of the Jews and Islam in this period see Paul Johnson, *A History of the Jews*. New York: Harper and Row, 1987, pp. 175-79 and 204-05.)

Jews prospered longer in Spain than they did in the Middle East where in the 13th century the Mongol hordes swept out of Central Asia destroying everything in their path. Hulegu Khan, the grandson of Genghis, in the 1250's destroyed the Ismaili Assassins and then besieged Baghdad. Here the Mongols killed hundreds of thousands of men, women and children, stacking their heads in neat pyramids all over the landscape. The Arabs were being repaid with an even greater ferocity for their own earlier butcheries in India and in the Christian lands of the Middle East and North Africa. The Mongols continued into Palestine toward Egypt where they were finally soundly defeated by General Baibars and the Mamelukes in 1261 at Ayn Jalut. The Mamelukes had been an army made up of slaves, who one day would usurp the power of their Arab masters, and became the rulers of the Caliphate.

Many Jews moved westward into Europe where they were largely responsible for inspiring a thirst for knowledge of the ancient works of the Greek and Latin writers and also of Arabic philosophers. One would not err by saying that Jews had a lot to do with stimulating the Renaissance or the rebirth of classical knowledge in Catholic Europe. Education had always been their secret and their strength. In fact, their presence and influence preceded the influx of the multitudes of Greek Christians from Constantinople after its defeat by the Ottoman Turks in 1453, which has usually been cited as the prime cultural motivation for the Renaissance in Western Europe.

As Europeans themselves became more and more educated, however, they had little further use for the Jews who began to be persecuted in the West. Most of the latter then immigrated to Eastern Europe often by invitation from the political leaders who at first received them with enthusiasm for their learning and craftsmanship. The Jews lived apart by themselves, however, cooped up in closed communities called ghettos or shtetlach. These concentrated aggregates of Jews would one day become targets for major vilification, abuse, and persecution, which led eventually to many of them immigrating to Palestine.

Jews continued to live as *dhimmi* here and there throughout Muslim lands until the modern era. In the 20th century they had grown to about 900,000, living as second-class citizens from Morocco, across North Africa, and in all of the Middle East. After Israel's Declaration of Independence on May 14, 1948, and the war that followed against five attacking Arab armies, over 700,000 of these Jews living in Muslim nations fled as refugees to Palestine where they were absorbed as citizens into the newborn nation of Israel.

Chapter 3

ARABS AND JEWS IN THE MODERN WORLD: Part I—1890 to 1929

Modern History Leading to the Present Conflict

Anti-Semitism once again reared its ugly head in 19th century Europe. France, Germany, and especially Russia saw renewed persecutions of Jews. The pogroms in Russia resulted in many deaths and destruction of Jewish communities. Where Jews had lived comfortably in the Diaspora, they were content to call these and other nations home, but the renewed persecution awakened in the hearts of many Jews a yearning for a homeland of their own. Their ancient prayer was revived, "If I forget you, O Jerusalem, may my right hand forget its skill. May my tongue cling to the roof of my mouth if I do not remember you, if I do not consider Jerusalem my highest joy" (Psalm 137:5, 6). This yearning for rebuilding in Jerusalem and Palestine a homeland for the Jews became known as Zionism, which was distilled in the dream of one man, a Hungarian Jewish lawyer-journalist Theodor Herzl (1860-1904). A whole new era began at the end of the century which would bring Arabs and Jews into the major conflict, which continues to this day.

Herzl, a popular columnist for a newspaper in Vienna, covered the Dreyfuss trial in Paris, and was personally overwhelmed with anguish by the irrational anti-Semitism in France. Alfred Dreyfuss, a Jewish military officer, had been accused of passing military secrets to the Germans. Anti-Semitism had been growing in France in the 19th century, and, even though there was no substantial evidence of his guilt, the trial of a Jew for treason overwhelmed the emotions of the French public, and Dreyfuss was wrongly convicted.

Greatly saddened and incensed by the Dreyfuss fiasco, Herzl concluded that what the Jews needed was their own nation. He sat down and wrote *Der Judenstaat* (*The Jewish State*) in 1896. It caused a sensation. It gave voice to all the longings Jews had felt for centuries. The next year 1897 Herzl organized the First Zionist Congress in Basel, Switzerland, and international Zionism was born "to create for the Jewish people a homeland in Palestine secured by public law." Herzl's boast was, "At Basel I founded the Jewish state. If I said this out loud today, I would be greeted by universal laughter. In five years, perhaps, and certainly in fifty years, everyone will perceive it." Herzl's remarkable prediction came true almost to the very year.

The idea of the return of the "chosen" to the Promised Land caught fire among the poor, the ordinary, the persecuted, and the orthodox. A new "exodus" was begun. Herzl died in 1904 at only 44 years of age, but 50 years after the Basel Congress, the United Nations on November 29, 1947 confirmed the establishment of a Jewish state in Palestine. This vote took place in spite of an ongoing, deadly conflict between Arabs and Jews, which has continued unabated to this day.

Britain's Amazing Contribution to a Jewish Homeland in Palestine

For almost 300 years before the modern Zionist movement began, a movement called the "Restoration" had developed among evangelical Christians in England. It happened after the Bible had been translated into popular English and became widely read especially among groups like the Puritans. There was a reawakening on the part of British Christians that God had not just chosen the Christian Church and given up on the Jews as was believed by Catholic and Reformed theologians, a teaching called "Replacement Theology," but also God had no plans to abandon the physical remnants of his chosen people. After reading the prophecies in the Bible, Christians in England began to believe that Jews were without any doubt in the future going to be reclaimed by God from the Diaspora and restored to the Promised Land of Abraham, Isaac, and Jacob.

Before the year 1700 at least twelve separate publications had appeared in England promoting the return of the Jews to their homeland in Palestine based on the Biblical prophecies. This teaching was tied directly to both a belief in the return of Jesus Christ as promised in the Scriptures and the conversion of the Jews at His coming. Names of famous Brits who held this view included the poet John Milton and the Puritan leader Oliver Cromwell. Another supporter across the Channel in Holland was the founder of the modern theory of natural law Hugo Grotius. He was a Dutch theologian who had rejected Calvinism in favor of an Arminian position. Calvinism, in general, had retained the Roman Catholic doctrine of Replacement Theology. When he made his views known, he was threatened a number of times with imprisonment and had to flee Holland for either France or Germany.

The names of teachers and clergymen that held to the idea of the Restoration of the Jews to Palestine in these years are too many to record here. The words of one Bible teacher Thomas Brightman may summarize them all. In 1641 he wrote in his exegesis of Revelation 15:12 concerning the Jews, "What! Shall they return to Jerusalem again? There is nothing more certain: the prophets do everywhere confirm it." This became tied to the conviction that Jesus Second Coming could not take place until the Jews had been restored to their homeland.

Nothing concrete came out of all this teaching, but two hundred years later Lord Anthony Ashley Earl of Shaftesbury, an evangelical member of Parliament who was a great supported of social causes, had discovered from reports of visitors to Palestine the same phenomena that Mark

Twain found later; namely that the land was desolate and sparsely populated. There were only about 200,000 poor Arabs in an empty barren region that had a potential to hold millions. At the time of the Crimean War in 1854 Lord Shaftesbury wrote to Prime Minister Aberdeen. Calling the land Greater Syria he said, "There is a country without a nation; and God now, in his wisdom and mercy, directs us to a nation without a country." This became translated into the famous slogan, "A land without a people for a people without a land." Shaftesbury was an outspoken Zionist and even appealed to Queen Victoria for Israel's restoration. Just a few out of many other famous Englishmen who supported this cause in the 19th century were the literary lights Lord Byron and George Eliot and political leaders, such as Disraeli, David Lloyd George, Lord Balfour, Winston Churchill, General Smuts, and the Middle East adventurer and friend of the Arabs T.E. Lawrence.

These ideas spread during the time of the Puritans to the American colonies. Roger Williams, the Baptist founder of Rhode Island, was a Zionist. Our second president John Adams, who was from New England, expressed an emphatic wish that the Jews could have their own nation in Palestine. The most active promoter was William E. Blackstone, the famous businessman Bible teacher of the second half of the 19th century, who wrote the famous little book Jesus Is Coming. He compiled a document signed by over 500 prominent Americans, which was sent to President Benjamin Harrison and his Secretary of State James G. Blaine asking them to call a conference of European powers with America to consider the Jews' claim to the land of Palestine.

Although the rank and file of Jewish people were becoming excited about the prospect of Palestine and a few were already immigrating, many Rabbis were holding back. This was particularly true in America where Jews were prospering and were in no danger of persecution. The well-known Rabbi Emil G. Hirsch said in the 1941, "We modern Jews do not wish to be restored to Palestine . . . the country wherein we live is our Palestine . . . we will not go back to form again a nationality of our own." Their concept was that a concentration of Jews in one land would just become a huge ghetto. Orthodox Jews also believed that only the Messiah could return His people to their land and looked upon Jews who did return to Palestine as the Hebrew Goy (Gentiles). This was right before the Holocaust. How things have changed

One of the British Restorationists was William Hechler, an Anglican clergyman who was chaplain to the British Embassy in Vienna, Herzl's base of operations. Hechler allied himself with Herzl and introduced him to Queen Victoria and Kaiser Wilhelm whom he had known when he served as a tutor for some of the children of the German Royals. Both of these heads of state were favorable to Herzl's vision. Kaiser Wilhelm tried to intercede with the Turkish Sultan in favor of more Jewish immigration to Palestine but was rebuffed. The British responded enthusiastically, however, by holding the next World Zionist Congress in London in 1900 with the theme "Palestine for the Jews."

This eventually led indirectly to the Balfour Declaration in 1917, which demonstrated that there was support for this Zionist dream in some of the highest echelons of the British government. Coincidentally this was just before Britain was to take on the responsibility or mandate for the ancient land of Israel called Palestine following the victory of the Allies in World War I. (For an excellent summary of the history of the original British influence in stimulating the Zionist cause see Derek Prince, *Promised Land*, pp. 25-40.)

Jewish Settlement in Palestine

Before 1880 there were about 12,000 Jews in Palestine most of them in Jerusalem. By the time of World War I there were over 115,000. The Zion Jewish National Fund appealed for financial help from Jews all over the world, and they began to buy land in Palestine in spite of the exorbitant prices charged by the Arabs. They never settled on anything but unoccupied land. They used the slogan "A people without a land for a land without a people."

As much as $1100 an acre was demanded by the *effendis*, or nonresident Arab landowners, for land which might be desert, or filled with rocks, or covered with brambles, or even a swamp. At the same time the best farmland in Iowa was selling for about $100 per acre. In spite of the high cost, Zionists throughout the world eventually bought up over 250,000 unoccupied acres. This was all accomplished without disturbing or displacing a single Arab unless the Arab had voluntarily sold his land and was amply compensated with a huge amount of money.

In his memoirs King Abdullah of Jordan, the great grandfather of the present Jordanian leader of the same name, accused the Arabs of being reckless in selling their land and then prodigal in wailing and whimpering about it. Contrary to popular complaint, Jews did not displace any Arabs in their acquisition of any of this original territory.

About 350,000 Jews were settled in the land by 1936. They had drained swamps, irrigated deserts, threw out the rocks, built 233 villages, some of which became towns and cities, planted over 5 million trees, and covered the land with fields of crops and orange groves, whose fruit they exported to Europe. Then they built factories, even heavy industry, and employed many of the Arabs in their fields and factories. These included the dirt-poor peasants, the *fellahin,* who had been cheated and exploited by their Islamic brothers, the rich *effendi* or absentee landowners.

Jews paid Arab workers decent wages, which raised the whole standard of living for everyone in Palestine. The *fellahin,* whose average life expectancy had been only 37 years, for the first time got proper sanitation facilities and free medical care. This greatly improved standard of living eventually attracted thousands of poor immigrants from other Arab nations who flooded into Palestine to participate in the

Jewish run economy. Infant mortality rates for Arabs were cut in half, and by 1945 their average life span had risen to 49 years. Some Arab leaders, in fact, at first praised the Jews for making available a new economic opportunity and a higher standard of living for these Arab populations.

Between WWI and WWII 475,000 Jewish immigrants came to Palestine primarily from Russia, Eastern Europe and some Arab nations. At the same time, however, there were 588,000 Arab immigrants who had come from Egypt, Jordan, Lebanon, Syria and Iraq to take advantage of the greatly improved economy and healthcare. Not only are modern Israelis the descendants of these Jewish immigrants, furthermore, but also most of the Palestinian Arabs, who now reside in Palestine, are themselves the offspring of twentieth century Arab immigrants. The majority of the Arabs in Palestine today are not the descendants of the earlier residents who numbered less than 250,000. So most of Palestine's present population has had a very short history in the land. Jews and most of the Arabs came into Palestine during the same period of time.

It is a myth, therefore, that Palestine is the ancestral home of all of the Arabs who are either refugees or are living in the land today. That this land is an Arab inheritance that was stolen by the Jews is a lie.

Events of WWI That Forever Changed the Middle East
Partly because of the leadership of the dashing Britisher T.E. Lawrence, Arabs had fought on the side of England and France against the Turks—the Ottoman Empire— during the First World War. Palestine, Lebanon, Syria, Iraq, Arabia were all part of this Islamic Caliphate, which had been called "the old man of Europe." They hoped to be rewarded by the Allies with an independent Arab state when this Islamic empire was broken up. At the end of the war Arabia came under the rule of Arab Sheikhs. By 1932 one leader had emerged as the most powerful; namely, King Abdud Aziz of

the Saud tribe. From then on Arabia was called Saudi
Arabia.   Egypt remained for a time under British control.
When the Saudi's displaced the Hashemites in Arabia, the
former leader of Arabia King Feisal of the Hashemite family, who had been ruling in Mecca, was at first given the rule
of Damascus, but was deposed by the French and set up as
the King of Iraq in Baghdad by the British. This was in compensation for the Hashemites losing the custodianship of
the sacred cities of Mecca and Medina to the more powerful
Saud tribe. Feisal's brother Abdullah became Emir or King
of Transjordan.

Iraq like all the other Arab states was an artificial creation cut out of the lands of the Ottoman Empire and had a
majority of Shiites and Kurds. Today Iraqis number 25 million—15 million   Shiites, 5 million Kurds and 5 million
Sunnis. King Feisal was a Sunni, and the Sunnites ruled from
Baghdad, the ancient Caliphate capital, and controlled Iraq
up through the regime of Saddam Hussein. Although the
Kurds and Shiites were the majority of the country, the
Sunnis from the beginning dominated them. The Allies were
not sensitive to the differences in the Muslim populations,
and their arbitrary land divisions have resulted in major
problems in Iraq to this very day.

During WWI, a Jewish organic chemist Dr. Chaim
Weizmann was the head of the British Admiralty
Laboratories. He had created for Britain a formula for syn-
thetic acetone, a chemical necessary for explosives. Acetone
had previously been imported from Germany, and Britain
was in dire need of a new supply. Asked by Prime Minister
David Lloyd George what reward he wanted for his invalu-
able contribution to the war effort, Weizmann responded, "I
want nothing for myself, only a homeland for my people."
An enthusiastic Zionist, he proposed to the British government that they establish a protectorate in Palestine for the
Jews after the war. The result was the following declaration
made on November 2, 1917 by Lord Balfour, the British

Foreign Secretary in conjunction with Prime Minister David
Lloyd George:

*His Majesty's Government view with favor the establish-
ment in Palestine of a national home for the Jewish people.*

This statement of intent was put in the form of a letter
written to Lord Rothchild the Jewish financier. The Balfour
Declaration has been called "The Magna Carta of the Zionist
Movement." Although it had not been stated in just this way,
it gave Jews a genuine hope that someday this might develop
into their having a nation of their own.

Many British leaders at the time like Prime Minister
David Lloyd George, who believed the teaching of the Bible
that Palestine was still "the Promised Land of Israel," encouraged this decision. Lloyd George said that he was more familiar with the towns of Judea and Samaria than he was with the
villages of his boyhood land of Wales. He believed that the
prophets of the Old Testaments had foretold that God
would bring His people the Jews back to their ancient homeland in the "last days." Of the committee of ten on the War
Cabinet that deliberated on this decision, seven were evangelical Christians. Observers have said that at no earlier or
later time in British history could a Declaration like this have
been written. It was a logical step in the 275-year-old
Restoration movement among Christians in England, who
believed that God wanted to restore the Jews to the land
promised to Abraham, Isaac, and Jacob.

Some Arab leaders were enraged by the Balfour
Declaration because Britain had also promised them land if
they rebelled against the Ottoman Turks. The British had
encouraged Arab nationalism, and the Arabs looked forward
to their independence and a new national identity. This
promise had been forwarded to rulers in the Hijaz, or western Arabia, by the British High Commissioner of Egypt.
Although Palestine was not mentioned in the correspondence, the Arabs took it for granted that Palestine was to be

included because, after all, it had been under the control of
Islamic peoples since they conquered it in the 7th century. It
was considered by them to be part of Greater Syria, which
was called Syro-Palestina by the Romans. Also it is an Islamic
principle that if ever a land has been "ruled by Allah," it must
remain the property of the Islamic ummah forever. Besides
Palestine was the site of Jerusalem, where both the Dome of
the Rock and "the farthest mosque" or al-Aqsa were located
on the Temple Mount. Jerusalem had not been of great
importance to Muslims compared to Mecca and Medina, but
it gained in stature as they competed with the Jews for its
control. They have now declared it to be their third most
sacred city and, whereas Jews had lived there for centuries,
Palestinian Arabs now wanted it all for themselves.

The Hashemite King Feisal, whose family had controlled
the Hijaz and Mecca and Medina before they were ousted by
King Fahd of the Saud tribe, developed a relationship with
Chaim Weizmann. They met at the Paris Peace Conference
after the War in 1919. Feisal was open and friendly and
signed an agreement with the Zionists that expressed
encouragement for the Jews to develop Palestine west of the
Jordan. For him this was conditional on the Arabs getting a
single large, national state over which he hoped to become
the King. The French and British, however, had earlier divided the Arab lands that had been part of the Ottoman Empire
between themselves in a secret treaty in 1916 called the Sykes
Picot Agreement. There would be no single Arab kingdom,
which Arabs had hoped for. France and England had already
divided the Middle East between themselves as spheres of
influence or control called Mandates by the League of
Nations. Britain originally took direct responsibility for Iraq,
Palestine and Egypt, France for Lebanon and Syria.

Although the British made Feisal King of Iraq in
Baghdad, he regarded this as a kind of booby prize and
reneged on any agreement he had signed with Weizmann.
His brother Abdullah, who became the Emir of Transjordan

never did agree with Feisal's generosity toward the Jews. He was the grandfather of the present King Abdullah of Jordan.

The San Remo Conference and the League of Nations— 1920-22

The International Conference in San Remo, Italy in April 1920 assigned to Britain the Mandatory responsibility for Palestine. This was confirmed by the Council of the League of Nations on July 24, 1922. The text creating the British Mandate authorized the implementation of the Balfour Declaration:

> *Whereas the Principal Allied Powers have also agreed that the Mandatory should be responsible for putting into effect the declaration originally made on November 2, 1917, by the Government of His Britannic Majesty, and adopted by the said powers in favour of the establishment in Palestine of a national home for the Jewish people, it being clearly understood that nothing should be done which might prejudice the civil and religious rights of existing non-Jewish communities in Palestine, or the rights and political status enjoyed by Jews in any other country.*

The League of Nations recognized the historic connection of the Jewish people with Palestine as grounds for reconstituting their national home there. In numerous Articles the Council then set forth the responsibilities of Britain in administering the Mandate. Emphasis is mine.

1. Britain was given full legislative and administrative power for Palestine.

2. **Britain was directed to secure a Jewish national home in Palestine**.

3. A Jewish agency was to be set up to coordinate the settlement of those Jews who wished to live in Palestine. The Zionist Organization was chosen as this Agency.

4. **Britain was to facilitate Jewish immigration and settle-
    ment on State and waste lands**.

5. Jews were to become **citizens of Palestine or
    Palestinians** by law.

6. Britain was responsible for the Holy Places and **was to
    protect a free exercise of religion.**

7. Britain was to supervise all religions **in preserving public
    order and good government.** All holy days of each faith
    were to be recognized.

8. Three languages—English, Arabic, and Hebrew—were
    officially recognized.

9. The Mandate was to decide the fate of Eastern Palestine
    from the Jordan River to the eastern boundary **empha-
    sizing consideration for freedom of religion with no
    discrimination.** (This eastern part of Palestine became
    Transjordan where ironically, in contradiction to this
    Mandate, Jews were discriminated against by not being
    able to settle in this area, which was originally considered
    part of the Balfour Declaration.)

In the years to come, the British administration failed
miserably to implement most of these provisions in good
faith. In 1939 John Gunther wrote in Inside Asia, one of his
regional overview books, *"From the beginning Zionism faced not
only the political watering down of the Mandate but also deep-seated
antipathy from anti-Semitic British officials. The Jews were violently
discriminated against—in what was presumably to be their own
country."*

The first responsibility for the Mandate was given to a
British military government. Their personnel had fought
shoulder to shoulder with the Arabs against the Ottoman

Turks and were in no way disposed with favor toward the Balfour Declaration. They were on the side of the Arabs in their total rejection of allowing the Jews to have a homeland in Palestine. An example of this close relationship between the British military and the Arabs was the Jordanian army called the Arab Legion. It was staffed with British officers and its leader was a British Lieutenant General John Glubb who was known as Glubb Pasha. He had voiced the opinion that to sacrifice 100,000 Jews was legitimate if it could save the British Empire.

Major-General Louis Bols was appointed the first military governor of the Mandate. He was an avowed anti-Semite and represented the negative reaction of most British military officers to the idea of Jews in Palestine. The British military actually preferred that Syria and Palestine be united under an Arab ruler, which would fulfill their promise to the Arabs of an independent state. So they encouraged the Hashemite Sheikh Feisal, after he had been displaced from his leadership in western Arabia by the Saud tribe and before he was made King of Iraq, to declare himself king in Damascus. This intrigue was conducted in spite of the fact that France was supposed to have the Mandate for Syria. All of this was initiated by the British military in opposition to the policies of the civil government in Britain.

The details of this intrigue of British officers became known through the reports of Colonel Richard Meinertzhagen, the chief political officer appointed in 1919 by Whitehall, British headquarters in London, to oversee the military government in Palestine. His published diary records what happened.

When the San Remo Conference began in April 1920, Colonel Waters-Taylor, the Chief of Staff to the military governor General Bols, was convinced that Arab freedom could only be accomplished through violence. With King Feisal in place in Damascus, he suggested to a young Arab leader Hajj Amin al Husseini that now the Arabs had a wonderful opportunity to show the world and the Allied powers that they were opposed to an official Jewish presence in the land. They could become a new nation of Syro-Palestine under Arab rule.

Hajj Amin was encouraged to organize an Easter day riot in Jerusalem against the Jews. It was hoped that this agitation would discourage the Allied powers meeting at the San Remo conference from implementing Britain's commitment to a Jewish homeland. Both General Bols, the first chief administrator, and General Allenby, who had taken Jerusalem from the Turks, would advocate the abandonment of the Balfour Declaration and that any thought that Jews should have a home in Palestine be rejected.

Hajj Amin al Husseini, later to become Grand Mufti of Jerusalem and Hitler's pal, was assured by the British military that they would not interfere with such an uprising. Arab agitators stirred up the crowds in Jerusalem, and cries were heard, "We will drink the blood of the Jews. Don't be afraid, the government is with us." The Jews, in the meantime, had been disarmed by the British, and the Jewish police force in the Jewish Quarter of the Old City had been relieved from duty. Also while the riots were going on and Jews were being killed and women raped, a cordon of British troops surrounded the Old City of Jerusalem so that no one could go in or out. So it was actually the British military that from the beginning encouraged the organized opposition to the Jews by the Arabs. This is how the bad blood began to grow between Arab and Jew, which exists with such virulence today.

The British must be held ultimately responsible for these attacks of the Arabs on the Jews in Jerusalem in 1920, and in Jaffa in 1921 when over 40 Jews were killed, and then again eight years later in 1929, because they did nothing to interfere with these attacks. They also had disarmed the Jews so that they could not protect themselves. They completely ignored both responsibilities of the British Mandate, which required that the military government not only keep order throughout Palestine, but that it also implement the Balfour

Declaration and show no discrimination.

As a result of Colonel Meinerzhagen's report and a commission's findings, General Bols and the military government were immediately replaced with a civil administration. But with the exception of the first High Commissioner Sir Herbert Samuel, who was himself a Jew, all future British governors of Palestine were infected with this same antagonism to the Jews and Zionism.

Hajj Amin al Husseini had been given a sentence of five years in prison for his leadership of this violence against the Jews, but he escaped from prison under mysterious circumstances. Then the British administration recalled and pardoned Hajj Amin because they recognized that he was a natural leader of the Arabs, and they wanted to win his cooperation. He was appointed the Grand Mufti of Jerusalem, the religio-political leader of the Arabs in Palestine. This appeasement effort proved to be a major mistake. Hajj Amin would not compromise. He himself had a secret ambition to be king of the whole of Palestine.

The Command Paper of 1922—
The British Create the Arab State of Transjordan

In order to appease the Arab opposition to Jews in the Holy Land and find a possible solution to the conflict, Winston Churchill as Secretary of the Colonies with one stroke of his pen in 1922 created the first partition of Palestine. We often forget that three-fourths of Greater Palestine was east of the Jordan River. He assigned to the Hashemite family, former custodians of the sacred cities of Mecca and Medina in the Hijaz, all of this area of eastern Palestine, which comprised 77% of the land originally included in the Balfour Declaration. A large, exclusively Palestinian Arab state therefore was formed on the East Bank of the Jordan River. Originally it was called Transjordan, referring to the territory "across the Jordan" from Jerusalem. Called just Jordan today, it is an area three times larger than Palestine west of the Jordan River.

In the days when Israel settled in the land under Moses'
successor Joshua, this area east of the Jordan River had been
given to the tribes of Reuben, Gad, and one half the tribe of
Manasseh. Ammon and Moab, descendants of Lot's sons,
also occupied part of what is now Jordan as did the offspring
of Esau (Edom) to the south. Amman is the name of Jordan's
capital today, which is derived from the name of Lot's son
Ammon (Joshua 13:8-32).

It should be noted that both Winston Churchill and T.E.
Lawrence believed that the Jews should have a home in
Palestine extending from the Jordan River west to the
Mediterranean Sea. They worked together in sorting out the
allocations of territory in the Middle East following WWI.

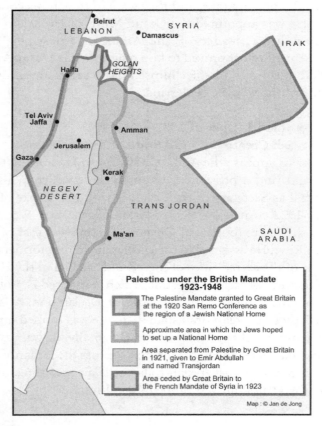

**Palestine under the British Mandate
1923-1948**

The Palestine Mandate granted to Great Britain
at the 1920 San Remo Conference as
the region of a Jewish National Home

Approximate area in which the Jews hoped
to set up a National Home

Area separated from Palestine by Great Britain
in 1921, given to Emir Abdullah
and named Transjordan

Area ceded by Great Britain to
the French Mandate of Syria in 1923

Map : © Jan de Jong

Lawrence as an adviser on the Middle East to Churchill in the Colonial Office traveled with him to the meeting in Cairo in 1921 when Feisal and Abdullah received their appointments. This was only four years after the Balfour Declaration, and no contradiction was seen between Arab independence and a Palestinian home for the Jews. Both Churchill and Lawrence were pro-Zionist and were committed to carrying out the Balfour Declaration in a suitable manner, which they hoped would pacify the Arabs. Hence, the compromise of 1922. What most westerners don't realize is that there is no such thing as compromise for Muslim Arabs when crucial issues of faith or Islamic law are involved.

It has not been widely known that T.E. Lawrence, who is identified with Arab independence, was also favorably disposed toward the Jews. The historian Sir Martin Gilbert has found evidence in notes written by Lawrence himself in the National Archives that in fact indicated he had developed an inner contempt for the Arabs and believed that the example of Jewish ingenuity and industry, in what he called the "Jewish National Home," would challenge the Arabs to make something of themselves.

This dividing of the land in the Command Paper of 1922, which sought a compromise solution to both Arab and Jewish ambitions and the promises of the British government, was in the tradition of the democratic method of settling disputes. It can be expressed in the maxim or slogan "give and take." Were the Arabs, however, appeased by receiving by far the major portion of Palestine as an independent Arab state? Absolutely not! Since there is really no tradition or spirit of compromise in Islam, it made no difference at all in the point of view of the Arabs toward Palestine and a Jewish homeland. It had no affect on the Arabs' intention to take all of Palestine for themselves and eliminate all the Jews. I cannot overemphasize that the Arab mindset is not inclined toward any kind of compromise in a matter like this. The Arabs have rejected all chances for compromise and a peaceful settlement over and over again.

They have had many opportunities to have their own Islamic
state in west Palestine alongside a Jewish homeland, but they
rejected each one. The Islamic point of view can be best
expressed in the slogan, "all or nothing at all."

1. Arabs could have had their second Palestinian state
    alongside of Transjordan in 1937 after the Peel
    Commission's recommendation for partition of west
    Palestine. At the time both Jews and Arabs rejected this
    solution.

2. This was also true in November 1947 when the United
    Nations proposed a partition of western Palestine
    between Jews and Arabs. This time the Jews accepted the
    proposal, but the Arabs rejected it.

3. Again in 1949 at the end of the first Arab/Israeli war, the
    Jews were willing to negotiate, readmit some of the Arabs
    who had fled as refugees, and establish the boundaries of
    two states. The Arabs refused again to negotiate, prefer-
    ring a state of truce, which would lead to more warfare
    and a potential conquest.

4. In 1967 the Arabs had another opportunity for a State,
    but they again responded negatively. The Jews were will-
    ing to give back all the land they had taken in the Six Day
    War, but the Arabs meeting in a council in Khartoum set
    forth their policy called "the three no's"—"no peace, no
    negotiations, and no recognition" of the State of Israel.

5. Then following negotiations at Camp David with
    President Bill Clinton, and Premier Ehud Barak of Israel,
    Yasser Arafat refused to deal at all even though the PLO
    was offered 98% of everything they had requested. Arafat's
    position represented the Arab immovable will that noth-
    ing would satisfy them except the total elimination of the

Jews, leaving the Arabs in control of all of western Palestine. It has seldom been pointed out that this would have given the Arabs two Palestinian states in both eastern and western Palestine—Jordan in the East and everything that includes Israel in the West.

6. So frankly it is a farce to even pursue the so-called Road Map For Peace, which is the present effort of the quartet—Russia, the European Community, the United Nations, and the United States—to find an answer to the problem of Palestine. Any Arab move in the direction of settlement is a deception motivated simply by a desire to buy time as they plan for a successful future conquest and annihilation of the Jews. They are looking to Iran and Hizballah right now as their best hope to fulfill their unbending purpose. The Iranian President Ahmadinejad is dedicated to wiping Israel off of the map, and he will likely try to do just that as soon as he acquires enough nuclear weaponry.

The original partition of 1922 gave 3/4ths of Palestine to the Arabs east of the Jordan River because they were the majority population. This is three times the size of Israel today, but it makes no difference because the Arabs will not be satisfied until they possess the entire area of what was called Palestine. Israel must be obliterated and all Jews driven into the Mediterranean Sea. There is no room for compromise on this. Another appropriate slogan for this prevailing Muslim Arab attitude might be phrased as "my way or the highway."

As part of this partition the rule was even established that no Jew could immigrate to Transjordan, meaning that eastern Palestine must be exclusively Arab. The obvious intention of this division was to encourage Jews to settle in western Palestine where they would establish their "home." Arabs would be encouraged to settle in Transjordan or eastern

Palestine. West Palestine would therefore be exclusively Jewish and East Palestine would be exclusively Arab. This, however, was a direct violation of the Council of the League of Nations' directive to Britain to effect freedom of religion with no discrimination throughout the Mandate, including Transjordan. As it developed East Palestine was exclusively Arab, but West Palestine also filled up with Arab immigrants to take advantage of the Jews' prosperity. Does anyone see any unfairness in this arrangement? Based on the directives of the Balfour Declaration, the San Remo Conference, and the League of Nations, the Jews were certainly getting a "raw deal" or "the short end of the stick!"

Nothing was ever stated specifically about a Jewish "home" developing into a nation state, but the idea was not rejected in 1922, as it was later in the British White Paper of 1939. This is when it became official British policy to create in West Palestine a territory held jointly by both Jews and Arabs. Two thirds would be Arab and one third Jewish. This new policy actually forbade the founding of a State of Israel. Any kind of arrangement like a joint state with the Arab majority in charge, however, would have surely led to a massacre of the Jews.

T.E. Lawrence of Arabia had admonished Abdullah, the new Emir of Transjordan, to control any possible Arab immigration to western Palestine. This, however, never happened. Although British restrictions were placed upon Jews immigrating to Arab territory, Arabs were never hindered from immigrating to Jewish territory. This also was a clear case of discrimination, violating the terms of the Mandate. More Arabs than Jews therefore moved into Western Palestine between WWI and WWII to take advantage of the thriving prosperity, job opportunities, and the higher, more comfortable, and healthier standard of living existing there because of the gifted diligence of the Jews in developing their territory.

This complete impasse continued even after the United Nations on November 29, 1947 partitioned Palestine west of the Jordan River. This second division of Palestinian territory allocated 56% of the land to Jews and 43% to Palestinian Arabs in West Palestine. A large part of the Jews' area was desert in the Negev. This division did anticipate an influx of Jewish immigration, however, and recognized that Arabs already had 77% of Greater Palestine in the existence of Transjordan. The Jews reluctantly accepted the partition, but the Arabs never acknowledged it. As we have seen, they passed up one opportunity after another for another Arab state alongside a Jewish state, spurning all offers in favor of the vision and goal of possessing all of Palestine for themselves and eliminating all the Jews. They wanted to take over all the territories that the Jews over many years had paid the Arabs high prices for and then developed out of swamp, desert, rock, and wasted land. Nor did the Arabs show any appreciation for the improved standard of living and health care that the Jews had provided. Does anyone see any expression of greed or selfishness here?

Almost five months after the United Nations' partition, Britain gave up the Mandate, and the Jews declared an independent State of Israel the very next day on May 14, 1948. Immediately five Arab nations—Egypt, Transjordan, Lebanon, Syria, and Iraq—whose armies were poised on the borders, invaded the new Jewish state. Miraculously the Arabs were soundly defeated that same year by the Jews who were fighting for their very existence. It was the first of five Arab/Israeli wars discussed in the chapter 6.

Chapter 4

ARABS AND JEWS IN THE MODERN WORLD: Part II—1929 to 1948

The Arab Riots of 1929 and the White Paper of 1930
From 1922 to 1929 there were no incidents in Palestine, and Arabs and Jews got along fairly well together. But all hell broke loose in Jerusalem in 1929. On August 15 Jewish youth held a celebration at the Western Wall singing the Zionist anthem Hatikva and raising the Jewish flag. Rumors circulated that Arab residents had been attacked by Jews. Arabs assembled at the Wall and burned the prayer request notes that had been inserted into cracks in the wall including pages from Jewish prayer books. At the Friday services in the Mosque the crowds were stirred up. It seems that pamphlets perhaps prepared by the Grand Mufti Hajj Amin al Husseini were distributed that claimed that that the Jews wanted to take over the Temple Mount, destroy the Dome of the Rock and the Al Aqsa Mosque and rebuild their Temple on the site. Some Jews may have wished that this could happen, but there was no Jewish plot to take over the area, and it was foolish to think that they would even be able to accomplish something so outrageous.

Arab riots based on these lies began in Jerusalem on August 23, when it was rumored that two Arabs had been killed. The riots spread to many other centers including Safed and Hebron where Jews were attacked by their Arab neighbors for the first time. There was a very old Jewish settlement in Hebron, which was the site of the graves of the Patriarchs Abraham, Sarah, and Isaac. This was a sacred area to both Jews and Arabs who had lived together peaceably for many years with little or no conflict. In fact, when the violence began in

73

Jerusalem, the Jews of Hebron refused the offer of the Haganah to come and protect them. Jews had lived there in confidence and believed that they would be protected by the A'yan or Arab Notables.

August 1929, however, saw the worst massacre of Jews in Palestine since the Crusades. Over half of the 139 Jews killed in these pogroms were from Hebron, 17 were killed in Jerusalem and 20 in Safed. A total of 339 were wounded. In comparing the size of populations with the United States, this was the same as over 200,000 being killed and almost 500,000 being wounded today in our country. The British who had never been enthusiastic about protecting Jews had provided little in the way of police supervision. There was, for example, only one constable in Hebron. It took the British several hours to arrive on the scene and stop the violence. Because the Arab mobs had killed 68 Jews and wounded 80 in Hebron, the British, instead of punishing the Arabs, removed all the Jews from their sacred center where they had had a presence for over 2500 years. This was for their own protection, but it seemed as if the British were blaming the Jews. The Arabs proceeded to take over all Jewish property and possessions. After all, Muhammad had promised booty for a successful jihad.

Colonel Meinertzhagen wrote the Colonial Secretary in Britain explaining that the British authorities in Palestine were failing to fulfill their responsibility to implement the Balfour Declaration. He pointed out that, as he understood it, the Declaration gave the Jews a most favored nation status in Palestine as long as Arab civil and religious rights were respected. He added that he had not known a single case where Jews had violated this requirement. No Zionist progress in Jewish settlements was being made at the expense of Arab rights. Arabs had made up stories claiming that injustice had been perpetrated, but there was no evidence that any of these trumped up charges were true. This was the testimony of the British official who was the on sight representative of the British government.

A British commission was organized to examine the problem behind the conflict. It produced the White Paper of 1930 that claimed that there was not enough land in Palestine to sustain any more immigrants. This was not true; nevertheless, Jewish immigration was greatly curtailed. But the British never stopped Arab immigrants from coming to Palestine—about 35,000 per year—to reap the fruit of Jewish prosperity in jobs, health care, and freedoms. This illustrates again the gross inequity of the British discriminatory policy and their blatant ignoring of the terms of the Mandate.

That Palestine was full, of course, was a false allegation. Every study of Palestine had indicated that the land was underdeveloped and underpopulated, and that there were large tracts of wasteland, which should be given to the Jews because they had proved to be adept at developing such lands. Greatly limiting Jewish immigration to Palestine was in direct contradiction to Britain's responsibility to help establish a Jewish homeland there. Both the British Parliament and the League of Nations were very unhappy. Prime Minister Ramsey MacDonald eventually wrote a letter to Chaim Weizmann and the Zionists promising that Britain would not abandon the Balfour Declaration. This began a whole new chapter in the conflict in Palestine. Arab response to was vicious. They called it the "black letter" and began turning against the British. It resulted in Arab riots and in their fighting both the Jews and the British in the next series of uprisings from 1936 to 1939.

The Arab Revolt 1936-1939 and the Peel Commission
In April 1936 the Grand Mufti Hajj Amin al Husseini called a general strike of Arab citizens. The Arabs were taking a stand against all Jewish immigration and further land sales or settlements. A month later the revolt expanded in a refusal to pay any taxes. Next the rebellion was extended to the bombing of the oil pipeline, which came into Haifa from

Kirkuk, Iraq and sporadic bombings of railways, Jewish settlements, and neighborhoods.

The revolt was temporarily called off while the British
again called for a Palestine Royal Commission in 1937 led by
Earl Peel to assess the causes of the revolt and suggest a possible solution to the grievances. Chaim Weizmann and Hajj
Amin al Husseini both appeared before the Commission representing the views of Jews and Arabs. Weizmann appealed
for the fulfillment of the promise of the Balfour Declaration
and Hajj Amin took a firm stand against any further Jewish
immigration and distribution of Arab lands to the Jews. The
Peel Commission could find no compromise to the
Arab/Jewish problem, and so it recommended partition—an
Arab state and a Jewish state with Britain maintaining control of Jerusalem and the surrounding area including a corridor across west Palestine to the Sea.

The Arabs refused to consider partition of the land that
they insisted belonged entirely to them. Jews were on the
fence in the matter, although David Ben Gurion, head of the
Jewish Agency, favored the plan because it gave the Jews complete control of Galilee. Residents of the two areas in the
number of 225,000 Arabs and 1,250 Jews would be transferred to their respective divided territories. This transfer of
populations had worked on Cyprus between Greeks and
Turks in 1922, and it was hoped it could succeed in Palestine
also.

The Arab revolt started again and continued from 1938
until March 1939. There were about 10,000 Arab peasant
fighters, which finally required a severe British crackdown.
The Haganah, or Jewish defense force, cooperated with the
British in trying to keep order. Under a British military
leader Ord Wingate the Special Night Squad of half British
and half Jewish brigades made a successful effort to protect
the oil pipeline. In the fighting 5,000 Arabs, 400 Jews, and
200 British fighters were killed. The British weighed in heavily by bringing in 20,000 more troops. Finally more than 120

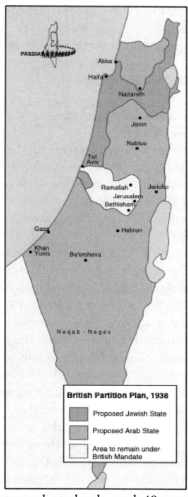

British Partition Plan, 1938

■ Proposed Jewish State

■ Proposed Arab State

□ Area to remain under
British Mandate

Arabs were sentenced to death, and 40 were hanged. Arab leaders were exiled, and the Grand Mufti Hajj Amin al Husseini fled to Egypt to avoid arrest. He later made his way to Germany where he joined Hitler in his campaign to wipe out the Jews in Europe.

One beneficial result of the uprising for the Jews was the disarming of the Arab population and the decimation of their leadership. Also the Jewish economy was separated from the Arabs making them more independent. A seaport, for example, was built at Tel Aviv whereas previously the Jews had been dependent on the Arab seaport at Jaffa. Both of these factors figured positively for the Jews ten years later during Israel's War for Independence.

British Policy Under the Mandate— The White Paper of 1939

In order to keep peace in Palestine under the Mandate, Britain had tended to favor the Arabs, who were in the major-ity. The Brits did seek to control Jewish immigration. This was not enough for the Arabs, however, who were absolutely opposed to any more Jewish immigration or the establish-ment of a permanent Jewish home in Palestine.

There were several other reasons why Britain tried to keep the Arabs happy by downplaying the Balfour Declaration. (1) Arab nations controlled most of the oil fields in the world, and without oil Britain and the industri-al nations could not survive. This was especially true in Iraq where British Petroleum had developed the Kirkuk oil field, one of the largest in the world, which supplied Palestine by pipeline. (2) The British also feared that offending the Arabs was not in the best interest of the Empire. Britain had responsibility for the Arab nation of Egypt, and India, "the jewel" of the British Empire, was also heavily Muslim. (3) Another undeniable fact was that there were those in the British administration who were not friendly to Jews. It has been asserted that there was an almost Nazi-like anti-Semitism existing among some British leaders in high places of influence. (4) Finally war with Germany was on the hori-zon, and Britain was afraid the Arabs would take the side of the Germans.

After the recommendation of partition by the Peel Commission had been rejected by both Jews and Arabs, the British Cabinet Committee on Palestine met to decide how now to handle the problem. Arabs had been in revolt since

1936. Lord Halifax of the Foreign Office warned the Committee that they had to make a choice between the Arabs and world Jewry. For obvious reasons he favored the Arabs. Malcolm McDonald of the Colonial Office offered a compromise, which became known as the British White Paper of 1939. A White Paper in the British system had no legal status but was simply a statement of policy on a specific issue for a specific period of time.

The most important and controversial part of this White Paper dealt with Jewish immigration. In deference to the Arabs' resistance to admitting more Jews to Palestine, the British suggested that only 75,000 more Jews would be allowed to enter the land averaging 15,000 per year for the next five years. This was based on an estimate that this number would increase the Jewish share to just one third of the total population. After 1944 therefore all Jewish immigration would cease.

The Arabs would not even accept this compromise. They labeled it the "Black Paper." The Arabs wanted all Jewish immigration to cease immediately. Considering the millions of Jews that were in danger in Europe from the Nazis, 75,000 was a ridiculously unrealistic and uncharitable figure. It seemed only a token assent that the British government had some responsibility for the Jews. It was certainly not a conscientious decision in the exercise of Britain's mandatory responsibility to establish a Jewish homeland.

In spite of the fact that the British Peel Commission on July 7, 1937 had recommended that western Palestine be divided between the Arabs and Jews, and that two separate states be established, the White Paper of 1939 rejected any idea of partition and favored no Jewish state at all. It envisioned a "homeland for the Jews in Palestine" only as a part of a future Arab/Jewish state where power was shared, and Arabs would outnumber Jews 2 to 1. This virtually negated the concept of a Jewish "homeland" and threatened a future civil war assuring a Jewish bloodbath. A major condition of the Mandate was violated and the Balfour Declaration might as well have been pronounced dead.

Winston Churchill and others in the British Parliament called this White Paper exactly what it was—a betrayal of Britain's original promise. All pledges and commitments had been broken. Even the Mandate Commission of the League of Nations accused Britain of a flagrant breach of its Mandate. It has been called shamefully "The Forsaken Promise," which is the title of a recent British documentary film that tells the truth about Britain's final refusal to implement the Balfour Declaration.

In Britain's defense, the White Paper was issued after the three years of Arab rebellion in Palestine against both the Jews and the British from 1936 to 1939. It had been the worst riotous uprising of Arabs since WWI. Hajj Amin al Husseini was even able to procure some arms from the Nazis, and Britain feared that the Arabs would join the Nazis in any future conflict. So the British arranged for several weeks of meetings with Arab and Jewish leaders in London to iron out their differences. None of the ideas presented, however, were agreed to by either Jews or Arabs. The conclusions the British drew from this conference, nevertheless, became the basis for Britain's official policy. The White Paper was thus issued unilaterally by the British Foreign and Colonial Offices as their best possible compromise. They didn't know what else to do, and it salved their consciences that they had tried something.

The White Paper appealed for its authority to the precedent of the Command Paper of 1922, which said that the Balfour Declaration did not indicate that the Jewish National Homeland should comprise all of Palestine, but that it might only involve a part of it. Following this principle, over 3/4ths of the total territory of Palestine had already been given to the Arabs to create the nation of Transjordan, which was off limits to Jews. It was apparent that it was Winston Churchill's intention, supported by his advisor in Middle Eastern affairs T.E. Lawrence, however, that the

Jewish homeland would be settled in all or most of Palestine that remained between the Jordan River and the Mediterranean Sea. I think that it can be assumed that since both men were Zionists and favored a Jewish homeland, it was their unspoken intention that the Jews should have virtually all of western Palestine since by far the larger portion, or 77% of the land of Palestine east of the Jordan, had already been given exclusively to the Arabs.

The White Paper, however, entirely ignored this original division of Palestine between Arabs and Jews and concentrated only on the territory where Jews had settled west of the Jordan. It therefore ignored the fact that the Arabs had already been given most of Palestine. It approached the problem as if the land west of the Jordan, or 23% of Greater Palestine, was all that comprised Palestine proper. The Paper speaks freely about a Jewish National Home that should be guaranteed by the world community, presumably the League of Nations. It made no provision for national defense, however, and the British refused to even provide the Jews with arms to defend themselves against the murderous attacks of militants among the Arabs. Also time after time as in 1920 and 1929 they were very slow or even refused to defend the Jews from Arab attacks.

We have already noted that the British actually were in charge of the principal Arab army, which was the famed Jordanian Arab League. Led by Glubb Pasha, a British General, it was staffed almost entirely by British officers. It was this very army that attacked the Jews, shelling Jerusalem and Jewish civilians in 1947-48, which was witnessed by Derek Prince and recorded in his memoir Promised Land. The Arab Legion also destroyed the Jewish quarter in East Jerusalem in 1948, including its revered, ancient synagogues, and imprisoned its entire male population.

All this aggression was carried out in spite of the White Paper's commitment to keep the peace between Arabs and Jews. Over and over again the British allowed Arabs to attack

Jews and stood by watching the slaughter. They also stood in the way of Jews defending themselves. This was true during the most murderous Arab uprising of all following the United Nations vote for Partition in November 1947. This neglect was not the fault of the average British soldier but was dictated by the policy of the British administration and the Foreign Office, which we already reported was led after WWII by Ernst Bevin, an avowed anti-Semite.

Arguments in the White Paper made it sound as if the Command Paper of 1922 supported their position. It ignored the obvious fact, however, that the unstated purpose of the creation of Transjordan in western Palestine by Winston Churchill was obviously to leave the small part that remained as a place where the Jews might find a permanent home and even identification as a nation. The British administration was trying to back out of its promise and its responsibility while at the same time trying to appear to support the precedents of the past. In carefully analyzing the While Paper myself, it is easy to see that it was typical diplomatic "gobbledygook." The Paper seemed to say one thing but left room for contradictory interpretations.

Finally the White Paper had declared that any further transfer of land to Jews would be restricted. In other words Jews could no long buy much land on which to expand. Only the acres, which they then occupied, would be their "homeland," and that was it. This policy again was another British attempt to please the Arabs, but it would be paid for with the blood of the Jews. All Jewish growth and expansion was being choked off. The British without apology had forsaken their original promise and commitment.

The Arabs Support Hitler
The Mufti of Jerusalem Hajj Amin el Husseini supported and encouraged Hitler from the beginning in his struggle against the Jews. The Palestinian Arabs received arms from the Nazis who acknowledged their common enemy. The Jews, on the

other hand, had been forbidden by Britain to import arms. This mutual hatred of Jews by both the Nazis and the Arabs fed on each other.

When the Mufti of Jerusalem opened his terrorist offensive in Palestine against both the British and the Jews in 1936, many Jews were killed. They fought back by first organizing a defensive army called the Haganah. What became known as "activist defense" is still practiced by the Israeli Defense Force (IDF) to this day. Radicals among them, however, believed that a good offense was the best defense and wanted to take the resistance to the Arabs and also to the British government. So an underground organization called the Irgun was founded as an offensive fighting force. One of its most infamous factions was the Stern Gang. They became guilty of reprisals that many regarded as terrorist acts. One of the early Irgun leaders was Menachem Begin who in later years became Prime Minister of the State of Israel and one of the principals in arranging peace with Egypt in 1979.

In explaining the policies of the Irgun, Begin explained that the Irgun was primarily concerned about bombing things and places. Their intent was never to kill people except where absolutely necessary or as unintended collateral damage. This is in contrast to Islamist terrorists whose chief goal has been to kill people—men, women, and children—as well as political and military opponents.

Whereas many Arabs sided with Hitler in World War II, as many as 137,000 Jews volunteered to fight in the British army against Rommel's German Afrika Korps. The British chose 30,000 of the volunteers, and they proved to be very effective soldiers. They made up 25% of the British forces at the crucial battle of El Alamein. Jews foresaw their own conflict with the Arabs escalating, so they used their experiences in the British army to enhance their own military training and experience. According to Pierre van Paassen in his book *The Forgotten Ally*, referring to Jews who supported the British during WWII, the Jews were "the defenders of Tobruck, the sappers in the desert, and the parachutists who descended behind Rommel's army. Jews provided thousands of doctors, nurses, medical supplies, food, truck drivers and trucks for the British Eighth Army." The production of 7,000 factories in Palestine were available to supply the British when no supply ships could get through the Mediterrranean. This helped to turn the tide against Hitler at a very critical time, and few realized it or even mention it.

The Arabs, on the other hand, were anything but a help to the British. The Iraqis declared war on Britain in May 1941, but Jews shut down the rebellion there. Syria and Lebanon were under the control of Vichy France, a German ally, but the Jews protected the pipeline from sabotage that ran from the Iraqi oil fields to Palestine. King Farouk and his family and ministers in Egypt were in touch with Rommel, and the Egyptian military personnel spied for the Germans.

The first engagement in which many of these Jewish soldiers participated was the battle of El Alamein on the border of Egypt in North Africa. General Erwin Rommel's German Afrika Corps had systematically pushed the British over 750 miles eastward in North Africa and were poised to invade Egypt. Rommel with his intelligence help from the Egyptians thought that all was over but the shouting. If the British lost this last line of defense at El Alamein to the German army, Egypt and Palestine would both have been overrun and tens of thousands of Jews might have been killed as they were in the Nazi holocaust. Historians, in fact, regard the battle of El Alamein as the turning point in World War II. It is the opinion of this author that the presence of Jewish soldiers made the difference because of the promise of God to them in Leviticus 26:7, 8?

You will pursue your enemies, and they will fall by the sword before you. Five of you will chase a hundred, and a hundred of you will chase ten thousand, and your enemies will fall by the sword before you.

This promise was to be fulfilled many times in the years to come as Jews fought to defend their lands, their families, and their very existence during five major Arab/Israeli wars in which the new nation of Israel faced grossly overwhelming odds following WWII.

A seldom told story of this crucial battle is about the new British commander General Bernard Law Montgomery, who had been elevated to his position by Winston Churchill over other candidates. Derek Prince who was in the British military at the time relates how earnestly he had prayed that new effective leadership be provided the British army, which had been badly mauled by the Germans. The choice of Montgomery was a surprise and not popular with the higher command in the Middle East. General Montgomery was the son of an Anglican clergyman, and was in his own way a devout believer. He gathered his officers and conducted what could only be called a prayer meeting. Then he visited all units under his command, which greatly increased the morale of the entire Eighth Army. Knowing the situation was "do or die," he destroyed the contingency plans for any retreat and meticulously planned for the battle with Rommel. It raged for 12 days, and the Allies, suffering 13,500 casualties, had their first land victory of WWII in October-November 1942. Montgomery was promoted to the rank of full general and knighted by the Crown. He was later to serve as Field Marshall under General Eisenhower's overall command in Europe, and was the Allied commander to receive the surrender of German forces in northern Germany on May 4, 1945.

The Evian Conference—July 1938

After Hitler came to power in Germany in 1931, the Nazis sought to make Germany *judenrein* (free of Jews). For the next ten years they tried to make life so miserable for Jews in Germany that they would leave the country. By 1938, 150,000 Jews had left Germany, which was 25% of the Jewish population. About 60,000 of these went to Palestine clandestinely. But as Hitler kept accumulating countries, he kept accumulating Jews. Hitler did not know what to do to get rid of these Jews. He wanted them to leave German lands for other nations but no other nations were willing to take them in as refugees. This is what led the Nazis to come up with their Final Solution. It resulted in the holocaust and the murder of 6 millions Jews in the gas chambers and crematoriums of Auschwitz-Berkenau and other death camps. But Germany was not the only nation that grievously sinned in this tragedy. Indirectly Hitler had accomplices. Many nations of the world, including Britain, which had closed the doors of Palestine, and the United States, which refused refugees, even 20,000 Jewish children, must share the blame.

In July 1938, the President of the United States Franklin Delano Roosevelt took the initiative in calling a conference of representatives from 32 nations at Evian-les-Bains in France to address the problem of Jewish immigration. The question was who will be willing to take Jews in as refugees to save them from Hitler and Germany's racism?

To the shame of the entire world, not a single nation would open its doors to receive any more Jewish refugees except Britain who took in 10,000 Jewish children ages 12 to 18. In fact, there was an agreement between Roosevelt and the British that if America would not bring up the subject of Palestine as a home for the Jews, the British would not mention that America was not filling its immigration quotas. Roosevelt only sent a businessman friend Myron C. Taylor as his representative. A possible reason for not sending an official American government delegate may have been because the State Department was already opposed to opening the gates of America to any more Jews. America was in the midst of the depression, jobs were scarce, and social services were overloaded.

Australia said bluntly that they had no racial problem, and they didn't want to import one. All other nations gave excuses. As in Jesus' story of the Good Samaritan, like the priest and the Levite, "they walked by on the other side." Chaim Weizman observed, "The world seemed to be divided into two parts—those places where the Jews could not live and those where they could not enter." Golda Meir, future premier of the nation of Israel, was there as an observer but was refused a seat at the table or permission to participate in the discussions. The Conference did not even issue any statement condemning Hitler's treatment of Jews, which prompted Hitler to conclude that no nation had any interest in opposing his racial policies. Hitler seemed to be given a free hand by world opinion.

Four months later the Nazi storm troopers conducted an assault on the Jews in Germany, which became known as "the night of broken glass," or Kristallnacht. About 1500 Jews were murdered, 30,000 were sent to concentration camps, 1574 synagogues were burned, and 7,000 Jewish businesses were looted and destroyed. It was a planned, systematic, nationwide devastation. "Crystal Night" was the first response by Hitler to the attitude shown toward the Jews by the nations at the Evian Conference. Hitler was just trying to find out how far he could go. There were some condemnations, but no sanctions, and no opening of any nation's doors, including Britain's Mandate in Palestine, to Jewish immigrants.

The Wagner-Rogers bill was introduced to the U.S. Senate that would have admitted 20,000 Jewish children under the age of 14 to the United States. Isolationists vigorously opposed the bill, and it was not supported by President Roosevelt. Without the support of the President it was defeated in February 1939. The wife of the U.S. Commissioner of Immigration, FDR's cousin, had expressed the opinion that 20,000 charming children would soon grow into 20,000 ugly adults. America was not lacking in its own share of anti-Semites. In retrospect the Evian Conference set the stage for the monstrous, inhuman tragedy that was waiting to happen, which the world also treated with virtual silence. So all the nations in the world participated in, or were stained by, Hitler's evil acts.

Anti-Semitism Runs Amok

World War II was a major milestone in the relationship of Jews and Arabs. The continuing Jewish immigration to Palestine greatly alarmed the Arab aristocrats or feudal barons who were fearful of losing complete control of the area. Because of their mutual hatred of the Jews, most Arabs supported Germany in the conflict with the Allies—Britain, France, and America, whom they called "the sons of Satan." Although the Jordanian army led by British officers fought on the side of the Allies, the Arabs of Palestine, Egypt, Syria, and Iraq took up Hitler's cause of anti-Semitism.

The ideological sympathy between the Arabs and Hitler concerning the Jews cannot be exaggerated. Even today Arab leaders identify the Allies attack on Germany both in WWI and WWII as an attack on Islam.

Hitler is a hero in the Arab world. Dr. Yahya al-Rakhaw of Egypt's Liberal Party said, *"We cannot help but see before us the figure of that great man Hitler. . who was the wisest of those who confronted this problem, and who, out of compassion for humanity, tried to exterminate every Jew."* The only complaint against Hitler is that he did not finish the job of killing the Jews—*"the most vile criminals on the face of the Earth."* (*Al Akhbar*, Egyptian Government Daily, April 18, 2001) Throughout WWII Arabs urged Hitler to extend the war into Palestine and bomb Tel Aviv or poison the water.

Hajj Amin al-Husseini, Grand Mufti of Jerusalem, who engineered the first uprisings against the Jews in Palestine in 1920, 1929 and 1936-39, was a close collaborator of Hitler and friend of both Himmler and Eichmann. On one occasion he dissuaded the Germans from exchanging as many as 15,000 Jewish children for German POW's. He insisted that they be sent to their deaths in the extermination camps. He helped train Bosnian and other Muslims in Europe as soldiers for

Himmler's SS, who were used to exterminate Jews in the Balkans. He exhorted the Germans on Berlin radio, *"Kill the Jews! Kill them with your hands; kill them with your teeth! This is well pleasing to Allah."* He was lodged by Hitler in a former Jewish mansion and was paid $20,000 a month out of funds confiscated from the Jews. Wanted for war crimes in 1945, Husseini along with many of the German SS officers, fled to Egypt where he was venerated as a hero in the Arab world until his death in 1974. His grand nephew Yasser Arafat later took up the same cause and led Palestinian Arabs in their terrorist attacks on Israel.

Both Syria and Iraq modeled their Baathist political parties after the example of the Nazi Party in Germany. Hitler was Saddam Hussein's hero from the time he was ten years old. He saw Hitler's portrait hanging in the kitchen of his uncle who was the mayor of Baghdad and idolized him. After the war, scores of Nazi leaders fleeing the Allies found asylum in Egypt where many became part of Gamal Abdel Nasser's staff and support. Many Nazis went to Syria, which, according to the famous Odessa Files, was a stopping off place before immigrating to South America. All of this collaboration of Nazis with the Arabs in their common fight against the Jews and the cancer of the aggressive Arab anti-Semitism that has grown since WWII is documented by Roy H. Schoeman, *Salvation is From the Jews,* San Francisco: Ignatius Press, 2003, pp. 254-302.

Britain's Final Effort to Thwart Jewish Immigration and a Jewish Homeland After WWII—The Precipitous Decline of Great Britain

In 1945 the liberal Labor Party won the elections in Britain in a surprise landslide. Sir Winston Churchill was replaced as Prime Minister by Clement Atlee. The new government had promised the Jews that they would be treated differently and that promises would be kept. The new Secretary of State for Foreign and Commonwealth Nations, however, was Ernst

Bevin, who was said to hate Jews as much as Hitler. During the war and after WWII, 1946 to 1948, before Britain gave up the Mandate, the British administration showed so little consideration for the Jews in Europe and Palestine it would have made Hitler proud.

In spite of the White Paper of 1939, which was official British Government policy, Jews continued to filter into the land violating that policy. More than 60,000 German Jews had fled from Hitler and come to Palestine before 1939 bringing with them skills as scientists and engineers of every kind. Many more thousands of Jews, however, would have immigrated to Palestine from Europe and would have been saved from obliteration in the crematoriums of the holocaust—Hitler's Final Solution to the Jewish problem. The White Paper had laid down the rules, but even these were not kept by the British officials. The White Paper was supposed to allow 75,000 immigrants over a period of five years, which would cease completely in 1944. Official printed Certificates were issued for these 75,000 souls, but by the end of WWII in 1945 there were 36,000 of these Certificates that had never been used even though there had been many requests that they be released.

This whole scenario of the British treatment of the Jews has its conclusion in the fulfillment of God's words to Abraham at the time of his calling in Genesis 12:3:

> I will bless those who bless you; and whosoever curses you I will curse. And all peoples on earth will be blessed through you.

For over 200 years leaders in Britain supported what was called "the Restoration," referring to the return of the Jews to their Promised Land, which culminated in the Balfour Declaration in 1917. During these years Britain became the most far-flung empire in the history of the earth controlling one third of the world. As a nation she was blessed beyond measure. It was said that "Britannia rules the waves" and "The sun never sets on the British empire." She was just a little island nation, but had been blessed by God to become one of the major powers in the world—not just in the 20th century, but also in all of human history. It was a kind of miracle.

Then the attitude toward the Jews began to change as the official national self-interest of the British government caused a tilt toward the Arab world. They gradually reneged on their promise to the Jews, allowing thousands who could have been saved by immigrating to Palestine to die in the Holocaust. By the time the British were forced to leave their Mandate in Palestine, they had been pummeled by Hitler in WWII, parts of London were in ruins, hundreds of thousands of British soldiers were dead, and Britain had lost its entire empire. Britain became a second rate power, a mere shadow of its glorious past. The glory of Britain was only a memory. It has been said that the most serious retribution inflicted on the British was the transformation of the British Lion into a cowardly, ungrateful beast. A once noble nation had degenerated into the spiritual heirs of Hitler.

Today the Muslims whom the British supported are boasting that they will take over Britain. There are more mosques than churches in London, which some are calling Londonistan. Gradually whole cities are being taken over by Muslim majorities with the threat of Islamic terrorism hanging over the nation. Most recently two huge car bombs were found in London's Haymarket and Picadilly Squares, which if they had exploded would have killed hundreds of people. It was a plot of 8 or 10 Muslim medical doctors. The mantra was "Those who cure you will kill you." This was just the latest in a string of terror events promised in the future by militant Muslims in Britain.

Today the irreligious Brits regard evangelical Christians with disdain considering them "insane." Prince Charles looks forward to becoming King someday when he will declare himself to be "The Defender of the Faiths" including

Islam. Near where the largest evangelical church in England, the 12,000 member Kingsway International Christian Center, is going to be torn down to make way for the Olympic stadium, Muslims have been granted permission to build the largest mosque in Europe on an 18 acre plot 500 feet from the Olympic centerpiece. The Mosque complex called the London Markaz is supposed to hold 70,000 people. This is certainly symbolic of what is going on in Britain today. The Markaz will dwarf St. Paul's Cathedral and every other major Christian center in the country. God is surely going to use Islam to bring a final judgment on the British nation.

Chapter 5

THE ORIGIN OF THE STATE OF ISRAEL

After Hitler's holocaust there was tremendous pressure on Jews, who still were unwelcome in Europe, to immigrate to Palestine. President Truman called on the British to admit 100,000 Jewish refugees from war torn Europe, but they refused. Britain had limited official immigration into the British mandate between 1939 and 1944 to only 15,000 Jews per year, and they hadn't even allowed that many. After this time all Jewish immigration was forbidden. Refusing to accept this limitation, the Zionists responded by smuggling in 113,000 more of their people. One event in this saga was celebrated in the famous book and movie *The Exodus*.

The Saga of the Exodus
The Exodus was the name of a large wooden ship that was transporting 4515 Jews to Palestine from southern France. Nearing the Palestinian coastline in July 1947, the ship was intercepted by 7 British warships—a cruiser and 6 destroyers. At 2 A.M. the Cruiser Ajax turned on a searchlight and commanded the Exodus, which was 20 miles out in the Mediterranean, to stop, warning them that they were in territorial waters, which was not true. When the Exodus ignored the warning, the refugee ship was rammed on its sides by two of the destroyers opening gaping holes in its wooden structure. If the pumps had not been adequate, the Exodus would have sunk with a great loss of life.

British sailors then boarded the ship, took over the wheelhouse, and slowly proceeded to Haifa. Here the Jews were forced to debark and immediately climb aboard three smaller British ships. Ernst Bevin, the British Foreign

Secretary, was determined to make an example of these violators of British immigration policy and ordered the British ships to return the refugees to France. When they got to France, the Jews went on strike and would not leave the ships. For 24 days the French supplied them with provisions. Finally Bevin ordered the ships to Hamburg in Germany where most of these Jews, who were survivors of the holocaust, had been interned in concentration camps. The British proved themselves to be little better than the Nazis as these 4515 Jews were forced back to detention camps like those from which they had been rescued a couple of years earlier.

There were two positive results that issued from this human disaster. First, the entire world witnessed the cruelty of the British and called for an end to their Mandate in Palestine.

Secondly, on the wharf watching the Jews, most of whom were being herded off the Exodus on to three smaller British ships loudly wailing and crying bitter tears, were representatives from UNSCOP, the United Nations Special Committee on Palestine. The British had thrown the whole problem of Palestine into the lap of the United Nations, and the UN had formed this commission to study the problem.

Jews Resist the British with Force and the UN Partition Plan

In spite of years of Arab attacks on the Jews since 1920, the British had disarmed the Jews leaving them defenseless. The Jews therefore smuggled into Palestine all kinds of small arms to defend themselves. Most of their supply of arms came through Czechoslovakia. Later this even included a few badly needed Russian MIG fighters. The Jews also ingeniously set up small factories in kibbutzim that were disguised as bakeries or laundries on the surface, but which manufactured ammunition underground. If the Jews responsible had been caught, they would have been hanged by the British.

Incidentally, at this time no arms came from America, which had imposed an arms embargo on the Middle East so that no American weapons would be responsible for killing either Jews or Arabs.

The extremist Irgun, in reaction against the stubborn resistance of the British to Jewish interests, went on the offensive and bombed the British headquarters at the King David Hotel on July 22, 1946. The Irgun claimed that they had called the hotel and warned its occupants who ignored the warning. This terrible attack killed 80 British officers and administrators and wounded 70. A total of 91 people died. From then on every arrest and execution of a Jewish leader by the British was avenged by executing a worse fate on some more important British officer. Under this pressure of Jewish terrorism, coupled with Arab aggression and a negative world opinion, Britain washed its hands of the whole mess, and in 1947 dropped the problem into the lap of the United Nations.

We have seen that members of the United Nations Study Commission on Palestine were in Jerusalem just when the Exodus had arrived deliberating as to what should be done. The seriousness of the situation had been dramatically demonstrated to some of these members of UNSCOP on the wharf at Haifa. They recommended a solution similar to that which had been suggested in 1938 by the British Peel Commission. Discontinue the Mandate, and settle the problem by dividing west Palestine between the Jews and the Arabs. So they drew up a Plan of Partition.

The General Assembly of the UN, in a very heated, divisive, tense atmosphere, took up the recommendation of UNSCOP and with Resolution 181 declared the division of west Palestine between Arabs and Jews on November 29, 1947. The vote was 33 to 13. Eleven of the "no" votes were cast by Muslim nations. Ten nations abstained. The Jews accepted the decision with great rejoicing, but the Arabs emphatically rejected it.

So the Arabs could have had a Palestinian state much earlier in west Palestine, but again they were adamantly opposed to an independent nation of Israel coming to exist on what they considered all their land. East Palestine called Transjordan had already been granted to them in 1922 by partition, but land from this new partition in west Palestine plus the other 77% of Greater Palestine east of the Jordan River was not enough. The Muslims wanted everything.

There really had been no concept of a Palestinian state among most of the Arabs, because a Palestinian state had never ever existed. Palestine had been considered from Roman times to be a part of Syria, and what was now Israel had never been governed by Palestinian Arabs but by the Ottoman Empire and later by Syria, Jordan, and Egypt. Arabs really had no consciousness of being Palestinians because they considered Palestine as Syro-Palestine, and so, if anything, they had regarded themselves as Syrians. It was the Jews who were originally called by the name Palestinians. The Jews were granted "Palestinian citizenship" in the British Mandate. Those Jews who fought for the British in WWII were known as the Palestinian Brigade. Arabs who fought with the British when offered the shoulder patch identifying them as Palestinians refused it saying, "We are not Palestinians, we are Arabs."

The British Mandate came to an end less than six months after the United Nations decision to partition the land. The last British officer departed from Jerusalem for Haifa at 8:00 A.M. on May 14, 1948, and the last British flag was lowered from over the city a few hours later. The Jewish Agency led by David Ben Gurion met immediately in Tel Aviv at 4:00 P.M. and declared the existence of the independent State of Israel on that same day. The new state had a population of just over 640,000 Jews plus about 100,000 Arabs, but Israel's army was miniscule—only about 20,000 soldiers. The total Arab population in Palestine was about 1.2 million or twice the Jewish population, because thousands of Arabs had immigrated to Palestine unimpeded during the British mandate from nations all around.

Arab armies from five neighboring nations invaded Israel immediately. Only hours old the new little nation was already at war. General Montgomery had studied the logistics a year before and concluded that the Jews could only hold out against the Arabs for about three weeks. Everyone, however, had underestimated the Jews, and both Arabs and Jews had underestimated each other. There was a fierce nationalism, which drove both sides, but Arabs were only fighting for their pride and a religious principle. Jews were fighting for their very existence. Arabs could escape to other countries, but the Jews had nowhere to go.

Five major Arab/Israeli wars were fought over a period of 35 years beginning in May 1948. By winning all of these wars the Jews tripled the size of their original territory, took over the dominion of hundreds of thousands of Palestinians, and established new borders, which had to be defended. Each war ended with a truce, but a truly permanent peace with all the Arab states has not been achieved to this day. Arabs have never accepted their defeats or the existence of the State of Israel, and look forward to the day when they will be able to return again with overwhelming deadly force to kill all the Jews or, as they say, drive them into the Mediterranean Sea.

Arab and Jewish Claims to Palestine

Arabs had lived amicably side-by-side with Jews for genera-tions, but it was a new world. The idea of a Jewish state exist-ing on land that Arabs had conquered and made their own since A.D. 638 was a sacrilege. A Muslim principle states that all land once conquered by Islam can never be given up. Islamic law demands that it will always and forever be considered the property of Islam. The land of Palestine is considered a per-manent part of the Dar al Islam—the House of Islam.

The Jews, on the other hand, have a claim going back to as early as 1200 B.C. According to their traditional history recorded in their sacred writings from 1000 to 2000 years earlier than the founding of Islam, the Israelites following God's command conquered the Promised Land under the leadership of Moses' successor Joshua. Several hundred years earlier God had promised Abraham this land of Canaan now called Palestine. It actually included land, which is today part of Iraq, Syria, Lebanon, Jordan, and Egypt. The covenant was then passed on through Isaac to Jacob (Israel) and his sons. This was the reason that after a 400-year absence the chil-dren of Israel returned from Egypt to this particular land of their ancestors. There is no mention in the ancient text of the Bible that Hagar or Ishmael, who had been banished to the Sinai desert, were to inherit anything.

In God's command to Israel to possess the land recorded in Deuteronomy 1:7-8, we get a picture of the extent of the territory promised to Abraham, Isaac, and Jacob.

> *Break camp and advance into the hill country of the Amorites; go to all the neighboring peoples in the Arabah, in the mountains, in the western foothills, in the Negev, and along the coast, to the land of the Canaanites, and to Lebanon, as far as the great river, the Euphrates. See I have given you this land. Go in and take possession of the land that the LORD swore He would give to your fathers—to Abraham, Isaac and Jacob—and to their descendants after them.*

Notice that the extent of this inheritance seems to include much of Lebanon and part of Syria and even Iraq to the Euphrates River. The southeastern boundary is the "river of Egypt," which was the waterway that became the Suez Canal. So at least part of the Sinai was part of the Promised

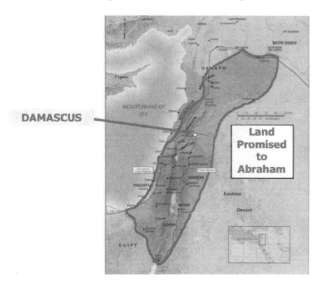

Land. The Israeli flag has two horizontal blue bars separated by a Star of David. The bars represent the two rivers—the Euphrates in the north and the river of Egypt to the south. Arabs who know the symbolism hate this flag

Abraham had actually purchased some land that included a cave called Machpelah in Mamre near modern Hebron from Ephron the Hittite. Here Abraham, Sarah, Isaac, and Jacob were buried (Genesis 23 and 25:1-11).

King David also bought land from Araunah the Jebusite that underlay the Temple Mount and some of the Old City of Jerusalem (I Chronicles 21-22). In both instances the Hittites and Jebusites wanted to donate the land, but Abraham and David both refused to accept the land as gifts. The Bible specifically emphasizes that the inhabitants or owners received appropriate payments for these parcels of land. This established a concrete historical basis for supporting an ancestral ownership handed down to succeeding generations of Jews.

King Solomon ruled an area that encompassed most of the land that God had told Joshua to occupy. It includes

Solomon's Kingdom c. 990 BC

Modern Day Israel 1999

DAMASCUS

much of east Palestine and is much larger than the land Israel occupies today.

Palestinian Arabs claim today that since the Israelites took the land from some of their ancestors, the Canaanites, Muslims were simply trying to recover what was originally theirs. There is absolutely no evidence at all, however, that the modern day Palestinian Arabs are descendants of the Canaanites or of any of the other non-Semitic nations of Moses' and Joshua's era. Canaanites were Hamites. Palestinians are primarily Semitic Arabs whose ancestors came from the Arabian Desert to conquer the lands of the Middle East in the 7th century A.D. They include the descendants of the Ishmaelites, the Midianites, the Edomites, and probably the Ammonites, Moabites, and other western Semitic peoples.

Also the vast majority of the Arabs in Palestine today are newcomers from neighboring Arab states, whose families have been in the land less than 100 years. Never in history has there ever been an independent Arab Palestinian nation nor was there ever any ancient Palestinian people as such who are the ancestors of today's Palestinian Arabs. Before 1900 according to a famous visitor Mark Twain, Palestine was a barren, almost deserted land. After the Jewish dispersion at the time of the Roman Empire, Palestine was governed by the Romans, the Byzantine Empire, the Parthians, Arabs from Arabia, the Crusaders, the Ottoman Empire, and following World War I by the British Mandate, the Jews, Syrians, Egyptians and Jordanians. That a Palestinian nation of Palestine ever existed is revisionist history and only a convenient myth, or more appropriately, we should call it a convenient falsehood.

Most of the Palestinian families today are descended from immigrants to the land as recent as the Jews. As many as 35,000 Arabs came into Palestine each year during the British Mandate to participate in the new prosperity and improved standard of living which had been provided by the

Jews due to their industrious reclamation of the land.

The Palestinians in reality have less of an official claim to the land than do the Jews. The Jews purchased hundreds of thousands of acres and with an inspired labor created a successful and prosperous society. Most of the Arabs came from neighboring lands for jobs, for greater liberty, and to share in the growing prosperity. They still supply most of Israel's unskilled labor, and without these jobs they are unemployed. Both modern Jews and Arabs were populating the area at the same time. To say therefore that the Jews displaced Arabs, who were the ancient settlers of the land, is another Palestinian myth.

Muhammad's strong stand against the Jews had included the promise that Muslims would obliterate them before the end of the age. His words are recorded in the Hadith: *"The last hour will not come before the Muslims fight the Jews, and the Muslims kill them."* This is the time Jews will hide behind trees, and the cry will be *"Oh Muslim, Oh servant of Allah, here is a Jew hiding behind me. Come here and kill him."* Arab antagonism to Israel is built into their religious teaching and historical heritage. An ancient maxim states that Ishmael will never give up trying to take Isaac's inheritance.

Documenting Islam's Hatred of the Jews

A former head of the Al-Azhar University Fatwa Committee responded in March 2004 to a question in an *IslamOnline.com* chat room, "What, according to the Qur'an, are the Jews' main characteristics and qualities?" Sheikh 'Atiyyah Saqr listed the following according to *MEMRI* (The Middle East Media Research Institute):

> *Fabricating, listening to lies, disputing and quarreling, hiding the truth and supporting deception, rebelling against the prophets and rejecting their guidance, hypocrisy, wishing evil on people, feeling pain at others' happiness and feeling happiness at others' afflictions, rudeness and vulgarity, murder*

of innocents, mercilessness and heartlessness, breaking promises, cowardice and miserliness.

He added:

We would like to note that these are but some of the most famous traits of the Jews as described in the Qur'an. They have revolted against the divine ordinances, distorted what has been revealed to them and invented new teachings, which, they claimed, were much better than what has been recorded in the Torah. . All this gives us glad tidings of the coming victory of Muslims over the Jews, as soon as Muslims cling to strong faith and belief in Allah and adopt modern means of technology.

There seems to be no compromise or solution to this point of view, which is deeply ingrained in many Muslims from the time they are children. In 1948 the Arabs verbalized their deep hatred for the Jews. The following statements of Arab leaders confirm an almost utter hopelessness for the future:

The entire Jewish population in Palestine must be destroyed or be driven into the sea. Allah has bestowed upon us the rare privilege of finishing what Hitler only began. Let the Jihad begin. Murder the Jews. Murder them all.
—Hajj Amen el Hussein, Grand Mufti of Jerusalem, Head of Palestinian Arab resistance—1948

The Arab nations should sacrifice up to ten million of their fifty million people, if necessary, to wipe out Israel. Israel to the Arab world is like a cancer to the human body. And the only way of remedy is to uproot it.
—King Ibn Saud of Saudi Arabia

The power struggle between Israel and the Arabs is a long-term historical trial. Victory or defeat are for us questions of

existence or annihilation, the outcome of an irreconcilable hatred.
                              —Al Riyadh Saud

This will be a war of extermination and a momentous massacre which will be spoken of like the Mongolian massacres and the Crusades. No Jew will be left alive.
            —Azzam Pasha, Secretary General of the Arab League

The Jews in Palestine must be exterminated. There can be no other option for those of us who revere the name of Allah. There will be no Dhimma. There will only be Jihad.
                              —King Farouk of Egypt

The Jews are destined to be persecuted, humiliated, and tortured forever, and it is a Muslim duty to see to it that they reap their due. No petty arguments must be allowed to divide us. Where Hitler failed we must succeed.
            —Sheikh Tamimi— recent Mufti of Jerusalem

We shall never call for nor accept peace. We shall only accept war. We have resolved to drench this land with Israel's blood, to oust the Jews as aggressors, and to throw them all into the sea.
            —Hafez al-Assad, former dictator of Syria

All Arab leaders in the Middle East were of one mind, *"There can be no compromise until every Jew is dead and gone."*

In doing research for his book *Salvation is of the Jews*, Roy Schoeman discovered that the link between the Nazis and the Arabs in their common hatred and fight against the Jews was a firm and lasting bond. Hitler's *Mein Kampf*, which means "My Struggle" and is translated *My Jihad* in Arabic, is still a best seller in Arab lands and especially in Palestine. He writes:

The anti-Semitic slanders that permeate much of the press in the Arab world are often indistinguishable from those of the Third Reich. Persistent themes that had been previously used by the Nazis include the intrinsic inferiority of the Jews as a race, the degenerate nature of the Jews as a source of moral corruption and sexual degeneracy, the 'blood libel' that the blood of non-Jewish children is a necessary ingredient in Passover matzos, that there is a worldwide Jewish conspiracy to take over the world, that the wars of the world are started by Jews for profit, and that the Jews are behind any and all acts of mass violence." This includes the 2001 World Trade Center attack (Schoeman, p. 271).

Here are some more recent statements by Muslim clerics and leaders:

The Arab people declare: We shall not be satisfied except by the final obliteration of Israel.
—Egyptian foreign minister Muhammad Salah al-Din

We demand vengeance and vengeance is Israel's death.
            —President of Egypt Gamal Abdel Nasser

Have no mercy on the Jews. Kill them and those Americans who established Israel here in the beating heart of the Arab world.
—Statement in a sermon on 10/14/00 at the Al Nahyan mosque in Gaza

The Jews must be butchered and killed. Have no mercy. No matter where they are kill them and those Americans who are like them.
—Dr. Ahmad Abu-Halabia from the Islamic University of Gaza, January 15, 2000

Allah willing, Israel will be erased. The United States will be erased. Britain will be erased. Blessings to whoever waged

Jihad for the sake of Allah. Blessings to whoever put a belt of explosives on his body or his son's and plunged into the midst of the Jews.
—Sheikh Ibrahim Mahdi on Palestinian TV, June 2001

Our objective is simply the liberation of the Palestinian soil and the establishment of a Palestinian state over every part of it. Thus, the Jews must be removed and Israel must be annihilated. We can accept nothing less.
—Yasser Arafat, Late Chairman of the PLO

The struggle with the Zionist enemy is not a struggle about Israel's borders, but about Israel's existence.
—A deputy of Arafat in 1994 after the Oslo Accords

A prayer was offered in the Grand Mosque in Mecca in April 2003 by chief cleric Sheikh Abdul Rahman al-Sudais in which he asked Allah "to terminate the Jews." He called them, *"the scum of humanity, the rats of the world, prophet killers, pigs and monkeys. . . evil, a continuum of deceit, tyrannical and treacherous."* This same cleric participated in Islamic conferences in Kissimmee, Florida and Ottawa and Toronto, Canada in January 2004:

Those young people who explode themselves to kill the Jews were not committing suicide but jihad. They are mujaheddin (holy warriors) *because there is no way to struggle and fight the Jews except that way. . Allah bless those martyrs.*
—Egyptian cleric Sheikh Wagdy Ghunaim at a Muslim Arab Youth Association conference in Ontario, California on December 29, 1997. He was also a speaker at the recent "Islamic for Humanity" conference in Kissimmee, Florida, January 2004.

Jews are accused of being responsible for almost all the calamities, injustices and immoralities in the world including

AIDS in Africa, Satan worship, the undermining of values and basic principles, all wars, corruption, and destruction, disrespect of religion, the undermining of monotheism and the desecration of the dead.

The Syrian author Dr. Salah Khalidi wrote in his book *The Jewish Mentality Based on the Qur'an* (Damascus, 1987):

> *Jews are liars, corrupt, jealous, crafty, treacherous, stupid, despicable, cowardly, and low life. They violate agreements and contracts and cause all evil in the world. . The Jews are a mortal danger threatening the world, a lethal plague that dismantles and destroys it. They are a hateful Satan. The Jewish message is hatred and jealousy, lies and deception, vilifications, duplicity, etc.*

The most heinous, unbelievable state of affairs of all is that the above teachings and hatreds expressed toward the Jews and Israel are being taught to little children 3 to 7 years of age in their homes and in school throughout the Muslim world, especially in Arab Palestine and by the closest neighbors of Israel. Because America is believed to be responsible for the existence of the nation of Israel and Jews being in the Middle East, the same kind of hatred is directed against this nation. Therefore, as the Ayatollah Khomeini proclaimed, Satan's home is in America on this Earth and both Israel and America must be destroyed. The fact that America had nothing to do with the founding of the nation of Israel is irrelevant because today America is Israel's most important ally.

Long standing friendships and amicable relations between Arabs and Jews inevitably had to come to an end. The Mufti of Jerusalem was adamant that Jews were interlopers, usurpers, and occupiers in Palestine and must be eliminated as Muhammad had taught. After the first major Arab terrorist action against the Jews in 1929 and again in 1936, Arab-Jewish relations were never the same. Hitler and the Second World War added to the hatreds and mistrust.

Arab leaders had forced the division and provoked the Jews to defend themselves. The defensive arm of Israel in these struggles was the Haganah. It became known as the IDF or the Israeli Defense Force and is on the job today.

When the United Nations voted to partition Palestine, giving the Jews perhaps only about 8,000 out of the 45,000 square miles of territory, which had originally been promised by the League of Nations in 1922, conflict was continuous. The armies of five Arab states, who had been preparing for war, attacked Israel immediately after the evacuation of the British and the declaration of an independent state of Israel on May 14, 1948. Brief descriptions of this invasion and the other four wars between Israel and the Arab states are given in the next chapter.

Israel's Declaration of Independence and Israel's Arabs
The Declaration of Independence for Israel, drawn up principally by David Ben Gurion, who was to become Israel's first Prime Minister, sought to extend a hand of friendship to the Arabs in their midst. The Preamble reminded them that the Jewish presence in the land had been *"bringing the blessings of progress to all the country's inhabitants."*

The Declaration promised that the development of the country would be for the *"benefit of all its inhabitants."* *"Freedom, justice, and peace, as envisaged by the prophets of Israel,"* would be its foundation. There would be *"Complete equality of social and political rights to all its inhabitants, irrespective of religion, race or sex."* Freedom of religion, conscience, education, and choice of language and culture would be guaranteed.

Then the declaration appealed to the Palestinian Arabs to *"preserve peace and participate in the up-building of the State on the basis of full and equal citizenship"* which included *"representation in all its provisional and permanent institutions."* This allowed the Arabs living in Israel the right to vote and to be represented in the Knesset, to hold office and potentially to share in all areas of civil life. More freedom was offered to Arabs in the new State of Israel than they experienced in any Muslim nation. To this day Israel is the only really free democracy in the Middle East

Finally the Declaration reached out a hand to the Arab neighbors of the new state promising *"peace and good neighborliness."* The new State of Israel promised to do its share in the common effort for the advancement of the entire Middle East. There were 38 signatories to this offer of friendship to the Arabs both inside and outside of Israel. The contrast between the attitude of the Muslim nations and the Jews could not have been greater.

Arabs, or Palestinians, a name they have finally accepted, living within the boundaries of the nation of Israel do have the right to participate in full citizenship—sharing in the economic, educational, and social well-being of the nation. As we have noted the term Palestinian was always used for the Jews living in the land since Arabs always considered the land to be Syro-Palestine and themselves as Syrians or just Arabs. After the 1967 Six Day War and the formation of the PLO, however, Arabs have usurped the term Palestinian as applying exclusively to themselves. This ties in with their claim that all of Palestine really belongs to them. A nation of Palestine never existed in history, however, nor was there ever a nationality called Palestinian until the 20th century. Both are pseudo designations.

Some Concluding Observations

1. Arabs in 1947 had totally rejected the idea of coexistence with a Jewish state. This attitude has never changed and Arabs and Jews live separate lives in Israel. Arabs are estranged from Jewish public culture. They have never wanted to be identified in any way as Jews. They have their own language although most are bilingual in both Arabic and Hebrew. They shop in different stores, have different schools and do very little socializing together. It

is a self-imposed apartheid. They will never consider themselves a part of the nation of Israel or Israelis.

2. As a result most Israeli Jews are suspicious of Israeli Arabs as a potential "fifth column" in their midst. This has been particularly true since Israeli Arabs took the side of Saddam Hussein against Israel in the Gulf War and the side of the PLO and the Palestinians in the Intifada of 2000.

3. One of the most outspoken opponents of the Jews among the Israeli Arabs has been Azmi Bishara, a Knesset member and head of the Arab political party Balad, which has at this time only 3 seats in the Israeli legislature. He has called for a completely secular, democratic but non-Jewish state. The argument is that in order to be truly democratic as Israel claims there must be a strict separation of church and state, and Israel must reject its Jewishness. This is exactly the opposite from the teaching of Islam. The separation of church and state is considered a pagan, secular doctrine and is in violation of Islamic law. Would the Arabs reject their Arabness? Besides, although the sensibilities of orthodox Jews in Israel must be acknowledged and even catered to, there is a fixed separation of church and state in Israel already. What Bishara probably meant was a separation of the state from Jewish culture and tradition, which would hardly be possible.

Israelis reply that Egypt, Jordan, Syria, Iraq, Saudi Arabia and a new Palestinian state, if it should exist, are all Arab states. Why should there not be one Jewish state? In recent plans to consider a Palestinian state, furthermore, Arabs have committed themselves to prohibit any Jews from living in their land in spite of the fact that Arabs live freely in Israel. This includes the territory of Gaza from which 9,500 Jews were recently evacuated giving all this land to the Palestinians as a gesture of good will. There is overwhelming proof of the fact that Arabs never have had any intention of permitting a Jewish state to exist if they can help it.

4. Some liberal Israelis would like to completely integrate the Arabs into Israeli society. This ideal, however, would have to have the concurrence of the Arabs, would it not? Right now this is completely unrealistic—a fanciful dream. Israel's Arabs, in fact, have come to deplore being part of a Jewish nation, but it is not so much the religious difference as it is a cultural contrast that offends them.

5. Most Israelis are willing to give Arabs complete civil equality including the sharing of economic wealth and tax revenues for Arab communities, but this still does not satisfy the Arab prejudice, which cannot accept at all, or ever, the existence of a nation of Israel in the land of Palestine.

6. In spite of differences and seemingly insoluble problems, the Arabs of Israel are far and away more free and prosperous as a whole than in any other nation in the Middle East. It is unlikely, however, that even the gift of freedom will ever solve the problem of the divide that separates these two people, religions, and cultures. (See Peter Berkowitz, "Israel's House Divided—Israeli Jews, Israeli Arabs, and Identity Politics," *The Weekly Standard*, April 12-19, 2004, pp. 32-35.)

End The Unjust Jewish Occupation of Arab Land!

A Satire

The above map satirizes the selfishness and unreality of the Arab's claim to Israel, which is only a small sliver of land of just over 10,000 square miles in a sea of Muslim nations whose lands encompass over 3,000,000 square miles. Israel is smaller than the State of New Jersey. Picture all the other 49 states as enemies of New Jersey seeking to take over all their land and to kill their people. For Israel to give up land for peace would be like the all the States asking New Jersey to give up half of the state's territory to New York, Pennsylvania, and Delaware in order to remain alive in this US land mass of 3 million square miles that comprises 49 surrounding enemy States.

Chapter 6

THE FIVE ARAB/ISRAELI WARS
1948-1982

Arabs vs. Jews Before the Formation of the State of Israel
Conflict between Jews and Arabs had boiled up many times in Palestine for almost 30 years before the fledgling State of Israel was invaded by the five Arab nations after Israel's Declaration of Independence on May 14, 1948. There had been riots and killings in 1920-21, 1929 and especially in 1936-39 when Hajj Amin al Husseini, the Mufti of Jerusalem, led widespread insurrections against Jewish settlements.

None of these Arab uprisings, however, equaled the ferocity of Arab outrage, which followed the United Nations partition of Palestine between the Arabs and the Jews beginning in November 1947. Some of the bloodiest encounters ever seen in the world were provoked against the Jews by the Arabs who were motivated by a vehement hatred against any thought of legitimizing a Jewish presence in what they considered their land and theirs alone.

The British who had been given a mandate to administer Palestine following the break up of the Ottoman Empire following World War I, had been under terrible pressure for years trying to placate the Arabs by resisting the Jews. The Mandate meant that they were responsible to keep the peace, enforce order, and administer justice. On all three counts the British failed miserably. Dependent on Arab oil and responsible for administering other Muslim nations, they were careful not to offend Arabs. As we have seen they virtually forsook their promise expressed in the Balfour Declaration from the very outset of the Mandate.

Britain finally turned the insoluble problem over to the

113

United Nations. The General Assembly voted to partition the land on November 10, 1947. The UN suggested three parcels: (1) The new Jewish state would be 60% Jewish and 40% Arab; (2) The new Arab state would include only 10,000 Jewish residents; (3) Jerusalem would be administered by the United Nations as an international city with 100,000 Jews and 100,000 Arab residents. The Jews accepted the plan because they thought that it was the best they could do. Arab leadership, however, violently objected and rejected the United Nations proposal. The British made plans to withdraw from Palestine in May 1948. Then from November 1947 to May 1948, the strife between Jews and Arabs was the most vicious and bloody of any internecine conflict before or since in Palestine, or almost anywhere else in the world for that matter.

It all began when the Arab High Commission called a three-day general strike against partition, and Arab mobs attacked Jews all across the country. Within the first 12 days 80 Jews were killed and during the entire time of the rebellion a total of 769 Jews lost their lives. Buses and even ambulances were ambushed. A mob of 200 Arab youths terrorized a commercial center in Jerusalem looting and burning Jewish businesses. The hellish nightmare that unfolded then continued to erupt from time to time in terrorist events to this very day.

The Jewish Haganah army had been formed as a defensive force. One of its most famous youth divisions was the Palmach. A squadron of this group was totally wiped out by the Arabs as they patrolled the Negev on December 10, 1947.

The British stood back and simply watched as Arabs drove three stolen British vehicles into Ben Yehuda Street, a commercial neighborhood in Jerusalem, and blew them up. Fifty-two Jews were killed as they slept.

The British also stood by as Arabs over a period of for four hours massacred 77 doctors, nurses, and patients in busses on their way up the Mt. Scopus road to the Hadassah hospital. These medical personnel had served both Arabs and Jews in treating diseases, injuries and saving lives for many years. This made no difference to their Arab attackers who just wanted to kill Jews, any Jews. To their eternal shame, the British refused to stop the carnage.

The Jews had formed a provisional government. The Council was meeting at the Jewish Agency Building when a car of a US Consul General drove up. The Arab driver on a suicide mission detonated a bomb which blew up the car and 13 people were killed—twelve Jewish leaders and one child.

The British were notoriously lax in maintaining either order or equal justice for the entire duration of their Mandate. Throughout the whole period of their administration they obviously favored the Arabs over the Jews. These commands came from the top. We have noted that Ernst Bevin, who after 1945 was head of the Foreign Office, which administered the Mandate, was no less anti-Semitic than Hitler himself. This antagonism showed itself many times during the period of British jurisdiction, but it is no better illustrated than in the British refusal to keep order or defend Jewish lives during this period just before they gave up the Mandate and left Palestine.

The Jews Go On the Offensive: Deir Yassin

In anticipation of the war to come, a group of Iraqi fighters in March of 1948 had infiltrated the area and taken up a position in a village above and near the vital road, which was the supply route between Tel Aviv and Jerusalem. This was the only route that could be taken by convoys bringing supplies to the Jews of West Jerusalem who were sometimes on the verge of starvation. More than 100,000 Jews were in danger of being besieged there by the Jordanian Arab Legion. The offensive arm of Jewish armed forces called the Irgun took charge of the problem on their own.

The village was Deir Yassin. Its name was to become a watchword and a chant in the months to come. Arabs claimed that Jews had committed a massacre there. The Irgun said that they had warned the civilian population with a loudspeakers on a truck that they were coming, and that people should flee. The Jews had left them three escape routes out of the village. The Irgun were after the foreign Iraqi troops that had taken over the town to use it as an arms depot and a site for attacking the convoys on the Tel Aviv/Jerusalem road.

On April 9, 1948 the fierce Stern Gang of the Irgun invaded the village. They found the Iraqi militants dressed in women's clothing, hiding their weapons under their robes, and mingling with women and children. Using this sub-terfuge the Iraqis killed or wounded 40% of the Jewish forces. The battle that ensued cost the lives of 107 Arabs—all the Iraqis and over 30 women and children who had not been allowed to leave. It wasn't the first or last time that Arab fighters would hide behind the skirts of civilians using them as human shields.

Arabs called Deir Yassin a massacre and greatly exagger-ated the numbers of dead not only to put the Jews in a bad light but also to encourage the Arab armies to hasten their attack and to wreak revenge on the Jews when they invaded Israel.

False reports of rape were issued on the Voice of Palestine radio in East Jerusalem. They later admitted that they had broadcast this propaganda to urge the surrounding nations to speed up their attack on the Jews. But the broadcasts struck fear into the hearts and minds of the Arab population in Palestine. The lying report of rape and a massacre caused resi-dent Arabs to flee their homes. The Arab armies actually encouraged their flight, so that civilians would not interfere with the invasion. In fact, according to Yasser Arafat himself, the Egyptians were able to herd thousands of Palestinian Arabs into refugee camps in the Gaza Strip in order to clear the way for their armies. This invasion of Deir Yassin became a rallying cry for Arab militants and an excuse to commit every kind of massacre and atrocity against the Jews. It proved to be a very successful campaign of bold and perverse lies perpetrated by the Arabs.

The Red Cross, however, had immediately been invited into Deir Yassin by the Irgun, and they found no evidence of a massacre. Later Beir Zayyit University in Ramallah did a study and found that there was no massacre. It was a military mission in which civilians unfortunately were part of the collateral damage. The Arabs had lied ferociously about the atrocities at Deir Yassin, which were supposed to have included mutilation of pregnant women, multiple rapes, and mass murders. To tell the truth Arabs were describing what they themselves would do and have done many times under similar circumstances.

A 1993 PBS documentary *The Fifty Years of War* interviewed survivors of Deir Yassin, and they testified that none of what Arabs claimed had happened, and that the Arab leadership had simply made it all up. Who is the "father of lies?" Arabs used the name of this village as a rallying cry to commit their own holocausts against the Jews, such as the massacre 4 days later of 77 unarmed and defenseless nurses, doctors, and patients on their way by bus up the Mt. Scopus road to the Hadassah hospital described above. This tragedy is almost never mentioned as the Arab retaliation to the Jews' attack on Deir Yassin.

The War for Independence—1948

Almost immediately following Israel's Declaration of Independence, five Arab armies attacked Israel. Their intention in the words of Azzam Pasha, Secretary-General of the Arab League, was to conduct *"a war of extermination and a momentous massacre, which will be spoken of like the Mongolian massacres and the Crusades."* He had said earlier, *"If the Zionists dare establish a state, the massacres we would unleash will dwarf anything which Genghis Khan and Hitler perpetrated."* It appears that the Arabs were accusing the Jews of doing what they intended to do; namely, massacre the citizenry.

To the amazement of the world the Arab armies, however, were all turned back by Jewish resistance, and a temporary truce was called by the United Nations. In that brief initial encounter of Jews against Arabs (May 14 to June 11, 1948) and throughout the months to come, a poorly equipped Israeli people miraculously defeated armies from Egypt, Jordan, Lebanon, Syria, and Iraq. Israel's first premier David Ben Gurion observed correctly that without any doubt the Jews' victory had to be one of the major military miracles of history.

On the very first day of Israel's independence the Egyptian air force bombed Tel Aviv. No one was injured, but most of Israel's air force, consisting of a few single engine Piper Cubs, Austers, and Fairchilds, without night flying capabilities, were severely damaged. Mechanics quickly cobbled them back together with spare and makeshift parts and got them airborne. Until Israel was able to procure some war surplus Messerschmitt fighters through Czechoslovakia over two weeks later, these little airplanes dutifully carried mail, dropped medical supplies, and flew reconnaissance missions. The pilots even carried small bombs, which they dropped by hand on some of the Arab armies causing amazement, fear, and confusion among their enemies.

The first foray against the new Jewish state was by an Iraqi force that attacked the village of Gesher on the west side of the Jordan River just below Galilee. As was true for most of the kibbutzniks, the settlers fought like tigers, and the Iraqis were unable to take the village even after a siege of seven days. This pattern, with very few exceptions, was repeated again and again in fights with the Lebanese, Syrians, and Iraqis in the north and against the Egyptians in the Negev in the south. The truth of the matter is that the Jews had nowhere to flee. They were fighting for their very existence.

Coming down from the Golan Heights with 30 armored

vehicles, a Syrian army overran two Jewish settlements on the east side of the Sea of Galilee, but were held up for two days by only 42 Jewish defenders in the small kibbutz of Zemach. The Syrians were headed for the kibbutz of Deganya, the gateway to northern Israel. By the time it took the Syrians to get by Zemach, Moshe Dayan was able to bring in two 65 mm cannon to face the Syrians. If Deganya at the southern tip of Galilee had fallen, the Syrian army could have cut Israel in half. The Syrians had tanks and flamethrowers. But when the two 65 mm guns, which have shells two and one-half inches in diameter, opened up on them, they fled. The siege of Gesher a few miles south was also relieved.

When you read the account of the War for Independence which lasted just a little more than a year with intermittent cease fires demanded by the United Nations, you are amazed by the Israelis hanging on by the skin of their teeth, facing one crisis after another. The Egyptian army tried to get by the Jewish settlements in the Negev south of Gaza. They wanted to march on up the coast and take Tel Aviv about 100 miles away. They were stopped time after time, first at the little kibbutz of Kfar Darom, which had only 30 defenders. The Israelis had only one antitank weapon with which they took out the first two tanks. The rest of the Egyptians fled.

The Egyptian army then by-passed Kfar Darom and went on to the next kibbutz called Nirim, where 40 defenders also held them off. Then the Egyptians elected to by-pass Nirim and attack Yad Mordechai, which was more strategic in that it guarded the road north. The Jewish kibbutzniks held out for five days against two infantry battalions, one armored battalion and one artillery regiment. They were finally forced to retreat, but not before they had given Tel Aviv time to strengthen its defenses and send reinforcements to hold the coastal road.

The Jewish village of Negba again proved the Jews to be fierce fighters. Out of 145 defenders, the Jews of Negba only lost eight killed and twelve wounded, whereas the attacking

Egyptian army lost six tanks, two Bren carriers, 100 killed and wounded and a Spitfire brought down by a machine-gunner. It was astonishing!

The Egyptians were turned back again and again and never did make it more than about half way to Tel Aviv where they were stopped at the Ashdod Bridge by the Messerschmitt fighters, which Israel had received in the nick of time on May 29. One Jewish fighter in evaluating what happened said that the Egyptians lacked a clear idea about the purpose for their fighting. The Jews, on the other hand, were fighting for their homes, their families, their future hopes and dreams, and the protection of all of their Jewish brothers to the north. When I look at the miraculous events of the War, however, I have to say that just as in the days of the Old Testament, it was the God of Israel. The victory was the Lord's. *"The horse is made ready for the day of battle, but victory rests with the Lord"* (Proverbs 21:31).

The Struggle For Jerusalem
In Jerusalem, however, the well-trained Arab Legions of Jordan led by the British commander Glubb Pasha and British officers, pounded the Old City of Jerusalem with thousands of artillery shells killing 1200 Jews and destroying 2,000 homes. Because of Jordan's overwhelming superiority in numbers and armament there was no hope, and the old rabbis of the Jewish quarter surrendered. All the able bodied Jewish men of the Old City were then taken to a prison camp in Amman, Jordan. This Jewish quarter of Jerusalem, which was the ancient site of Jewish worship and learning, and which included the most famous old synagogues in Palestine, was utterly destroyed by the Arab Legion. The most cherished Jewish house of worship was turned into a latrine for the Jordanian army. Then the tombs on the Mount of Olives, where hundreds of Jews had been buried through the years were desecrated, and the ancient tombstones were used to build another latrine for Arab soldiers.

Jews were also banished from the Western Wall, which was their place of prayer.

British officers leading the Jordanian Arab Legion must be held responsible for the outright massacre of 300 Jews in the settlements of Kfar Etzion south of Jerusalem. These were 4 villages on land that the Jews had purchased from the Arabs. The Legion led by its British officers also dropped artillery shells on the 100,000 Jewish civilians of West Jerusalem, shelling the university, the synagogues and even hospitals. It was an indiscriminate reign of terror.

The New City of Jerusalem with its 100,000 inhabitants miraculously held out against the Legion for weeks. The great fortress at Latrun, which was situated just above the Jerusalem to Tel Aviv highway, was held by the Arabs. From this vantage point the Arabs were preventing supplies and reinforcements from reaching the beleaguered inhabitants of the city. After two disastrous attempts to conquer the fortress, the Jews made a new route through the mountainous desert bypassing Latrun. They called it "the Burma Road" after the famous trail, which supplied Nationalist China during World War II. West Jerusalem was reinforced and remained Jewish, but the Old City including the Temple Mount with its Western Wall was taken by Jordan to be controlled by Arabs until after the 1967 war. Incidentally two of the soldiers in the Jewish army that tried to take the Latrun fortress later became prime ministers of Israel—Yitzhak Rabin and Ariel Sharon, who as a young platoon commander was almost killed in the battle.

Jews were banished and forbidden entrance to their holy sites for the next 19 years. The old Jewish quarter and the Temple Mount with its Western Wall were under Jordanian control. We cannot help but mention the overwhelming difference in attitude and behavior when Israel reconquered East Jerusalem 20 years later in 1967. Instead of retaliating for the destruction of their ancient synagogues by destroying the Al Aqsa Mosque and the Dome of the Rock on the

Temple Mount, they protected these Muslim sanctuaries from harm. They allowed the Arabs free access to them for their weekly services and prayer times and even gave the Arabs virtual control of the area. Although Israel claims ultimate sovereignty, the Temple Mount is supervised to this day by an Arab administration called a *waqf*, which is an inalienable religious endowment. Jews kept only the Western Wall as a place of prayer.

This showed from the beginning the significant contrast in the belief and value systems of Arabs and Jews. The Arabs, however, instead of admiring and learning from the restraint of the Jewish fighters, regarded it as inherent cowardice and weakness. They believed that Allah had intervened and prevented the Jews from desecrating their holy places. Arabs have taken every advantage of this freedom and have even banished Jews on occasion from visiting the Temple Mount, the ancient site of their Temples. Arabs from the top of the Mount have also attacked Jewish worshippers at the Western Wall during their prayers. No kind of civil response can ever be expected from militant Islam. "Give them an inch and they will take a mile" and even "bite the hand that feeds them." These maxims have been demonstrated over and over again.

The Arab Refugee Problem
The Jews were vastly outnumbered by these five Arab armies both in the size of their fighting force and their military armament. Palestine also had a large Arab population which in itself was a potential weapon aimed at the very heart of Israel. The Arab military leaders, however, had urged their Arab brothers to get out of the way, to flee their homes until Israel was conquered after which time they could return as victors for the spoils. Leaders of Syria, Iraq, and Glubb Pasha British Commander of the Arab Legion all urged Palestinian Arabs to get out of Israel temporarily so they would not get killed or hurt in the invasion. Tens of thousands of Arabs

heeded this advice and fled to the neighboring Arab countries much to the amazement of the British. This also caused much sincere concern in Jewish cities like Haifa and Tiberias. Many of the local Arabs had been friends with the Jews. In Haifa the mayor made every effort to get his Arab citizens to stay and continue their commercial contributions to his city. Those Arabs in Jewish territory who chose to remain eventually became citizens of Israel, where they are freer and more prosperous than Arabs in any Arab nation anywhere.

In some cases Arabs were forced by the invading army to move. We have noted that Egypt commanded thousands of their Arab brothers to get out of the way of the army, compelling them to flee into the territory of Gaza, where they still languish in refugee camps. The Jews, furthermore, for the strategic military purpose of establishing protected lines of defense had to force some Arabs to evacuate their villages either by direct order or by instilling in the villagers a fear of being massacred.

We have already noted the tragedy of Deir Yassin. Other tragedies blamed on the Jews took place at the villages of Kfar Kassem and Qibya. Whereas ruthless actions always struck fear into the hearts of Israel's enemies, they also promoted more than ever the smoldering hatred, which festers to this day, much of it, of course, kept alive and intensified by exaggerated stories and false propaganda.

The Israelis also had to displace thousands of Arabs especially in the coastal areas and in the south because the Arab presence threatened their supply lines and complicated their strategy in the war, which had been forced upon them. These towns included the 50,000 residents of Lod (Lydda) and Ramle, Khirbet Azzun, Ad Dumeira, an Nufeiat, al-Foqara, Miska, Khirbet as-Sarkas, and in the northern Negev, Najd, Sumsum, Zarnuga, Karkauba, Arab Rubin, Yibna, Huj and also several other villages in Galilee. I list these because little attention has been given to these innocent Arab victims of the first Arab-Israeli war.

As many as 170,000 Arabs had fled Israel before hostilities even got started with no pressure on them from the Jews. The wealthier Arabs who were the landowners and leaders left for places like Beirut where they intended to wait out the war that they knew was coming. Poorer Arabs were left without leadership and decided to follow their leaders out of the country especially in the direction of Lebanon and Syria. The Arab nations then met in a Council and, instead of absorbing them into their populations, decided to set up shelters for these refugees. These became the Refugee Camps that continue to exist to this day.

In all, over 500,000 Arabs were displaced from their homes, and instead of being assimilated into the populations of the surrounding Arab nations, which would seem to be the normal human response, they have languished for years in refugee camps like ghettos in most of the neighboring Arab nations and in Gaza and the West Bank. Over many years the numbers of refugees have multiplied to over 3.5 million souls. America and the European nations have tried to get Israel to take them back unilaterally, but for good reasons Israel has refused. To repatriate these millions of Arabs into Israel today would obviously destroy the Jewish state. Polls done among these refugees by Khalil Shikaki show that after 60 years, only 10% of the refugees wish to return to the land of Israel anyway. Most prefer to remain and become citizens of the lands where they are, but the Arab states have refused to assimilate them.

At the end of hostilities in 1949 at the Lausanne Conference when truces were made with the five Arab nations, the Jews did offer to accept 100,000 Arab refugees back into Israel and give up lands that they had taken in return for a negotiated peace treaty. They even offered to just take back some refugees with no peace treaty. The Arabs refused to even consider any of this, because they neither wanted to negotiate with Israel nor give even tacit recognition that Israel was a legitimate nation state. So the refugees languished. The Arab refugee problem from the beginning, therefore, was primarily created by the Arabs themselves. It has persisted because Arabs have refused to negotiate or compromise at all. Had the Arabs accepted the partition plan of the United Nations, in the first place, there never would have been any refugee problem.

Another reason why the Arab refugees have not been readmitted to Israel is that during this same period 700,000 Jews fled from persecution in Arab countries. They were welcomed by the Jews and became Israeli citizens. This mutual displacement of peoples was an almost even swap, but whereas Israel received and settled their Jewish immigrants, the Arab nations, except for Jordan, refused to admit their Arab brothers to become part of their own Muslim populations.

Of the several hundred thousand Jews that had been living in all of the Muslim nations eventually only 8,000 were left, except for larger populations in Iraq and Iran. When the Shah was the leader of Iran, the Jews were tolerated and safe just as they had been under the ancient Persian ruler Cyrus whom the Shah admired. Iran also gave de facto recognition to the State of Israel from the beginning. The Iranians then helped with Jewish immigration from Iraq in 1948 -1949 and had many connections with Israel in educational and technical fields.

Another refugee matter that is never mentioned is that during the 1948 war thousands of Jews were displaced by the Arab Legion in and around Jerusalem. Jews were evicted or massacred in the four villages of Etzion to the south where they had bought land. They were also ejected from their homes and synagogues in the Jewish Quarter of Old Jerusalem where they had lived for centuries. All this territory was controlled by Jordan, and no Jew was allowed to set foot on this land until after Israel reconquered the territory in the Six Day War.

These refugee camps have produced a severe environment,

fostering a fierce Arab hostility. They have provided bases for an unremitting terrorism of the fedayeen against Israel from then until now. No refugees were given permanent residence in any Arab nations except Jordan who granted the Palestinians citizenship. This is a travesty because their labor is needed, for example, in an underpopulated nation like Syria that has been begging for people to come and farm the arable land in the country that is sitting idle. Any immigrants would be welcome except the Palestinian refugees. The Syrians admitted in so many words that the refugees had to stay in their place to keep their hatreds "directed against Israel." It was the plan and purpose of the Arab states to keep these hatreds alive by refusing a haven for any of the refugees. It was also a way to stir up world opinion against Israel. To put the entire blame on Israel for all of this, however, is one of the biggest lies being told even to this day by their Arab enemies.

We can therefore conclude emphatically that the Jews are not responsible for the entire Arab refugee problem, which still exists and is being exploited in Arab propaganda. It is obvious that the Arabs have also kept the problem alive, because it gives them an excuse never to have to negotiate any offer made by the Jews for peace. They can always insist on the return of the refugees, which gives them an excuse to refuse any peace offer.

How long will it take well-meaning western arbitrators to realize that the Arab leadership does not want peace with Israel? This was clearly seen in Yasser Arafat's refusal even to discuss the extremely generous Barak/Clinton "land for peace" offer at Camp David in 2000. Arafat knew that he could stall any agreement by insisting on the return of all the refugees, because it was a demand that must always be refused. His goal, of course, was never to make peace at all, but to hold off until the Palestinians were strong enough with outside help to obliterate all the Jews and destroy the nation of Israel. Then they could have a Palestine that was 100% Arab. He said as much many times in Arabic never hiding his true purpose from his own people. I am sure that those who know the truth wonder how Yasser Arafat ever could have received the Nobel Peace Prize. It demeaned the honor of that venerable institution and cheapened the meaning of such a distinguished award.

The Palestinian refugees following the War for Independence in 1948 were variously estimated to number 520,000 to 810,000. We have noted that their Arab hosts did not absorb these refugees, but they were detained in camps to keep their protests alive before the whole world. By 1996 Arab Palestinians had grown in number to 1.8 million in Jordan, 372,700 in Lebanon, 352,100 in Syria, 880,000 in the Gaza Strip and 1.2 million in the West Bank.

The UN established the United Nations Refugee and Works Administration (UNRWA) to supervise the Arab refugee camps especially in Gaza and the West Bank and provide education, health and social services. Most of the budget of $85 million dollars a year has been covered by the United States. But we haven't received any thanks for this support from the Palestinians, who are being taught by their leaders to hate America because we support the Jews. It is unlikely that any of the Palestinians are even aware of America's provision for them. Muslims have proved that treating them with gentleness, honesty, kindness, and justice is almost never appreciated or reciprocated.

The nearby Muslim nations who are wallowing in trillions of dollars in oil profits have provided only a pittance to their Muslim brothers in the refugee camps. It is a calculated Arab strategy to keep the hatreds of Jews alive among the refugees, among Arab citizens in other nations, and throughout the rest of the nations in the world who have been deceived into blaming and thus hating the Jews for this problem.

The Aftermath of the First Arab Israeli War

As a result of the War for Independence Israel had increased the size of its territory by 30%. They had gained all of Galilee north to the Lebanese border. They had conquered the fortress of Acre and controlled the seashore from the Lebanese border to Gaza. They controlled land from the Mediterranean north of Gaza into the Negev east of the Sinai in a long triangle of land as far as the Gulf of Akaba. David Ben Gurion had sent a contingent of troops to secure the land on this arm of the Red Sea where the port of Eilat was established. This had been an original part of the UN partition in order to give the Jews access to the Sea. Israel withdrew from positions it had taken in the Sinai, and Egypt kept the Gaza Strip with its displaced Arab population. Jordan kept the West Bank, and Syria retained the Golan Heights.

The armistice with Egypt was signed on February 29, 1949. King Farouk had offered to recognize Israel if he could have the Negev, which comprised 62% of the Jewish nation. This was not realistic, and Israel had no guarantees. The armistice with Transjordan was concluded on April 3, 1949. Israel lost all of Old Jerusalem but retained the New City to the west. The West Bank, or Judea and Samaria as it is called in the Bible, remained under Jordan's control.

Hajj Amin al-Husseini, the Mufti of Jerusalem, had ambitions to govern all of Palestine. He made his claim to be king of Palestine from his exile in Egypt but was completely rebuffed by King Abdullah of Jordan who became the custodian of all of eastern Palestine including the Arab holy places on the Temple Mount. Abdullah had said that he "might" recognize Israel if he could have a corridor from Jordan to the Mediterranean Sea. This would have cut the country in half and again there were no guarantees.

Israel withdrew from southern Lebanon and armistices were signed with both Lebanon and Syria on March 23 and July 20 respectively. The Syrians had offered to take 300,000 refugees if Israel would give up all the area around Galilee. Syria's very unstable government gave no assurances that any promise would be kept. In fact, there were 16 regime changes in Damascus in 16 years.

Note that none of these were peace agreements. There was no sincere effort to have a final settlement. Israel and the Arab states were still potentially at war. This has always been the way of Islam. There is peace only within the Islamic *ummah* or greater Muslim community. Everything outside must always remain the "House of War." Truces or cease-fires are possible, but only in order to regroup, rearm, and live to fight another day. None of the Arab states were required to even recognize that Israel was a sovereign state. Technically Israel had no borders, and the Arabs kept up their terror and their boycotts. Israel continued to be attacked in intermittent guerrilla style warfare.

During the entire period of the War for Independence, Jewish immigrants kept arriving in Israel by the thousands. As many as possible were needed, and able-bodied men were immediately conscripted to fight the Arabs. Others established new settlements or kibbutzim all over the little nation even while the war was going on.

This first war, however, cost Israel enormously. Its crop fields were gutted and mined. Its famous citrus groves, the chief basis of its economy, were destroyed. The financial cost totaled $500 million, which would be comparable to America's spending $275 billion. Worst of all 6,373 Israelis were killed. This was about one percent of the population of 630,000 , which would be comparable to almost 3 million in America.

Neither the United Nations, America nor Western Europe had enforced the partition resolution nor did they give the Jews arms to defend themselves. The Jews were on their own under God. If the western powers had intervened, many Jewish lives would have been saved. It was the same story repeated over again as it had been during and following WWII. If the doors had been opened by the British to Jewish immigration into Palestine and if refugees had been accepted on the ships fleeing Europe, many would have escaped Hitler's holocaust or the tragedies of accidental death. But

Israel was a nation, Biblical prophecy was being fulfilled, Jews were returning to the Land of Promise from all over the world, and we are closer to the coming of the Messiah and the end of the age.

The Role of the United States

It was Britain and the United States that put pressure on Israel to end the war. Fighting had continued with many interruptions for truces and cease-fires from the United Nations. It wasn't until Britain threatened to get into the war defending Egypt against Israel, and President Truman gave Israel an ultimatum in late December 1948, that Israel relented, and the final cease-fire took place on January 7, 1949.

The United States had not been actively involved in the politics of the Middle East. This was Britain and France's territory. The United States had enthusiastically supported partition in the United Nations, but we became very alarmed by the resulting violence. On March 19, 1948 the United States proposed to the United Nations that a trusteeship be established instead of partition. In other words there would be only one nation with both Jews and Arabs, which would be administered by the United Nations. David Ben Gurion, who was to become Israel's first premier, absolutely refused this suggestion saying, "We will decide the fate of Palestine . . . A Jewish state exists because we defend it."

Finally there is a myth promoted by the Arabs that the United States was responsible for the founding of the state of Israel. Nothing could be further from the truth. Instead of sponsoring Israel, America on December 5, 1947 had imposed an embargo on shipping of any arms to the entire region. As we have seen the State Department did not want it said that United States' weapons had been used against Arabs or against Jews.

American Presidents varied in their interest in Israel. Harry Truman was friendly, because he was up for election the same year he recognized Israel. After winning the election in 1948 with the support of the Jewish vote, he hardly showed any more interest. Dwight Eisenhower held Israel at a distance. He was more concerned about friendship with the Arabs because of Arab oil. There were also no really pro-Israel people in his administration, and his Secretary of State John Foster Dulles was frequently critical of Israel especially during the 1956 war with Egypt over the Suez Canal.

JFK was the first U.S. President to show an overt friendship to Israel. He had several pro-Israel members in his administration. He broke the 1947 U.S. embargo on arms sending Hawk missiles to Israel when he heard that the USSR had supplied Nasser and Egypt with long-range bombers. It was discovered later that an agreement had also been made in 1960 to supply small arms to Israel through Germany.

LBJ, however, was even more openly friendly to Israel than President Kennedy. He surrounded himself with many Israel supporters in and out of government. The ambassador to the United Nations, the head of the National Security Council and the number two person in the State Department were all unabashedly pro-Israel. President Johnson credited his Sunday School training with preparing him for this favorable bias.

The arms embargo was now thoroughly shattered. Israel's Prime Minister Levi Eshkol had met with President Lyndon Johnson in 1968. The United States finally sent 200 Patton tanks and eventually 100 Skyhawk bombers and 50 Phantom F-4 supersonic jets to Israel partly because France, who had been Israel's main military supplier, had placed its own embargo on arms to the Middle East. Israel paid $285 million cash for the F-4's all of which were delivered by 1970. At the same time America tried to keep a military balance in the Middle East by selling some arms to friendly Arab states from Morocco to Jordan and Saudi Arabia.

It was soon after the Six Day War that Johnson gave a

speech outlining America's foreign policy in the Middle East called "Five Great Principles of Peace." A Jewish friend and neighbor Arthur Krim, head of the United Artists Corporation in Hollywood and chairman of the Democratic Party's finance committee, had helped him edit the speech at his ranch in Texas. Krim's wife Mathilde, a medical doctor, had been an agent for the Israeli Irgun in her youth. Johnson's speech established America's pro-Israel position for the next 20 years.

Then it was during Nixon's administration in 1973 that America began to transfer tons of weapons, crucial technology, and financial support to Israel. This was during and after the Yom Kippur war. It was part of the competition of the Cold War with the USSR in the Middle East. America has been Israel's enthusiastic ally since that time. We give more financial and military aid to Israel than any nation outside of NATO. We recognized that Israel is the only free democracy in the Middle East, and was surrounded by autocratic enemies many with the style and purpose of Hitler.

There is a fascinating true story of how America began for the first time to give Israel a large number of arms. It was in the midst of the Yom Kippur war in 1973. The Arabs had taken a major advantage with their surprise attacks and greatly outnumbered the Israelis. They were heavily armed with huge numbers of Russian tanks and armaments. The Israelis were hanging on for dear life, and Israel was even considering forming a government in exile. If the Arabs had pressed their advantage immediately and won, it is unlikely that many Jews would have been left alive and Israel would have ceased to exist. Golda Meir was Prime Minister of Israel. She had been begging President Richard Nixon's Secretary of State Henry Kissinger to supply Israel with some arms. Even though Kissinger was an Austrian Jew he refused, telling friends, "Let Israel bleed a little."

The Prime Minister's generals came to her and told her that everything was almost lost. In desperation Golda Meir picked up the "hot line" to President Nixon himself. It was 3:00 in the morning. He got up and received the call sitting on the edge of his bed in robe and slippers. Golda begged him for help telling him it was probable that Israel would be destroyed. Nixon said she sounded like his mother. He remembered that every afternoon when he had come home from school as a boy in Whittier, California, his devout Quaker mother would read Bible stories to him. On one afternoon when they were reading some story about the Jews in trouble, his mother said to him, "Richard, someday you are going to be a powerful man. If you have an opportunity to help the Jews, who are God's people, when they are in trouble, do it?" These words echoed in his memory. The Jews in America were liberals, however, and many had been among "Nixon's enemies." He was even regarded as one of our more anti-Semitic presidents.

Nixon also was in the midst of the Watergate scandal, and the Congress had warned him not to go off and start some big foreign policy adventure as he had done in China. In fact, they were considering impeaching him. In spite of the facts that he may not have been personally inclined to help Israel himself plus the possibility of hurting his own prospects with the Congress, Nixon responded to Golda's plea by commanding the Defense Department to send scores of American military cargo planes with all the arms imaginable to help the Jews. Without this help, Israel very likely could not have survived. Nixon threw caution to the winds because he really believed that he had come to the Presidency for just this moment, to respond to his mother's directive to him as a child that if he ever had the chance to help the Jews, he must do it!

The 1956 Sinai/Suez Campaign: Israel, England, and France vs. Egypt

The second Arab Israeli war in 1956 centered on Egypt. The dictator Gamal Abdel Nasser nationalized the Suez Canal in

July of that year in order to use the revenues to support the construction of the Aswan Dam, which the Russians were helping him build. Also he wanted to prevent any Israeli shipping reaching Haifa or Tel Aviv from the south. At the same time he blockaded the Straits of Tiran at the mouth of the Gulf of Akaba preventing Israeli shipping from even using their own port of Eilat at the southern tip of the Negev. A naval blockade, of course, has always been considered an act of war.

Britain and France were enraged because they owned the company that ran the Canal. So these two nations secretly negotiated a plan with Israel to work together to free the Suez. For years Israel had suffered from terrorist attacks on their settlements and farms from Gaza and Egyptian territory by terrorists called the *fedayeen* meaning "those who sacrifice themselves for a cause." Nasser had received considerable military armament from the Soviet Union, which emboldened him to make belligerent speeches against Israel. He had developed a vision for some kind of Pan Arab Union with himself as its leader. For a time he had joined with Syria in a loose union called the United Arab Republic. He had also made an alliance with Jordan. This was all in preparation for another invasion of Israel. It was only going to be matter of time until he broke the truce of 1949 and renewed the war.

France, which was struggling in a conflict with Muslim revolutionaries in Algeria, showed sympathy to Israel in secretly providing arms to counteract the Soviet arms sent to Egypt. This included Mirage fighters. Part of the plan was that Israel would strike first through the Sinai toward the Suez Canal as a counterattack to the terrorist invasion of the *fedayeen*. The British and French would demand that all parties withdraw ten miles from either side of the Suez. When Nasser refused they would declare him the aggressor and then would rush in and retake the Canal.

The Israeli army led by Moshe Dayan began the attack on October 29, 1956. Incredibly this Sinai campaign was won in one week. Paratroopers surprised the Egyptian forces in the Mitla pass. The Egyptians essentially fled leaving even their shoes behind so they could run faster in the sand. Examining the deserted headquarters of the officers, Israelis found copies of Hitler's *Mein Kampf* translated into Arabic as *My Jihad*. This showed the long association of the Arabs with the Nazis. Within a few days the Israelis were on the bank of the Canal. Israel had 172 fatal casualties, but the Egyptians lost many hundreds of fighters.

The British and French landed at Port Said at the head of the Canal on November 5th and marched inland into Egyptian territory. They had taken control of two thirds of the Canal when the United States, backed by the United Nations including just about every other nation in the world, intervened. The British and French involvement seemed like a resurrection of colonialism of an earlier era, which was in disrepute. Secretary of State John Foster Dulles, supported by President Eisenhower, had also expressed the fear that it was a war, which could have no ending. He said that the western nations must not get bogged down in an interminable war with the Arabs. These words of advice may be prophetic for our own time. It should be noted that the United States at this time was not supporting Israel.

The United States and the Soviet Union successfully pressured Britain and France to halt their attack. Then Britain, the United States, and the Soviets together threatened Israel whose armies stopped their advance. The war had lasted only 100 hours. The goals of the alliance, however, were accomplished. Actually everyone but the Arabs got what they wanted. The Israelis withdrew their forces, which could easily have marched on into Cairo, in exchange for (1) the promise of a United Nations peace keeping force (UNEF) to stand in the way of further Egyptian aggression and (2) assurances that the Straits of Tiran at the mouth of the Gulf of Akaba would be kept open to Israeli shipping. The Egyptian blockade of the Straits was removed.

In the final agreements with Egypt, the Egyptian military withdrew from the Gaza strip, which was really part of the territory the United Nations had given the Palestinians in their 1947 plan for the partition of west Palestine. The Suez Canal was retained by Egypt but was to be kept open to all shipping including Israel's. Because of the presence of the United Nations peacekeeping force in the Sinai, the terrorist raids of the *fedayeen* on Israel's homes and villages virtually ceased for the next ten years.

An indirect result was that Egypt and the Soviet Union moved closer together. Actually there had been a major sea change in the policy of the USSR in 1954. The Soviet Union had been the second nation after the United States to recognize the State of Israel in 1948 because Israel was organizing itself into *kibbutzim*, which were socialist enclaves. Israel's early leaders were socialists and the Soviets therefore felt a kinship with Israel and wanted a foothold in the Middle East. They also believed that Israel could be an example to the world of successful socialist communes. When socialism in Israel took a different turn with free elections in a free society, they felt rebuffed. So the Soviet Union began to cultivate and support the Arabs.

In spite of what was really a defeat, Nasser was now a hero to the Arab world because he had taken the Canal. In spite of Nasser's blockade, which was an act of war, Israel was looked upon as the aggressor because the Israeli Defense Force had been the first to move its armies toward the Canal. This began Israel's downhill plunge in popularity in the United Nations. In later years the majority of resolutions in the United Nations Assembly have been declared against Israel for one reason or another. Of course, the presence of about 57 Muslim nations out of about 180 countries making up the UN would often find the pot stirring against the Jews.

The Incredible Six-Day War—June 5-11, 1967
In their hearts the Arabs never gave up their commitment to

eliminate the State of Israel. For years the Palestinian refugee camps had been a source of constant terrorist raids across the borders of the Gaza Strip, Jordan, and especially from Lebanon and Syria. These were indiscriminate attacks on the Jewish civilian population. The United Nations never condemned the Arabs, but when the Jews retaliated, the UN hastened to condemn Israel. The double standard was cruel, and it has continued to this day.

An Arab summit led by Syria had urged the use of Palestinian Arabs in the refugee camps to destabilize Israel. The Palestinian problem that exists to this day in the Middle East therefore was really promoted by virtually all the Arab states surrounding Israel. The formation of the Palestinian Liberation Organization, encouraged by Syria and Jordan, was a response to this request. The PLO was formed by Arab nations of the Arab League at the Palestine Congress in East Jerusalem in May 1964. It became an umbrella organization for several other groups, such as the terrorist group Al Fatah.

In January of 1965 the Movement for the National Liberation of Palestine or *al-Fatah*, meaning "Victory," had been organized. Its leader Yasser Arafat, who would also become leader of the PLO, was to become a thorn in Israel's flesh until his death. Al Fatah carried on a continuous infiltration and bombing of civilian targets across the Syrian, Lebanese, and Jordanian borders for years. Al-Fatah was the first major terrorist organization. Arafat therefore became viewed as the modern initiator of terrorism in the Middle East. During the Yom Kippur War, Lebanon was known as "Fatahland." (Today Al Fatah's leadership of the Palestinians has been rejected by Hamas as not aggressive enough. Hamas has taken over the Gaza Strip and also wants to wrest control of the West Bank from Arafat's old group.)

Arafat was related to the former Grand Mufti of Jerusalem Hajj through a cousin on his grandfather's side. His name was Amin al Husseini-Abd al-Rahman Abd al-Raul Arafat al-Qudwa al-Husseini. He became chairman of the

PLO when it was formed under Egyptian President Nasser's supervision by the Arab League. As leader of the terrorist group al-Fatah he had taken the name Yasser Arafat to indicate a fresh start and perhaps to disassociate himself from the unpopular Hajj Amin. The goal of the PLO from the beginning was the liquidation of Israel. It immediately established the Palestinian Liberation Army. This move also had the support of Egypt. President Nasser soon placed the Gaza Strip and the Sinai at the disposal of the PLO and closely associated himself with its purposes and principles.

Serious saber rattling on the part of the Arab states began again in November 1966. Egypt had renewed its alliance with Syria and Iraq in April 1963, placing their armies under a unified command. Its stated purpose as always was the "liberation of Palestine." Jordan then allied itself with Egypt again in 1967 to prepare to avenge the Arab defeat in the war of 1948. They all mobilized their armies in anticipation of invading Israel. Demonstrations by howling mobs of Arabs in major cities, such as Cairo, Amman, Damascus, and Baghdad cried out for Israel's destruction. It was obvious to all that the Arabs were preparing for another invasion of Israel.

The Six Day War really had its origin on May 16, 1967 when Nasser demanded that the United Nations Emergency Force (UNEF) be removed. The UN had installed this buffer military presence in the Sinai between Egypt and Israel ten years earlier as a part of the Suez War settlement. What most did not know is that from the beginning a secret commitment had been made in 1956 by then Secretary General of the United Nations Dag Hammersjold that Nasser only had to ask and the force would be removed. So Secretary General U Thant in an act of appeasement meekly bowed to Nasser's demands removing the UN buffer force, and the Egyptian army moved into the Sinai to fill the void.

Tens of thousands of Egyptian troops and many tanks provided by the USSR then encamped along Israel's southern border. Nasser committed another act of war by once more blockading the Straits of Tiran, which had been declared an international waterway in 1957. This prevented Israeli ships from leaving the port of Eilat on the Gulf of Akaba. On May 26, 1967 Nasser gave a speech in which he declared essentially that war with Israel was again inevitable, and that the Jewish state must be obliterated once and for all. He stated unequivocally, "Our basic objective is the destruction of Israel."

Israel today has been condemned as an occupation force in west Palestine because the Golan Heights, the West Bank and the Gaza Strip are under Israeli control. This has been offered as a reason for ongoing Arab aggression. This needs to be seen for what it is; namely, a deceptive piece of junk propaganda. None of this so-called "occupied territory" existed when the Arab armies were aggressively gathering on Israel's borders from May 16 to June 4, 1967 preparing again to attack and murder all the Jews. No matter what excuses Muslim nations give to this day for wanting to eliminate Israel, we come down to only one ultimate reason; namely, Muhammad's virtual command that all Jews must be killed before the Day of Resurrection can take place, and that any land on earth once controlled by Muslims must always belong to Allah and Islam.

Together the Arabs had over 200,000 men, 1750 tanks and 700 airplanes poised to invade Israel. Moshe Dayan was Chief of Defense and Yitzhak Rabin was Chief of Staff. Together they agreed that Israel had little choice but to strike first. So at 7:45 A.M. June 5, 1967 in a rapid whirlwind attack Israel's air force of only 300 airplanes immediately took control of the air, destroying over 400 Arab planes most of them on the ground. The Arabs had only 280 planes left but were afraid to use them for fear that they too would be destroyed. The Israeli Defense Force decimated the Egyptian army in the Sinai killing 15,000 and taking 6,000 prisoners.

Jordan had been slow in responding so Nasser called

King Hussein and said that Egypt had destroyed the Israeli air force. We know about Nasser's deceit because the Mossad, Israeli intelligence, intercepted the call. It was an outright lie, but Nasser's claim encouraged the Jordanian army to attack. Later Nasser lied to Hussein again telling him that it was the Americans and French that had come and destroyed his airplanes on the ground. Arabs are notorious liars where infidels are concerned, and it seems that some of them also have no difficulty in telling outrageous lies to each other.

Israelis were less than eager to engage the Jordanians because the Arab Legion had been so strong and well trained in 1948. The IDF occupied the hills around Jerusalem, however, and finally entered the Old City. With tremendous pent up emotions, devout Jews rushed to the Western Wall to pray and praise God. It was the first time Jews had seen this meager remnant of their sacred Temple site for over 19 years. Jordan had driven all Jews out of East Jerusalem in 1948, and Jews from then on had been forbidden any access to the old Jewish quarter or the Wailing Wall.

The 1967 War changed Israel, and in many ways, it changed the world. Christians remembered Jesus' prophetic words, *"Jerusalem will be trodden down by the Gentiles until the times of the Gentiles are completed"* (Luke 21). We had all entered a new era in human history. From now on Jerusalem and the Holy Land would become a major focus of the entire world.

Moshe Dayan hesitated to attack Syria because he was afraid that the Soviet Union might come to their defense. He heard, however, that the Syrian army was already in flight, and so the Israelis occupied the Golan Heights even though Dayan had not been authorized to do so. This high ground was strategic because it had been used by the Syrians to shell Israel's settlements in Galilee. The Israeli army now had a clear field to advance into Syria and take Damascus. This was true also for Cairo in Egypt and Amman in Jordan. The Israelis refrained from further conquests, however, because they felt that they already had too many Arabs within their own boundaries to rule and almost too much territory to defend. They also feared armed intervention by the USSR and other non-Muslim nations.

According to Shimon Peres the war was really won in the first two hours, but it continued for six days until it was stopped by a resolution of the United Nations. The United States had remained officially neutral throughout the Six Day War, but the sympathies of President Lyndon Johnson and most Americans favored this one and only little democracy in the Middle East.

Israel miraculously had taken all of the Sinai Peninsula and the Gaza Strip from Egypt, Jerusalem and the West Bank from Jordan, and the Golan Heights from the Syrians. The war tripled the size of Israel's territory and made them the

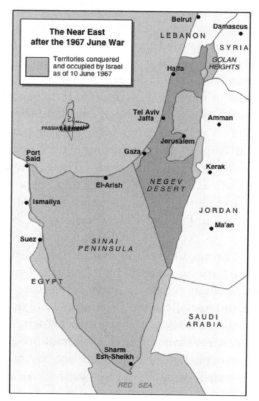

rulers or caretakers of hundreds of thousands more Palestinian Arabs. Only 777 Israelis had been killed, a little more than one tenth of those slain in the War for Independence.

A Six-Year Hiatus and the War of Attrition with Egypt (1969-70)

The Muslim world was in shock from the results of the Six Day War. Arab pride was shattered. They had been humiliated before the world, and their belief system and faith had been shaken. It was unthinkable that Jerusalem, Islam's third most sacred center, which for 1329 years had been under Muslim control, was lost to of all people in the world, the Jews. This jihad was not over. This struggle could never be abandoned until the nation of Israel was eradicated.

Israel's leaders now had more land than they wanted. What they really wanted was peace with their Arab neighbors. Maybe they could now exchange "land for peace," which became the mantra heard to this very day. So Israel made an offer of peace in exchange for territory taken in the war. Israel was willing to give up all this land they had taken in the Six Day War in exchange for a genuine peace with her neighbors. In August an Arab Summit Conference was called in Khartoum to decide what to do. Their answer to Israel became known as the three "No's" and set a pattern for almost all future efforts to find a solution to the problem of Israel's presence in Palestine. The decision was "No peace, no negotiations, no recognition." This concise formula was greeted with cheers all over the Arab world.

The Arab nations were still bent on the obliteration of all Jews and absolutely refused even to recognize the existence of the State of Israel. Because the Arabs would not negotiate, Israel kept the three territories under their supervision. Except for conservative and orthodox Jews, who considered these territories part of the land promised to Abraham, Isaac and Jacob, which they therefore wanted to settle, most

Israelis would have preferred to exchange the land for a permanent peace. The "land for peace" idea was always only an American or western premise. It was really never accepted by the Arab nations. There was one exception. The Sinai desert was returned to Anwar Sadat and Egypt in the peace settlement with Israel in 1978, but land was only one factor in these negotiations mediated by President Jimmy Carter.

There was a major change and concession to come in the future. We will see later that, hoping for peace and recognition, Israel almost thirty years later at the time of the Oslo Accords (1993-95) gave the Palestinians virtual self-rule of two of these territories taken in the Six Day War; namely, the Gaza Strip and the West Bank. The Palestinian authority had been the PLO, but a new official political entity was formed called the Palestinian National Authority (PNA). Both were under the control of chairman and president Yasser Arafat. After Arafat's death in November 2004, the more moderate Mahmoud Abbas was elected to the presidency of the Palestinian National Authority. He is the Palestinian leader that Israel and her allies have been trying to deal with, but now Hamas hard-liners have taken Gaza and destroyed President Abbas' offices. The only authority the PNA retains is over the West Bank, but Hamas is in the process of trying to force a takeover there also. So there is no solution in sight. All peace initiatives at this point were dead. They are being resurrected, however, around a new proposal by the Saudis. Negotiations are being conducted in secret. It is very likely that all these efforts will also prove to be as meaningless as the Oslo Accords and the Camp David meetings in 2000.

Immediately following the Six Day War, the Soviets began rearming Egypt and Syria more massively than ever before. Russia did not want this democracy and ally of the United States in the Middle East. They sent military advisors to train the Arabs. Military action began again almost immediately. Egyptian gunners sank the Eilat, an Israeli destroyer

13 miles out in the Mediterranean, killing 47 Israelis on October 21, 1967. (This event is really what triggered America's resolve to arm Israel with supersonic Phantom F-4's.) Israel retaliated by bombing and strafing all along the Suez Canal destroying oil refineries and a power station. Egyptian and Israeli forces facing each other across the Canal remained in constant conflict for three years, which became known as the War of Attrition.

There were many air battles. Scores of new aircraft provided by the Soviets were destroyed in both Egypt and Syria. Russians themselves piloting five planes in Egypt were shot down. Finally the Israeli air force was commanded by Israel's leaders to carry a punitive destruction into the interior of Egypt. The city of Ismailia where the Muslim Brotherhood had been founded was as completely destroyed as any German city during the bombing in World War II, and the principal Egyptian military commander was killed. In this three year conflict Israel lost 1424 soldiers and 100 civilians, twice as many as during the Six Day War.

In 1963, Israel had received its first arms—Hawk missiles—from America. While on vacation in Florida that same year, President John Kennedy had met informally with Israel's Foreign Minister Golda Meir. Only a few months before his assassination Kennedy assured her *"Don't worry, Mrs. Meir. Nothing will happen to Israel."* It was not until the Soviets stepped up their support of the Arabs, however, that American military aid to Israel developed in earnest. The arms buildup in the Middle East had become a competition between the United States and the Soviet Union. America had decided that Israel, the only democracy in the Middle East, would not be destroyed. This assured the future Arab mistrust and hatred of the United States.

After the 1967 war, Israel found herself in charge of over 1 million more Palestinian Arabs plus the 400,000 that already lived within the boundaries of Israel. The question was what to do with the Gaza Strip, the West Bank, and the

Golan Heights. Most wanted to allow the Arabs to rule themselves under an Israeli administration. Others saw the West
Bank as Judea and Samaria, the historic land of Israel, and
began to establish settlements beginning in the Jordan Valley
and moving westward. A settlement was established near
Hebron, the sacred site of the Tomb of the Patriarchs—the
graves of Abraham, Isaac, and Jacob—but at first little effort
was made to develop the Gaza Strip, which had originally
been controlled by Egypt. On the other hand, all Syrian villagers had fled the Golan Heights in the north, so Jewish settlements filled in the gap virtually annexing that territory.

Arab and Jewish communities within Israel were maintaining a more or less amicable relationship under an
enlightened, democratic policy. Under the slack, negligent,
and uncaring Jordanian rule, the West Bank had languished
economically. Now many Arabs found jobs in Israel and
thousands had passes to freely visit Jordan to trade. The area
was more prosperous and freer than it had ever been. Moshe
Dayan, and others, however, at that time were absolutely
opposed to granting the Arabs autonomy for fear that the
Palestinians would be taken over by the militant PLO, which,
of course, is exactly what eventually happened at the time of
the Oslo Accords in 1993-94.

Arabs in Israel proper were already allowed to vote and
had elected some representatives to the Knesset or parliament. It was unthinkable, however, that these other
Palestinian territories should be annexed. To grant one million more Arabs Israeli citizenship would virtually destroy
the identity of the Jewish state. Israel did not want to absorb
either the Gaza Strip or the West Bank. In retrospect, maybe
Israel should have annexed these lands as they did the Golan
Heights.

Now finally many Arabs within Israel finally began to
agitate for a separate Palestinian state. Such a state in west
Palestine had been possible in 1948 but had been rejected by
the Arabs. It was argued that there really was no need for a

Palestinian state because Jordan, which made up two thirds of what was Greater Palestine, already existed with a population of only 70,000 Palestinian Arabs. One could argue that with such a sparse population, Jordan could have absorbed and made a home for many of the 1.5 million Palestinians that were in Israel, Gaza and the West Bank.

This was actually the goal of Yasser Arafat and the PLO and other even more radical Palestinian groups who were based in Jordan. They wished to take over Jordan and extend its boundaries to the Mediterranean Sea creating a single Arab state eliminating Israel. The Palestinians had been very disappointed by the failure of the Arab states against Israel, and decided to take over the task with guerrilla warfare from their base in Jordan. Eventually the Palestinian guerrillas, or the PLO, rebelled against King Hussein.

Although conflicts with the Jordanians had been festering since the Six Day War, the actual armed rebellion began in what is called "Black September" 1970. The Palestinians tried to assassinate King Hussein. The 60,000 strong Jordanian Bedouin army ruthlessly put down this rebellion of 16,000 armed Palestinians. It had actually been an attempted *coup d'etat*. More than 2,000 Palestinian Arabs were slaughtered. Most of the rest fled to Lebanon, which then became a principal haven for militant Palestinians under the leadership of Yasser Arafat. Here they continued to raise havoc and also tried to take over Lebanon, until they were expelled by the Israeli Defense Force in 1982. We shall see that this just awakened a new enemy, which had been living peacefully next to Israel; namely, the Arab Shia who lived in south Lebanon whose radical arm became Hizballah—the Party of Allah—Israel's most skilled and dangerous adversary today.

Arafat had proved duplicitous and treacherous even in his dealings with fellow Arabs:

For Yasser Arafat, Black September was a test. He was asked to honor agreements, and repeatedly violated them; he was asked to rout out the extremists in his camp, and he didn't rout them out; he was asked to opt for realistic strategic goals, and he didn't opt for them. From Jordan he continued to Lebanon, from Lebanon he was expelled to Tunis, from Tunis again to Gaza and to Ramallah, where he found himself, 32 years after Black September, once again causing chaos, and once again besieged by armored forces which he will not be able to subdue (*Haaretz Newspaper*, May 28, 2002).

Golda Meir, an American Israeli who had been born in Milwaukee, Wisconsin, unexpectedly became Prime Minister of Israel in March of 1969. She proclaimed, "We are ready to discuss peace with our neighbors all day and on all matters." The Arabs showed her no respect and mocked her as a "grandmother telling bedtime stories to her grandchildren." This kind of response could have been predicted considering Islam's prejudiced attitude toward women whom Muhammad called "deficient in intelligence." Nasser declared, "What was lost by war must be restored by war" and there is "no call holier than the call to war." He, of course, was speaking of "Holy Jihad."

The Six Day War and Israel's continuing domination militarily had been such a humiliation for President Nasser of Egypt that he resigned, but he was implored by the Egyptians to stay at the helm until his death in 1970. His dreams of uniting the Arab nations under his leadership ended in failure. His greatest accomplishment, the Aswan Dam, was completed soon after he died. Anwar Sadat, one of the military officers who had participated in the overthrow of King Farouk I in 1952, succeeded Nasser as the President of the United Arab Republic. He proclaimed himself military Governor-General during the Yom Kippur war, and said that he was willing to sacrifice one million Egyptians to regain the Sinai.

The Yom Kippur War—October 1973
Yom Kippur, the Jews holiest holiday, the Day of Atonement,

arrived in 1973 on the eve of October 5th. Many of the military were on leave for the holiday. The air force was always ready, but most of the reserves had not been alerted. Israel had a standing army of no more than 80,000 whereas Egypt alone had 800,000 full time fighters. Most of Israel's army was in the reserves, which added up to virtually every able-bodied man and woman in the working population. Full-scale war naturally meant therefore that Israel's entire economy ground to a halt.

By the time Israeli intelligence was alerted to the fact that Egypt and Syria had planned a two front attack on Yom Kippur 1973, it was too late. Syria had massed 1200 tanks on the borders of the Golan Heights, and Egyptian forces easily crossed the Suez Canal in several places into the Sinai to face off against a much smaller Israeli military force. The Israelis as usual fought like tigers and held back the Arab armies. The Jews' experience was that they needed only one-fourth of the forces of the Arabs and could still defeat them with better strategy and greater determination. This time, however, the overwhelming force of Soviet supplied arms of the latest and best manufacture placed Israel in much greater jeopardy than ever before.

The tank battles of the October War were the most extensive ever seen in the history of warfare. Hitler had invaded Russia's 1,000-mile front with 1400 tanks. Syria alone had 1400 tanks and was eventually joined by Iraq with over 300 and Jordan with 50 more. Egypt had as many as 4,000 tanks plus the latest Sam missiles to knock planes out of the air. The Israeli air force could not get within 20 miles of the fighting for fear of losing all their planes. As it was, during the conflict they lost 100 planes, one third of their air force. The Arab's antitank weapons also were of the latest design.

In studying the progress of the war, one can only describe it again by one word— "miraculous." Syria's 300,000 troops and Egypt's 850,000 man army outnumbered Israel's 6 to 1. At the beginning of the war the Arab armaments outnumbered

Israel's by 4 to 1, and the Soviet resupply of the Arabs upped that ratio sometimes to 10 to 1.

The simultaneous attack began at 2 P.M. on October 6. Egypt crossed the Canal with a force of 80,000 men, 240 warplanes, and fired 10,000 shells from 2,000 guns in less than an hour. They did not realize that they were facing less than 500 Israelis. Israel lost 208 men but tenaciously held the Egyptians back until the reserves arrived. The acts of heroism on both fronts were legendary and too many and too agonizing to tell. But the names of the defenders have become legendary in Israeli history. Egyptian observers were amazed at the unbelievable tenacity of the Israeli soldier. They were fighting for the very existence of their homes, their families, and their nation.

On the Golan Heights Syria attacked with 1,400 tanks. They faced only 170 Israeli tanks but were unable to break through to Israel's territory. An Israeli tank force of only 20 destroyed over 500 Syrian tanks in the north. A main thrust of 600 Syrian tanks was stopped by 57 Israelis. Over 237 Iraqi tanks were destroyed without the loss of a single Israeli machine. When Jordan tried to come to the aid of Syria, Israelis destroyed 28 of her British Century tanks. In all Syria lost 1,150 tanks and Israel lost 100. The Israeli army was only 14 miles from Damascus and could have gone on to occupy the city, but again they feared the intervention of the Soviet Union.

Tank battles in the Sinai showed similar figures. Egypt threw 2,000 tanks into the battle. In one engagement 264 Egyptian machines were destroyed to only 10 for Israel. The Russians, who were pouring arms into Egypt and Syria with hundreds of planeloads and even shiploads, were greatly distressed at the unbelievable losses of these armaments. The United States did not begin to rearm Israel until October 13, or a week into the war. The competition of the Cold War had come to the Middle East with a vengeance.

Ten days after the first Egyptian attack, the Israeli army

established a bridgehead on the East bank of the Canal and counterattacked across the Canal to the West. The Israelis destroyed many artillery and antiaircraft bases and the Third Army of the Egyptians that had crossed the Canal into the Sinai began to be isolated. Israelis also cut off several roads to Cairo and advanced to within about 65 miles of the city.

Things looked bleak for the Arabs, so General Sadat asked the Russians to seek a cease-fire resolution from the United Nations. It was actually Henry Kissinger who arranged the end of hostilities before Israel could capture or kill the entire Egyptian Third Army that was caught in the Sinai backed up against the Canal. Kissinger figured that Arab honor had to be protected, and he saw an opportunity for peace. A complete Israeli victory and total humiliation of the Arabs again would only harden them against any kind of permanent settlement. It was on October 22 that the Security Council passed Resolution 338 ordering a cease-fire within 12 hours, the beginning of negotiations, and a try for "a just and durable peace."

One wonders how many years it will take for the Western Democracies, whose system is built on compromise, to understand the Islamist mind and culture, which does not know the meaning of compromise or conciliation with infidels. The West stubbornly adheres to the hope that it can broker a permanent peace, refusing to face the fact that militant Muslims understand only one course—ultimate victory or death. Orthodox Islam is a culture of death.

Six years later Anwar Sadat finally did enter into a more or less extended truce, which was called a peace, with Menachem Begin and Israel, which was mediated at Camp David by President Jimmy Carter in 1979. As a part of these negotiations Egypt received the Sinai back. They wouldn't have had to fight for it in the first place because Israel did not want to keep it. Israel only wanted security for their shipping from their port of Eilat through the Gulf of Akaba and the Straits of Tiran.

For this solution all three of these leaders eventually received the Nobel Peace Prize. Sadat, however, paid for this compromise with his life. A radicalized member of the Muslim Brotherhood assassinated him two years after the peace. This same Brotherhood influenced the founding of both Hamas and Islamic Jihad about ten years later. Radical Islamists want no peace under any circumstances with either Israel or the United States.

The Yom Kippur War was the last major attack on Israel by the Arabs until the two *Intifadas* of the Palestinians in 1987 and 2000. There are no statistics for the Egyptian dead but Syrian casualties numbered 3,500. Israel lost a total of 2,522 fighting men and women on both fronts. This would be comparable to a loss of over 100,000 American troops as a percentage of population. Israel had spent an entire year's GDP on the war, comparable to 10 trillion dollars for America, and became completely dependent on future American economic aid. It has remained so until this day. Egypt also receives a couple of billion dollars a year in aid from the U.S., which was probably a necessary plank in the peacemaking process of 1979. It appears that America and Jimmy Carter paid handsomely for this peace treaty. Can we say the America bribed Egypt to make peace?

How can we comprehend the incredible superiority of Israel even when immensely outnumbered both in men and armaments by their Arab enemies? I was in Israel in 1973 after the Yom Kippur War, and I was visiting with an Israeli soldier who had fought on the Egyptian front. I expressed that I believed it was a miracle of the Lord. The soldier, an agnostic, however, scoffed and said that the Arabs were cowards and just did not know how to fight. He attributed all Israel's victories to the superiority of the Jewish fighting forces. It came to me that this was exactly what Ezekiel had prophesied. Most Jews would return to the Promised Land in a state of unbelief—the dry bones described in Ezekiel 37.

Later that evening in Jerusalem, I thought again of God's

promise to Israel in the Torah: *You will pursue your enemies, and they will fall by the sword before you. Five of you will chase a hundred, and a hundred of you will chase ten thousand, and your enemies will fall by the sword before you* (Leviticus 26:7-8). Then I thought of the twenty Israeli tanks in the north Golan Heights that destroyed 500 Syrian tanks, of the 57 that stood against 600, of the 80,000 soldiers in the standing army of Israel against 850,000 Egyptians and 300,000 Syrians, and of the 2,000 Egyptian tanks standing against a handful of Israeli tanks in the Sinai and losing 274 tanks to Israel's 10. However you try to explain what happened, the only best answer is that it was all superintended by the promise, purpose, and plan of the God of Abraham, Isaac, and Jacob.

The War in Lebanon—1982

In 1949, the United Nations admitted Israel as a member of the General Assembly. All the Arab states surrounding Israel voted against this resolution—Egypt, Saudi Arabia, Transjordan, Libya, Syria and Lebanon. An armistice or indefinite truce had been declared following the 1948 war, but there were no peace treaties.

We have seen how Syria, Jordan and Egypt in 1964 encouraged the formation and activity of the Palestinian Liberation Organization and the terrorist group al-Fatah. The Palestinian Arabs while in Jordan formed an army and committed many terrorist acts including the hijacking in 1970 of four civilian airliners, which were landed in northern Jordan and then destroyed.

In what has been called "Black September" of 1970, we noted that the PLO felt strong enough to attempt a revolution against King Hussein of Jordan whom they had tried to assassinate. The Jordanian army killed thousands of the rebel fighters and thousands more Palestinian civilians. The PLO and Fatah then fled to Lebanon where they had Syrian support. Syria had actually fought with the Palestinians for a brief time against Jordan. The Palestinians then did in

Lebanon what they had done in Jordan. They tried to take over the country and a civil war began, which continued for fifteen years (1975-1990).

Lebanon had been a half Christian, half Muslim nation for years with the Maronite Christians running the government. This had been mutually agreed to years before in a Constitution, which was drawn up by the many different sects in that country. Israel supported the Christian Arabs in Lebanon, called the Phalangists, in their civil war in order to prevent a complete Palestinian or Syrian occupation of the country. Arafat and his al-Fatah, however, had virtually taken over the southern part of Lebanon and the district of West Beirut, and the al-Fatah terrorists began conducting commando raids on the northern settlements in Israel.

After an especially bloody attack on March 11, 1978 by Fatah commandos on two busses on the Haifa/ Tel Aviv road, killing 37 and wounding 76 Israelis, Israel retaliated by invading south Lebanon. They occupied all the territory to the Litani River displacing 100,000 Lebanese in their quest to destroy the PLO/Fatah bases. The United Nations demanded an immediate Israeli withdrawal and sent a peacekeeping force called the United Nations Interim Force in Lebanon (UNIFIL) to replace the Israelis.

The United Nations peacekeepers, however, were either powerless or indifferent to the PLO/Fatah shelling of northern Israel with Russian made Katyusha rockets. So Israel's army of 60,000 troops under General Ariel Sharon invaded Lebanon again with a firmer purpose on June 6, 1982. Prime Minister Menachem Begin called the attack "Operation Peace for Galilee."

This time Israel's armies in a lightning strike went all the way to Beirut in seven days. Most members of the PLO were rooted out of their hiding places by the end of August. It took only 70 days to complete "Operation Peace for Galilee." The PLO lost all its southern Lebanon bases and its headquarters in Beirut. As a part of the cease-fire agreement, which was brokered by the United States, 7,000 PLO fighters agreed to evacuate Lebanon for eight other Arab countries including Tunisia, where Arafat set up an international headquarters.

The terribly destructive shelling and bombing of Beirut had been seen on television screens all over the world, and Israel was almost universally condemned. The Israeli leaders were determined, however, to stop all attacks on their northern settlements by the terrorists. They pulled back to create a buffer zone in the South and stayed for three years. What happened during those three years was to change things forever. This second phase of the war was even very unpopular in Israel and caused much disapproval, even condemnation, of Israel's leadership.

Israel had wanted to set up the Christian Phalangists in a government of Lebanon which would be at least neutral, if not favorable to Israel as an ally. The Phalangist leader Bashir Gemayel, a Maronite Christian, who was scheduled to be the new president of Lebanon, however, was assassinated by a huge bomb that took out his headquarters and killed over 200 people in September 1982. It was presumed at the time to be the work of Palestinian terrorists, but it was later discovered to have been carried out by a member of the Syrian Socialist Nationalist party who was a Syrian intelligence agent. Syria has continued to this day to interfere aggressively in Lebanon. This has included assassinating other Lebanese leaders like Rafik Hariri, a former President of Lebanon, who opposed Syria's meddling in Lebanese affairs (February 14, 2005). They are now supporting Hizballah in an effort to take over the government still run by Maronite Christians.

There were two Palestinian refugee camps near Beirut called Sabra and Shatila. It was believed that there were some "nests" of Palestinian fighters hiding there. The Israeli army surrounded the camps and sent in about 150 Phalangists or Arab Christian Lebanese fighters. The Lebanese commander

Elie Hobeika had been directed by Israel's commander Ariel Sharon to act like a dignified army, but the Phalangists went berserk and took out their frustration and vengeance for the massacre of their leader Gemayel. It is uncertain how many were killed, but estimates range from many hundreds to a few thousand, including about 35 women and children.

These killings were declared by the United Nations to be an act of genocide, which was not really an accurate description of what happened. (It was a massacre, not a genocide, which is the destruction of a whole race, national or ethic group.) Again Israel was blamed and condemned. No mention was made that it was the Arab Lebanese Phalangists who had done the killing. Israel and Ariel Sharon were blamed because they had allowed it. On the surface it might seem that the United Nations was just doing its job until we find that in the same year the Syrian army massacred over 20,000 Syrian citizens, rebels in a town called Hama. This raised hardly an eyebrow and motivated no UN resolutions. Inequalities and inaccurate evaluations in UN resolutions happened time and time again until the United Nations has lost all credibility as an honest broker.

Reaction against Jews, who were equated with Nazis in the European press, was severe. It provided an excuse for another wave of anti-Semitism to sweep the Continent. It could never be proved, however, that this was Israel's or Sharon's intention or that he was really to blame. Many to this day, however, consider him a "war criminal," because he gave the Phalangists permission to enter the camps knowing what they might do to avenge the murder of their leader Bashir Gemayel.

More than 6,000 Palestinians and 600 Syrians had been killed in this first phase of the War in Lebanon with the loss of only 368 Israeli soldiers. The United Nations arranged an agreement between Lebanon and Israel and commanded that all military forces withdraw. Syria refused and the United Nations as usual was impotent. Israel therefore left

30,000 troops in southern Lebanon to protect her borders. Since this was a militia army, such a permanent outlay of troops was very hard on Israel's economy, a fact that was not lost on Syria. Syria kept 40,000 troops and 1,200 tanks in the Bekaa Valley in west central Lebanon. Also there were still 10,000 PLO supporters in the country. It was a temporary stand off that left an unresolved situation ripe for potential conflict for more than a generation to come.

What has not been reported much was the reaction of the Shia whose homes were in scores of poor villages in South Lebanon. They had been abused by the Sunni PLO when they came into the area to set up bases from which to harass northern Israel. When the Israelis marched into the territory in 1982, therefore, they were welcomed by the Shia as liberators. Actually the Shia had been good neighbors and had accepted the Jewish state for all the years the Israelis were south of their border. During the years of the Shah, Iran had been one of the few nations that had fair and friendly dealings with Israel. So the Shia in Lebanon had not been responsible for the military incursions or the rockets. It was the PLO, who after they were expelled from Jordan had set up what became known as "Fatahland." This was the name Israelis gave to these aggressive Palestinian military bases run by al-Fatah in South Lebanon, which was really Lebanese Shiite territory.

When the Israelis returned to south Lebanon with their 30,000 troops, they tried to organize the Shia villagers into National Guard units to provide protection for northern Israel. They were not very persuasive or very gentle. This was something they had done with a league of villages on the West Bank. They wanted to create a buffer in southern Lebanon as a "North Bank." The Shia had wanted to live and let live, but they did not want to be pushed around; and they did not want to become part of a Jewish run military band.

The Shia began to regard the Israeli Defense Force as an occupying enemy and fought back. The Israelis employed a policy they called the "Iron Fist." It backfired. The Shiites had no militia and few arms, but they had a tradition of suicide attacks as part of their history and tradition. They began to put these tactics into practice against the Israelis, who found themselves at war with an elusive enemy that took 600 lives. This was almost twice as many as the IDF had lost in the first phase of the war. It was proportionately equivalent to the 30,000 lives that America lost during half of the Viet Nam war. Southern Lebanon became Israel's Viet Nam. The Israelis were not prepared to fight this kind of a conflict. It was time to withdraw and take their chances with rockets and incursions. The war became intensely unpopular with the Israeli people and Prime Minister Shimon Peres accepted a lopsided 16-6 vote in his cabinet to withdraw the troops to a narrow security zone.

As the Israeli troops moved out, hundreds of Hizballah moved in from Beirut and now Israel would be attacked by Shia militants, who would now get their arms, their training, and their support from Iran. The Iranian revolution had spread to Lebanon. There began a long struggle by the Shia to try to take over the Lebanese government and turn Lebanon into an Islamic Republic, which is still going on.

So the Lebanese War of 1982-85 was Israel's first failure. They had defeated the PLO but had failed to stop the Arab attacks on northern Israel, which were continued by a new enemy, the Lebanese Shia and the Party of Allah (Hizballah), which was founded by Hassan Nasrallah in 1982. But that is not all.   In December 1983 a bomb had exploded on a Jerusalem bus killing six Israeli civilians. Credit was taken by the Palestinian Liberation Organization. From then on Arabs began using suicide attacks, which had proved to be a successful tactic in Lebanon, and against which there was little defense. It was a new beginning of continuing terrorist attacks throughout Israel for over 20 years from that day until now. The new enemies were Hamas, Islamic Jihad, and Hizballah—all supported by Iran.

Chapter 7

CONFLICTS WITH THE PALESTINIANS
THE FIRST INTIFADA
AND PEACE INITIATIVES: 1987-2000

The First Intifada and Pressures for Peace

By 1987 Israel had controlled the territory in Palestine taken in the Six Day War for twenty years. Many Palestinians in Gaza and the West Bank were being integrated into the Israeli economy and were dependent upon Israel for their livelihoods. Israel kept the peace as much as was possible and retained all power and control over what was becoming a joint society.

Neither the Muslims nor the Jews were comfortable with this arrangement. Israelis did not want to lose their identity as a Jewish state; therefore, there was never any thought that all the Palestinians would become citizens of Israel. Muslims also did not want to speak Hebrew or become Jewish. Although Arab living conditions in Israel were far superior than they had in any of the nations from which they and their families had come, they chafed under Israel's authority. The pent up rage of twenty years finally erupted into what became known as the Intifada.

Whose Land Is It Anyway?

We have seen that in the Six Day War, Israel acquired by conquest the portions of Palestine called the Gaza Strip, the West Bank, and the Golan Heights. Conservative Jews regarded all this territory, and more, as part of ancient Israel or the Promised Land that had been given to them by God through the promises made to their father Abraham. The West Bank had been Judea and Samaria, and the Golan

Heights was the region of Bashan.

According to Joel, one of the earliest prophets, God called all of Greater Palestine "My land," in other words it was a small section of the Earth that He had specifically reserved for His own personal use and distribution (Joel 3:2). Throughout the Diaspora conservative Jews never gave up the hope or the goal that this land would contain a new nation of Israel. This was a promise recorded many times by the Major Prophets, especially Isaiah, Jeremiah, and Ezekiel, that God in the last days would restore the Jews to their Promised Land (Appendix 1):

> *Therefore say: This is what the Sovereign LORD says: I will gather you from the nations and bring you back from the countries where you have been scattered and I will give you back the land of Israel again (Ezekiel 11:17-18).*

Orthodox Jewish believers therefore began to build settlements on their lands, which had been acquired in the Six Day War, believing that God was fulfilling His promise.

Secular or liberal Jews, on the other hand, were not concerned about what were supposed to be Israel's ancient lands. They were willing to work out a resolution with the Arabs. They were willing to exchange these newly acquired lands immediately for a promise of a lasting peace so that there could be a secure nation called Israel in at least part of the land of Palestine. "Land for peace" was their principle, and it still is. This exchange could have taken place immediately following the end of the Six Day War. Israel indicated a willingness to give back these lands, but as we have seen the Arabs had a "summit conference" in Khartoum and came up with the "3 No!" formula "No negotiations! No peace! No recognition!"

Just as they had rejected the UN partition in 1947, the Arabs absolutely refused again to even consider negotiating a peace with Israel in 1967. They might have welcomed the return of the three territories that Israel acquired in the Six Day War, but they really were not even thinking at the time of a Palestinian state separate from a Jewish state. Their conviction was that all of west Palestine belonged to Allah and thence to them. That the Arabs do not have a separate Palestinian state in west Palestine today, therefore, as they already have in east Palestine (Jordan), is their own choice and hence their own fault as we have already presented in detail. All this agitation for a Palestinian state today is a smoke screen obscuring their real purpose of totally eliminating Israel, killing all the Jews, and taking all the land for themselves.

According to the rules of warfare worked out in the West as a part of International Law over many years, any settlement concerning lands acquired during a war is to be made at the peace table. No peace table means no negotiations and no settlement! Arab stubbornness therefore made any solution for the disposition of these territories impossible, and therefore Israel has kept supervision of the land. These territories were already part of what had originally been designated as the "Jewish homeland" anyway according to the Balfour Declaration, if it had been implemented as intended. Most Israelis, however, would much rather have exchanged these lands for peace and Arab recognition of Israel as a nation.

After the Oslo Accords in 1993 Israel turned the immediate supervision of the West Bank over to the PLO. They even provided arms for their police force with the help of the United States. They wanted to show their good will and "prime the pump," so to speak, to encourage some kind of peaceful settlement. They followed the same plan with the Temple Mount. They then later unilaterally withdrew from the entire Gaza Strip, taking down all the settlements and removing the 9,500 Jews who were living there. They just turned it all over to the Arabs. They did this, of course, at the urging of the United States and other mediators who were hoping for some positive reciprocation on the part of the Arabs. Westerners, however, have no conception and don't even seem to want to understand the Arab mind, culture, philosophy of life, or religious beliefs. They refuse to accept the fact that compromise with infidels is not in the Islamists' vocabulary. They continue therefore to be "ripped off" and disappointed to this very day. Why will these well meaning but brainless appeasers never learn?

The Arabs, however, were not motivated to any kind of reconciliation. Their response to Israel's unilateral act of good will was to increase the Qassam rocket attacks on Israeli settlements such as Sderot in the Negev. They interpreted Israel's retreat from the Gaza Strip as a victory for their suicide bombers and their resistance. They credited Allah with giving them a military victory for which they owed the Jews nothing. They saw the Gaza withdrawal as symbolic of the expelling of all Jews from the rest of Palestine and fulfilling the final goal of creating a Palestinian state over every square mile of the land.

Now the Jewish settlers in Gaza had developed a unique and incredibly successful agricultural industry in greenhouses along the Mediterranean Sea, which supplied Israel with most of its produce. They left all of it to the Arabs, but instead of adopting this lucrative industry and feeding their own people, the Arabs destroyed everything. What a waste! How are we to reply to such folly and indigence? Jesus said, *"By their fruit* (what they produce) *you will know them"* (Matthew 7:15-16), referring to true and false prophets.

Is There an "Occupation"?

Israel has been accused of occupying Palestinian land. Israel's presence in Palestine is always described as "The Occupation." Many do not realize that Arabs include in this accusation the entire nation of Israel—all the Jews' land in Palestine. The occupied territories are not only the three lands in question—the Gaza Strip, the West Bank, and the

Golan Heights. In the mind of the Muslim, all of Palestine has been Allah's land ever since it was captured by the Arab armies in the year 638. The Jews are regarded as having usurped the rightful territory of Islam and are thus an occupying force wherever their feet touch the ground in west Palestine. This is in spite of the fact that (1) Jews from all over the world helped to buy at a very high price from Arabs, who claimed ownership, much of the disputed land that has been occupied by Jewish settlers for 70 to 100 years. (2) Furthermore, in 1917 the British, who were to be given responsibility for the territory after WWI, promised the Jews a homeland in the land of Palestine. How can the Jews therefore be occupiers in their own territory, which was promised to them by the conquerors and new owners of the land of Palestine. It was part of the spoils of WWI taken from the Ottoman Empire by the Allies. Even the Qur'an states that the spoils of war belong to the victor.

This is simply one of many outright lies propagated by Islam. It is a myth created by Arab propaganda. Here is more proof: (1) These lands were occupied by the Jews for centuries before there ever was an Islam. (2) Palestine had never ever been owned by Palestinian Arabs. (3) There had never, in fact, ever been a Palestinian state at any time in history. The only basis for the Arab claim, when you come right down to it, is a religious dogma—land once owned by Islam forever belongs to Islam. Islam, however, was a johnny-come-lately to that area. Arabs had no ancient roots in that part of the Middle East. Any claims to that effect are fraudulent. They are promoting a great deception more commonly called "a Big Lie."

After the Jews had been expelled in the 2nd century by the Romans, who named the land Palestine, the territory went through many hands—the Byzantines, Persians, Arabs, and Crusaders, finally winding up as part of the Ottoman Empire, the last Islamic Caliphate. Palestine was then considered part of Syria. The Arabs in Palestine in the early decades of the 20th century always identified themselves as Syrians. In fact, when the British founded the Palestinian Broadcasting Service in 1936, Arabs vehemently reacted to the use of the name Palestinian in the title, demanding that it be changed to The Southern Syrian, or Iraqi, Broadcasting Service. The term Palestinian was always at this time applied to resident Jews. Jews were called "Palestinians" by the British, and the identification was accepted by the Arabs, who refused to be called Palestinians until after 1967.

When the Ottoman Empire was defeated in WWI, Palestine came under the control of the British Mandate in 1920. All of Palestine, including what is now Jordan, was originally included in the promise of the Balfour Declaration to establish a "homeland for the Jews." As we have already learned, however, because of fierce Arab opposition, the British made the first partition of Greater Palestine in 1922, giving the Arabs the much bigger piece of the pie in order to keep the peace. What became the Arab nation of Jordan received 77% of Palestine on the east side of the Jordan River. It was declared to be the Arab state as opposed to a possible Jewish state on the other side of the river. No Jewish settlement was to be permitted in Transjordan.

What remained of Palestine west of the Jordan River was then considered to be the "homeland for the Jews." This it was decided would fulfill the promise of the Balfour Declaration of 1917. This was legally confirmed by the San Remo Conference and also the League of Nations in 1920-22. This means that the majority of the nations of the world accepted this arrangement. It was assumed that most of the Arabs would be encouraged to migrate to what was called Transjordan. This was the original Palestinian state. Jews then could establish their homeland in all the land west of the Jordan River.

This first partition of Palestine, has all but been forgotten in the midst of the Arab determined claims to West Palestine and their accusation of a "Jewish occupation," which is not only a false allegation but grossly unfair. The Allied Powers that were victorious over the Ottoman Empire in WWI had every right by International Law to dispose of the land of the Empire as they saw fit. Providing a "homeland for the Jews" on a small part of this land was perfectly legitimate or legal as is recognized by the fact that it was confirmed by the League of Nations in 1920-22 and by the United Nations itself 25 years later. It cannot be emphasized enough that the lands under the British Mandate had never ever been an Arab nation. Jews were not displacing Arabs. Therefore how could it be an "occupation?"

In the next few paragraphs let's briefly review what we have previously covered in detail. During this 25-year period (1920 to 1945) thousands of Arabs flooded into west Palestine from the surrounding Arab nations. They came because the Jews had made the land to prosper. Arabs got employment and health care and found a freedom that did not exist in any of their nations of origin. Winston Churchill estimated that Arab immigration averaged 35,000 people per year.

When the Arab population grew, they began to agitate against the Jewish presence. We have seen that the British in desperation, who had curtailed Jewish but not Arab immigration, formed a study group in 1937 called the Peel Commission, which recommended that another land partition be made west of the Jordan between Arabs and Jews. The United Nations seeing no other solution to the west Palestine problem made the same decision in November 1947. Jews were actually awarded a very small percentage of what had been Greater Palestine. Arabs could have had their own Palestinian state west of the Jordan River at that time in addition to all of East Palestine, but they rejected the partition plan. They were being disingenuous. They rejected all partition plans, because they wanted it all for themselves, refusing that the Jews be allowed any part of the land. So the Arabs had rejected a possibility for having their own state

twice in the partition plans made by both the British Peel
Commission and the United Nations.

Britain, in the midst of a severe conflict between Arabs
and Jews that they could not manage, finally gave up the
mandate in May 1948. The Zionist agency led by David Ben
Gurion immediately declared an independent state, and five
Arab nations, who were poised on the borders, attacked the
new nation of Israel from all sides. Their purpose was to murder or obliterate all Jews driving them into the Mediterranean
and forcibly take the lands of west Palestine. These five Arab
nations, however, had no intention of establishing a
Palestinian state on these lands even if they had defeated
Israel. A Palestinian state in west Palestine had never been considered even by the Arabs in Palestine themselves. As it was,
Jordan illegally kept the West Bank for itself, and Egypt kept
the Gaza Strip even though it was many miles away from their
country. Neither had ever owned these territories. They just
kept them, and the world made no outcry.

In light of Muhammad's teaching concerning the spoils
of war, the Arabs said that in conquering Israel they looked
forward to acquiring the largest booty that any Muslim
armies had ever achieved. They proclaimed that all of
Palestine belonged to them, and the Jews could have no part
of it. Most Arabs hold tenaciously to this position today as a
part of their religious faith, which makes any hope for a settled peace impossible. Both Hamas and Islamic Jihad, for
example, have this demand written into their original char-
ters, and the Palestinian Liberation Organization never recognized the legitimacy of Israel in any of its documents or
negotiations. In light of all this, it is baffling how the western mediating nations, including the United States, are so
blind to the realities of what is the true situation in the
Middle East. It appears that they all feel that they can force
their own vision of what should be on both Arabs and Jews.
When are they going to learn that it just won't work?

As we have seen in the previous chapter, the Arabs lost

all five wars in 1948-49, and the Jews acquired more territory than most Israelis wanted. The Gaza Strip was occupied and kept by Egypt, and the West Bank and East Jerusalem by Jordan. Each of these territories had large refugee populations, which neither Egypt nor Jordan wanted to assimilate. Syria held the Golan Heights as part of an early agreement between Britain and Franc. This was the status of west Palestine from 1948 to 1967.

All of these territories occupied by these Arab states had been part of the British Mandate. The only legitimate basis for their keeping the lands was conquest. The land was never historically theirs, but with the British gone and in the absence of any so-called Palestinian authority, they simply annexed the land. After 1967 when the Jews took these three territories—the Gaza Strip from Egypt, the West Bank from Jordan, and the Golan Heights from Syria—they had the same right of conquest. They acquired these lands in the same way that Egypt and Jordan had taken them 19 years earlier. International Law says these lands are "up for grabs" unless the Arabs will enter into negotiations and make some kind of compromise or peace to get them back. It is a total misconception to say that these lands were illegally "occupied" by the Israelis. They had just as much right to them as anybody else without a negotiated peace. It seems that the Arabs have sold the Americans and the Europeans a bill of goods, which is a fraud, a myth, and a Big Lie.

There is really no "occupation" as it is commonly defined. It is not a legal formulation. These territories—the Gaza Strip, the West Bank, and the Golan Heights—are the spoils of war. Until the issue is solved by negotiations these territories belong to Israel according to any rules of International Law. The problem has been a weakness or shortsightedness on the part of secular Jews who really did not want these extra lands, which were part of the original promise of God to Abraham, so they are in dispute by default. It is my opinion that considering Muslim intransigence, stubbornness and total disregard for truth, Israel should keep these territories. The Arabs cannot be trusted under any circumstances. It is too late for the Gaza Strip, which Sharon foolishly vacated, but not too late for the West Bank, which is the area of ancient Judea and Samaria, which belong historically to the Jewish nation.

When the Syrians completely vacated the Golan Heights, the Jews swiftly settled the territory, which was the ancient land of Bashan, called the inheritance of half of the Hebrew tribe of Manasseh in the records of the book of Judges (13:29-31). Its strategic overlook of Galilee, had been used by Syria to shell Israeli towns and settlements. For the protection of northeastern Israel, the Heights had to be fortified by Israel and could not be given up. With Mt. Hermon, also called Sirion, as its northern boundary, the Golan also controlled some important sources of water for much of Israel, which came down out of these northern mountains. Syria has wanted all the Golan Heights returned before peace negotiations can even begin. That this is a transparent hoax ought to be clear to anyone knowing the past history of negotiations with Arab Muslims who follow the treacherous example of their Prophet. Some Israeli leaders like Prime Ministers Rabin and Barak were willing to give part of the Golan back to Syria, but felt they must retain a fortified buffer zone for Israel's protection. No agreement has ever been reached, and it is unlikely that Syria would ever negotiate in good faith anyway considering the teachings of Muhammad and Islam. At the moment the Syrians show every indication that they are preparing for another war.

Without any doubt, if Israel gave the Golan Heights back to Syria it would once again become the launching pad for some new attack against Israel in the future just as the Gaza Strip is being used today as a base for rocket attacks against Jewish communities in the south. It would be foolish, to say the least, for Israel ever to return the Golan Heights to Syria, which will never truly consider peace with a nation that they won't even admit has a right to exist.

Many Jewish settlements have also been founded on what is called the West Bank (of the Jordan River). They have always been accused of stealing Arab land for these settlements. This is another outright lie. The lands the Jews settled on the West Bank were either (1) state lands, which Jordan had previously claimed as a national reserve, or (2) land which the Jews purchased from the Arabs, or (3) uninhabited, even uninhabitable, land where there were no Arabs. These settlements have almost always been established by orthodox or conservative Jews who want to make the statement that this is land that was promised to them by God through His covenant with Abraham. It is the land of ancient Israel—Judea and Samaria. As long as Arabs have refused to negotiate a peace, according to International Law, there really are no legal restrictions that should be able to stop this land development where Arab residents are not displaced. Finally how can Arabs even make the accusation that it is these settlements that stand in the way of peace, when the Arabs refused to make peace even when there were no settlements? It is simply an excuse—another part of the Great Arab Deception.

The original plan of American and European negotiators in the Middle East has been to follow the principle, "Land for peace." This was the reason behind the unilateral evacuation of Jewish settlers and the relinquishing of the control of the Gaza Strip to the Arabs in September 2005, which was supervised by Ariel Sharon, then prime minister of Israel. Sharon was incapacitated soon after this decision by a severe stroke, and the former mayor of Jerusalem and member of the new Kadima Party Ehud Olmert became Sharon's successor. It was Olmert's intention to continue Sharon's new policy and also give the West Bank to the Arabs removing all Jewish settlers. Arabs will be very willing to take the land, but they will never exchange the land for peace. They will instead use it to promote more intense terrorist attacks against Israel. How long will it take American and European negotiators to learn this fact? Why are they so blind and stubbornly hanging on to a false hope? How many times does the West have to be duped before we wake up to the fact of the treachery built into the very fabric of orthodox Islam?

The Israeli Defense Force earlier had unilaterally withdrawn from southern Lebanon to appease the Arabs. Instead of showing gratitude for this olive branch, the Shia Hizballah backed by Syria and Iran built rocket sites from which to bombard northern Israel with Katyusha rockets. Also instead of accepting Israel's withdrawal from the Gaza Strip as a peaceful gesture, the Arabs dug tunnels under the walls to attack Israel's military and kidnap her soldiers and set up rocket launchers to send a daily barrage of Qassam rockets into Israeli settlements.

Because of the tragedy in Gaza and the negative response of the Arabs, who looked upon the Israeli withdrawal as a reward for terrorism, Jews have begun to change their minds about letting go of the West Bank. They realize that it could become an armed camp of Palestinian terrorists fed with arms from Syria and Iran, a deadly dagger aimed right at the heart of the Jewish nation. Artillery and rocket launchers could be placed in the mountainous heights, and all of Israel would be at their mercy.

At the present time, al-Fatah has strongholds on the West Bank and is being armed by the United States as a buffer against a militant Hamas, conquerors of the Gaza Strip, who want to invade the West Bank and take over the Palestinian National Authority. It is a very dangerous time, because neither Hamas nor Mahmoud Abbas and al-Fatah want a Jewish state to exist. Israel has no choice now, however, but to work with Abbas and their al-Fatah terrorist enemies. The choice is between the lesser of two evils. I would predict, however, that because of their common enemy Hamas and al-Fatah will get back together and unite in further aggression against Israel, or Hamas will defeat al-Fatah and take over the control of the West Bank. It was Israel's misplaced faith and false hopes that allowed them to give the autonomy of the West Bank to Arafat and the Palestinians in the first place. It should never have happened. It was a foolish, hopeless gesture of generosity on the part of Yitzhak Rabin and Shimon Peres made at the time of the Oslo Accords.

There is only one place in west Palestine where the argument could be made that Jews were occupying Arab land. These are the 14 settlements, with almost 25,000 inhabitants, near Jerusalem and Bethlehem called the Etzion Block. The original Gush Etzion settlement of 4 kibbutzim was made on land purchased by the Jews from the Arabs. Then during the 1948 War, the Arab Legions led by British regulars massacred all Jews in this settlement. It was an obvious war crime, which was never accounted for. When the Israeli armies in the 1967 war reacquired the land, therefore, Jews vigorously established ten additional villages that now have a substantial, growing population 50 times the size of the original settlements. Again this acquisition resulted from a war. To give up any part of the Etzion Block would require extensive negotiations, and the Arabs refuse to negotiate.

The Beginning of the First Intifada

Up until 1987 unrest in Israel had been expressed by Arab mobs made up principally of children and teenagers throwing stones or even Molotov cocktails. Now guns were used for the first time. On December 6, 1987 a 45 year old Israeli Jew Schlomo Sakle was stabbed while shopping in a Gaza market. Two days later a semi-truck with an Israeli driver turned carelessly into a line of oncoming traffic and four Arab workers from a Gaza refugee camp were killed. It was rumored to be revenge for the stabbing of the Jew. Israeli soldiers on patrol began to be attacked. Palestinian mobs in the thousands raged against their tormentors. Shots were fired in defense. Arabs were killed. Within five days the uprising in Gaza had spread to refugee camps on the West Bank. All of Palestine was aflame with passions. It was the beginning of the first Intifada.

There were almost one and one-half million Arabs in the Palestinian territories. Over 800,000 Palestinians were the refugees of the 1948 war plus their descendants. They lived in squalor in 27 refugee camps in Gaza and the West Bank. In the rest of the world refugee problems in the past had been solved by some kind of resettlement of the people. No Arab nations had offered to absorb these homeless Palestinians into their countries. But these displaced Arab populations were allowed to fester on purpose, keeping alive the animosity against the Jewish presence in Palestine.

Within the boundaries of the land of Israel itself there were another 700,000 Israeli Arabs who joined their brothers at least in spirit by proclaiming Peace Day on December 21, 1987, which was the beginning of the Intifada within Israel proper. This first Intifada explosion was not planned. It just happened. The journalist Thomas Friedman, now with the *New York Times* was an eyewitness. He writes in his award-winning book *From Beirut to Jerusalem*,

> *I always think of the Intifada as an earthquake—an eruption of twenty years' worth of pent-up geothermal steam—raw Palestinian rage—that opened the Palestinian-Israeli fault line and created a physical chasm between the two communities. But it didn't open a chasm wide enough to totally disconnect the two communities. That would take time and much effort, because Israelis and Palestinians were simply too intertwined* (p. 376).

The term Intifada is sometimes defined as "the shaking." The concept is a shaking loose from something or someone, wanting nothing to do with what is being shaken off, to be finished with something, or to break with someone and refuse to have anything to do with that person. It was the Palestinians' primal scream against what they considered an Israeli occupation of their land. They sought some kind of separation, which would give them their own identity. They wanted Israelis and the world to know that they were not Jews. They were refusing to be absorbed into a Greater Israel.

Yasser Arafat, the PLO chief, who had fled from Beirut to Tunisia during the 1982 War in Lebanon, was as much surprised by the Palestinian uprising as anyone else. The Intifada, however, gave him a new lease on life. Originally he had been the recognized leader of the Palestinian refugees outside of Palestine. In 1973, the PLO had been declared by the Arab nations to be the official representative of the Palestinian people. Now Arafat was to become the recognized leader of all Arab Palestinians including those living within the boundaries of Israel.

Arafat had been labeled the original terrorist, but now he turned the tables and told the world that the Israelis were the real terrorists. The Palestinians at first had used mostly stones and rocks as weapons. The Israeli soldiers responded with rubber bullets, tear gas, and occasionally real ammunition. The Palestinians may have initiated the rebellion, but unfortunately, or maybe conveniently, it was seen by the world as a totally one-sided conflict, and this changed the equation.

Two things were to happen that have continued to frustrate all sides to this day; namely, (1) The desire for a separate Palestinian state was finally born and its fulfillment insisted upon. Earlier opportunities had been there for the Arabs to have their own state in west Palestine, but they had rejected it. Now they have changed their minds and are clamoring for it. It is obvious to me that it is simply a Palestinian effort to get incrementally or little by little what they have not been able to get by jihad. Israel will continue to give and give and give and the Arabs will take and take and take until they have a base from which they can try to take the rest by force. This is no secret; they have said as much. (2) Nations of the world began to intercede and try to seek out a peaceful solution to the immediate hostility of the Intifada, and then finally resolve once and for all the entire conflict between Jews and Arabs.

A few Arabs within Israel had been elected as representatives in the Knesset, Israel's parliamentary body. Some of them formed for the first time an all Arab Democratic Party, which recognized the PLO as the official representative of the Palestinian people and called for a separate Palestinian state and the return of all former Arab lands to their original Arab owners.

On December 22, 1987, the United Nations Security Council issued a resolution condemning Israel for overreacting to the uprising—for violence, harshness and brutality in putting down the insurrection. The United States did not veto this resolution, and it immediately gave Arab states a basis to call for Israel's withdrawal from the territory won in the 1967 War and the establishment of a Palestinian state. This was something that the Arabs would not even have considered twenty years earlier.

The New Peace Initiative and the Rise of Hamas

In February 1988 the United States began a peace initiative to try to persuade Israel to negotiate with the Palestinians. Undersecretary of State Richard Murphy was the first representative sent to the Middle East. Eventually after seven months of further shuttle diplomacy by James Baker and three years of negotiations, a formula was worked out for a preliminary peace conference between Israel and representatives of the Arab States and the Palestinians. It was to be sponsored by both the United States and the Soviet Union and was to be held in Madrid, Spain in October 1991.

At the same time as this effort for peace was launched in 1988, a new radical, hard-line organization was formed in Palestine called Hamas, the Arabic word for *zeal*. (In Hebrew *hamas* means "evil.") It grew out of the influential welfare and educational Islamic Association formed by a Gaza leader Sheikh Ahmed Yassin, who as a student at Al Azhar University in Cairo had joined the Muslim Brotherhood. He came to share the Brotherhood's belief that the entire world should be ruled by Islam. As efforts for peace with Israel were being launched, Yassin transformed his association into "The Islamic Resistance Movement" for which the name Hamas is the Arabic acronym. Hamas took the hard line that rejected any peace with Israel and claimed all of Palestine for Palestinians. Its goal was to eliminate all Jews from Palestine. Its method was acts of terror leveled against all Israelis and any Palestinians who opposed its principles.

For the Palestinians in Gaza, Hamas provided welfare schools, hospitals and clinics and also funds for refugees in other areas. Some of the money for this charity was raised in the United States. Hamas thus became a competitor with the PLO for the hearts and minds of the people. Hamas became the most active terrorist group to promote suicide bombings, and because of its aggressiveness threatened to replace the PLO as the sole representative of the Palestinian people. Yassin not only ordered suicide bombings but also kidnappings of Israeli soldiers. He had been imprisoned twice and released in prisoner exchanges. Both times he went right back to promoting terrorism against Israelis, preaching that Israel had no right to exist. We shall see in the next chapter that Israel finally responded to the hard line of Hamas by assassinating its founder and leader Sheikh Yassin in March 2004.

Hamas was joined in Palestine by four other terrorist organizations: Islamic Jihad, Al Fatah, the Al Aqsa Brigade and Hizballah, which have headquarters in Lebanon or Syria. These radical Islamists have provided a continuing resistance to any efforts for peaceful negotiations between Israel and the Palestinians. They are the major reason there was no hope that Yasser Arafat could ever really come to a settlement with the Israelis. He not only feared ouster from his position as PLO chief, but also knew he could be in grave danger of assassination himself. Terrorist organizations in Israel have been responsible for the murder of any Palestinian caught collaborating with Israel or taking any kind of aggressive stand in favor of peace. More hundreds of

Palestinians have been killed by these terrorist militants than by the Israeli Defense Force. The militants will sacrifice any human life including their Muslim brothers in order to advance their cause.

Enter Saddam Hussein

In the meantime the Intifada continued. By the time of the first peace conference in 1991 at Madrid, 1225 Arabs had been killed including 78 children. Of that total almost half were killed by radical Palestinians themselves because they were considered to be collaborators with the enemy. Thirteen Israeli soldiers had also lost their lives.

At this time one of Israel's most implacable and dangerous enemies was Saddam Hussein of Iraq. One of his goals was to take Jerusalem back from the Jews. He called his army "The Jerusalem Army," and hoped to duplicate the 6th century B.C. victory of Nebuchadnezzar over the Jews. In fact, he fancied himself a reincarnation of this Babylonian monarch.

Saddam's other hero was Adolf Hitler. We noted that when he was a child, Hitler's portrait hung in the kitchen of his uncle who was mayor of Baghdad. He had major ambitions for himself emulating Hitler. He envisioned a kind of United States of the Middle East by which he could dominate the area and become a world player. His Baathist party had been modeled after the Nazi party in Germany, and one of Saddam's goals was to follow in Hitler's footsteps in eradicating all the Jews.

Saddam had for nine years (1980-88) tried to conquer his Shiite neighbor Iran. Muhammad had taught that Muslims should never fight each other because they were brothers; however, this did not seem to apply to the age-old conflict between Sunnis and Shias. Most Sunni states like Saudi Arabia were doubtless glad to see Saddam engage Iran; however, they also feared his ambition to extend power over the entire Middle East including the coveted Saudi oil fields.

Because Iran had taken hostages from our embassy in Tehran in 1979, holding them for 144 days, and because Saddam was a secular state and seemed a safer ally, the United States favored Iraq in this war and had extended some friendship and military help to Iraq. Even with some clandestine help from America, however, the Iraqis after years of conflict had to settle for a draw with Iran, a nation that is three times their size.

Eventually we discovered that we could not work with Saddam Hussein. On August 2, 1990, he launched his second major aggression. Saddam ordered an attack on Kuwait claiming that it had formerly been the 19th province of Iraq. He was using the same tactic that Hitler had used to take the Rhineland, then Austria, and then the Sudetenland before World War I. His ultimate goal was to take over the oil countries of the Middle East and establish a new Muslim Caliphate with himself as its leader. America responded immediately with Operation Desert Shield to protect Saudi Arabia, which seemed to be next in line for occupation by Iraqi troops. The American military stationed itself on land in Saudi Arabia and on sea in the Persian Gulf. Eventually there were 500,000 troops involved in a coalition from many nations. Our military was only the first of 30 nations to respond in resisting Saddam's aggression. To tell the truth, it was all about oil. Over 60% of the world's oil supply came from the Middle East, and it had to be protected.

The United Nations immediately demanded that Saddam withdraw from Kuwait and imposed sanctions. When Saddam declared Kuwait to be the 19th province of Iraq and refused to withdraw, however, the first Gulf War was begun on January 17, 1991. The coalition that was formed against Saddam by many of the world's nations included many Arab states, including Saudi Arabia and also Israel. The Israeli Arab political party, however, sided with Saddam. He threatened Israel with rocket attacks on August 31, which he later carried out with Scud missiles. Forty Scuds fell on Israel during the Gulf War. Few Israelis were injured but one Israeli was killed.

The United States, which led the effort to liberate Kuwait, urged Israel not to participate in the conflict because Arab states, such as Saudi Arabia, were a part of the coalition. No Arab state could dare be in any kind of an alliance with the Jews. Israel complied and did not retaliate for the missile strikes, although their fighters were on the tarmac ready to fly to Iraq and take out the missile sites if necessary. Israeli citizens huddled together with gas masks expecting incoming rockets armed with chemical warheads. Fortunately this never happened, and Israel never entered the war.

On January 17, 1991, an American army of 120,000 troops and a large British force invaded Kuwait from bases in Saudi Arabia. A massive air strike was begun which saturated strategic targets within Iraq for almost a month, giving the war its popular name—Operation Desert Storm. Sometimes there were 1,000 sorties in one day using precision bombs and computer guided rockets. The military entered in force into Iraq early in February and by February 22, 1991 a cease-fire proposed by Russia had been agreed to. Within 100 days Kuwait was liberated, Saddam had been subdued, and things returned to a measure of normalcy. It may have been the unexpected overwhelming domination of the Iraqis by the United States military which cowed the nearby Arab states into beginning to think of pleasing the superpower by moving in the direction of some kind of "arrangement" with Israel. The presence of the infidel nations' military forces on the sacred soil of Arabia, however, motivated the beginning of continuous terrorist attacks against the United States and later Europe.

Continuing Efforts for Peace—Madrid and Oslo (1991 to 1993)
On October 30, 1991, Israel sat at a negotiating table for the

very first time with Arab foreign ministers from Syria, Jordan, and Lebanon in Madrid, Spain. There was even a Palestinian delegate in attendance. There was also a Palestinian delegate in attendance. Prime Minister Yitzhak Shamir represented Israel. President George H.W. Bush and Premier Mikhail Gorbachev were the joint sponsors overseeing the proceedings. It was just at the time that the Soviet Union was dissolving, which finally took place on Christmas Day 1991. The Arabs would soon lose their major champion, and Gorbachev would no longer continue to be a central figure in the negotiations.

It was a beginning. Talks continued in Washington D.C. from December 9, 1991 to January 24, 1992. Then many bilateral meetings discussing all of the issues that needed to be settled were held in other nations including in Moscow, the capital of the new Russian Commonwealth of Independent States. (CIS) Nothing concrete really developed out of these initial talks; however, one barrier had been broken. It was the first time that Jordan, Lebanon and Syria with a Palestinian representative had sat down at a negotiating table with Israel. The only permanent result of these talks was an eventual peace treaty signed between Israel and Jordan in 1994.

In the meantime Hamas was taking over the fight for the Palestinians against the Israelis with a vengeance. Many more were killed, and Israel captured and imprisoned hundreds of Hamas militants and deported their leaders, including a number of elderly Muslims, to Lebanon, which caused a world wide scandal. Strangely, in spite of the obvious Palestinian aggression, Europeans and the United Nations were constantly taking the side of the Arabs against Israel. This probably stemmed from the fact that the Palestinians were considered the little dog in the fight. This antagonism toward Israel probably also had roots in centuries of European anti-Semitism. Europe's favor for the Arabs doubtless also had a lot to do with Europe's dependence on

Arab oil.

In the midst of all this mayhem, the Soviet Union had collapsed and thousands upon thousands of Russian Jews were free to immigrate to "the Promised Land." Arafat had met this new threat with an order to his Palestinian followers to shoot on sight any immigrant coming to Israel. They were to do anything and everything they could to stop the flow of immigrants, which would increase the numbers of Jews in the land. Nevertheless, Israel's population quickly increased by at least five percent.

The Intifada conflict had gone from bad to worse, but in 1992 Israel elected a new Prime Minister who was utterly committed to solving the problem with some kind of peace. Yitzhak Rabin, who had been Israel's delegate to the Madrid Conference, headed up the new Labor controlled government. He urged the Palestinians to give peace a chance, to negotiate toward their own autonomy, and to cease all violent and terrorist activity during the peace process. He said that the Palestinians were to become partners, not enemies, and Palestinian rights would be restored. He asked only that the Arab countries recognize Israel's right to exist as a sovereign state in peace and security. This seemed a reasonable goal, but, in light of all the attacks and invectives Arab leaders had leveled against the Jews and Israel, and their adamant refusal to recognize the continuation of any Jewish presence in Palestine, it was certainly unfounded optimism on Rabin's part.

Rabin was definitely an incorrigible idealist. He did not want to face the fact that Palestinian leaders had committed themselves many times to the ultimate destruction of the Jewish state. Arabs had from the very beginning in 1947 rejected the idea of a divided land with two autonomous states. How could he hope to change their minds considering their religious convictions that the Jews were usurpers of Arab land and property? After all, Muhammad had spoken out vehemently against the Jews, and his vision for the last days must be fulfilled; namely, the total elimination of the Jews from the Earth.

It should have been no surprise that both Hamas and Islamic Jihad militants emphatically opposed Rabin's vision. They refused any compromise whatsoever with Israel. So the killings and the terror went on. Many terrorists continued to be imprisoned or deported. Rabin and Minister of Defense Shimon Peres, nevertheless, were determined to fulfill their campaign promise that the Palestinians should become autonomous or rule themselves.

The Farce of the Oslo Accords (1993 to 1996)

Behind the scenes Israel and the PLO, which had headquarters in Tunisia, were talking. Representatives from both sides were secretly invited to a villa just outside Oslo, Norway where negotiations began in January 1993. It was really a continuation of the series of conferences that had begun with the Madrid Conference in 1991 and followed the same kind of two step plan with the Palestinians: (1) Arranging for self government for the Palestinians, followed by (2) Negotiations for a permanent solution. The final agreement was called the Oslo Accords, which were signed in Washington D.C. on September 13, 1993. This was not at all a peace settlement but only as a Declaration of Principles for future action that would hopefully lay the groundwork for a peaceful settlement.

The major development of the day was that Yasser Arafat was recognized by Israel as the leader of the Palestinians. In a "revolutionary" gesture Rabin shook Arafat's hand with President Clinton looking on. The now famous picture was published around the world giving hope to many and provoking anger and resentment among hard line Muslims. Arafat was invited back to Palestine, and the Palestinians were promised eventual self-rule. A kind of Marshall Plan was also proposed where responsible nations in the world would supply the Palestinians with considerable funding to launch what was hoped would eventually become a peaceful Palestinian state existing alongside of Israel in the land. How Israelis, Americans, and anyone else could have fallen for the hypocrisy inherent in the dealings of Yasser Arafat is difficult to understand. It seems that the passionately intense desire for a permanent solution to the conflict had allowed all eyes to be blinded to what really was an impasse.

The Oslo Accords turned out to be a disappointing hoax. Arafat was putting on a big act for the entire world. It amazes me that he was able to carry out this hoax for almost ten years without producing one fruitful result for the Israelis while he aggrandized position, property, a headquarters in Palestine, and billions of dollars for himself and the PLO. In Israel and the West's desperate hope for peace, they all fooled themselves. Or was it a demonic inspired blindness and deception?

The Oslo Accords were launched to achieve a period of peace, better termed a truce, during which time negotiations on the details could be worked out. This agreement was not a peace plan but only an attempt to create an atmosphere of moral trust over a period of five years. Could a compromise be achieved? Western strategists should have paid more attention to the biography of Muhammad, who is considered the "Perfect Model" for Muslims, and the example of his famous ten-year truce of Hudaybiyyah with the Meccans, which he violated after 17 months.

The terms of the agreement were simple. Israel's responsibilities during the five years were as follows: (1) Grant recognition to the PLO as the authority for Palestinians, which included the return of Arafat as its leader; (2) Transfer control of the land on the West Bank and the Gaza Strip to the Palestinian Authority; (3) Educate the Israeli people to work toward peace; (4) Allow the creation of a 10,000 member Palestinian police force which would take over security duties from the Israelis; and (5) Supply the Palestinian Authority with arms or weapons for this police force.

The Palestinian's responsibilities were: (1) Bring an end to all terrorism; (2) Change the charter of the PLO, now renamed the PA (Palestinian Authority), to officially recognize Israel as a legitimate state; (3) Protect the Jewish holy places which were in the territories that were to be transferred to Palestinian authority and would no longer be protected by Israeli security teams; (4) Educate the Palestinian people, including the children, to work toward peace with Israel.

What actually had each side given up in what was called "the peace of the brave"? The Palestinians, on the one hand, were giving up the dream of destroying Israel in favor of recognizing Israel's right to exist. The Israelis, on the other hand, were risking the creation of a "terrorist" state in their own back yard, giving themselves indefensible borders. One area of their nation would have a width of only nine miles.

In looking back how did the Israelis and Palestinians keep their commitments? To summarize, the Israelis kept all of their commitments and the Palestinians kept none of theirs. No one should have been surprised, but most of the international community completely ignored the results and the awful contrast.

Israel's Response:

1. Israel recognized the PLO, inviting Arafat to set up headquarters in Palestine.

2. Israel transferred the supervision of 42% of the West Bank and 90% of the Gaza Strip, land that they had taken in the 1967 war, to the Palestinian Authority. This was the first time in modern history that any nation had given back strategic land won in a war without a peace agreement.

3. Israel supplied the 10,000 Palestinian security forces with small arms.

4. Finally Israel began an educational program for peace, which changed the minds of a large number of Israelis concerning the existence of a Palestinian state—from 28% of the people before Oslo to 51% after. Textbooks for children were even changed after Oslo to reflect the new effort for peace.

The Palestinian Response:

1. Palestinians, on the other hand, did not disband their terrorist organizations.

2. More Israelis were killed in terrorist attacks in the five years after Oslo than had been victimized in an entire 15 years before the Oslo agreements. The Palestinian Authority pretended to oppose these attacks, but documents were discovered later that showed Arafat was actually financing the terrorist organizations and praising the suicide bombers. The PA claimed that Hamas was an outlaw organization, but in Arabic to his followers Arafat praised Yassin, the founder of Hamas and called for Holy Jihad.

3. Article 19 of the PLO Charter stated that the partition of western Palestine was illegal, and Article 21 said that armed revolution was necessary, and that all solutions, which did not include the total liberation of Palestine for Palestinians, were to be rejected. The PLO never changed these statements. The Palestinian Authority never officially offered any legitimacy to the State of Israel. This was absolutely in direct violation of their signed commitment.

4. In spite of Arafat's assurances in the agreement, Israel's holy sites, which came under Palestinian control, were all destroyed—Rachel's tomb in Bethlehem, Jacob's tomb in

Nablus, and the old Jewish synagogue in Jericho. The violent Arab crowds trashed all holy items including scrolls of the Scriptures, vowing that Jews would never come back to those places. Palestinian security forces armed with Israeli supplied weapons, to their shame, did not interfere with these sacrileges. It seems that Palestinians couldn't wait to desecrate all Jewish sacred sites as soon as they had an opportunity. What a major contrast this was to Israel's treatment of Islam's holy places during the years that they controlled Jerusalem. Not a single Arab sacred sanctuary had been damaged or defiled in 26 years.

5.   As to educating the Palestinian people, there was continuous oratory each Friday in the mosques urging Palestinians to butcher and murder all Jews, to encourage the *shahid* or suicide bombers as holy martyrs, and to teach children to glorify the martyrs' death. Palestinian textbooks after Oslo never cited steps for peace and made no reference to Jewish lands. Maps never showed even a hint of the existence of Israel. As far as Palestinian children were concerned, Israel did not exist. In fact, children continued to be taught openly in the classroom to hate the Jews.

Arafat said in Arabic on a TV interview that the Palestinian boys and girls were the future generals and that a picture of a child with a stone in his hand facing a tank was the "greatest message in the world." Funds were given by Europe and America to send Palestinian children to summer camps, which turned out to be paramilitary camps training children to be Arab holy warriors. Polls in Palestine showed that 85% of the people supported terror, 73% rejected any kind of peace with Israel, and 72% of the children wanted to become suicide bombers. So much for educating Palestinians for peace!

From time to time Arafat made a show of calling on the

Palestinian people to renounce terror and violence although he obviously did not mean it in his heart nor could he enforce it. Negotiations, nevertheless, concerning the status of Jerusalem and the refugees did continue. Israel would establish commercial relations with an independent Gaza. At least 10 million dollars a year were pledged by America and the Europeans to fund the beginning of the new nation. Arafat put most of the money in personally controlled off shore bank accounts. He had over 5 billion dollars or more stashed away including $1.3 to $3 billion he allocated to himself. The reason Arafat wanted to control the money was that he thought it would assure his own protection as the leader of Palestine for years, because he held the purse strings. His untimely death left all solutions to this problem unresolved. I think that Palestinian officials are still searching for some of the money. Arafat's greed also extended to owning many businesses including the control of all the cement that was imported into the territories. His deceitfulness, corruption, and venality were unlimited.

Arafat, when confronting opposition from Arabs concerning the Oslo Agreements, pointed to the example of Muhammad and the false truce of Hudaybiyyah. Speaking in Arabic he had implied that he had no intention of honoring the Oslo commitments even as Muhammad had not honored the truce. This was not immediately understood by the world because journalists, who might have made this known, did not understand Arabic. Also few of them knew any details of Muhammad's history or his principles.

Arafat never officially in any PLO literature, including the PLO Charter and By Laws, ever recognized Israel's right to be a sovereign state. Arafat said he had changed them, and everybody believed him. Shimon Peres went on TV declaring it to be so and said that a new era had dawned. As usual Arafat was lying. So these Israeli/PLO agreements in which liberal Israelis, and the liberal Europeans and even some conservative Americans had placed so much hope proved to be a

cruel hoax and a farce. Negotiations, however, have continued as if an Israeli /Palestinian peace has a chance. They are
only going through the motions. We shall find that all of this
hopeless "noise and fury" was like treading water in a stream
moving toward a waterfall.

After months of further discussion in Bucharest and
Cairo, the principals met under the auspices of President
Hosni Mubarak of Egypt in Cairo on May 4, 1994.
Representatives of the Press from all over the world were
there. Finally, after much hedging on Arafat's part, as he
tried to withhold his signature from several maps and other
agreements, the PLO leader caved in to pressure and the
Cairo Agreement was signed. It amounted to nothing but a
piece of paper.

A Palestinian National Authority, however, had been
given legislative, executive, and judicial powers with its own
armed police force and control over health, education, and
welfare in Arab controlled Palestine. The PNA could negotiate with foreign powers concerning everything but foreign
affairs and national defense. Both Gaza and Jericho were
turned over to the Palestinian National Authority. Arafat
assured his followers on the side, however, that Holy Jihad
would continue until Jerusalem lay in Palestinian hands.
What he really meant was that jihad would continue until all
of Israel was under the control of the Arabs in a Palestinian
state free of Jews. He was a walking-talking contradiction.
Was Arafat ever sincere? Could he have ever really been trusted? The answer is obvious. His Nobel Peace Prize was the
scam of the century.

Faysal al Husseini, Minister for Jerusalem Affairs in the
June 24, 2001 edition of *Al Arabi Daily* said, *"The Oslo Accords
were a Trojan Horse to get inside Israel and weaken her. The strategic
goal is always the liberation of Palestine from the Jordan River to the
Mediterranean."* The Palestinian goal has been and always will
be *"the elimination of the Jewish State. The entire land is Arab. We will
not give up Haifa, Joppa or Galilee. All the land is Palestine."* The

Arab world was bombarded with this kind of rhetoric in spite of the Oslo Agreements that required a Palestinian promise to recognize Israel's right to exist as a nation. Now lets face the facts and be real. How can anyone even begin to deal with people like this? Frankly, it is proving foolish to even try! How can anyone dredge up adequate words to express our frustration with these transparent frauds?

Another part of the Oslo agreement was a commitment by Israel to dismantle some of the settlements Jews had built in the West Bank, the ancient Judea and Samaria, and also cease the building of any more settlements. Israel then promised to withdraw from the Gaza Strip within five years. Conservative Israelis felt that Rabin and Peres had sold them out. Yitzhak Rabin was warned that he might be assassinated, but he dismissed the warning as some kind of propaganda. As usual he was wrong!

Peace with Jordan and Rabin's Assassination

Israel next completed a peace agreement with Jordan officially ending their 47-year-old state of war. Rabin and King Hussein flew to Washington to sign the agreement on July 25, 1995. The barbed wire fence was removed and a gate was opened between the two nations. Unfortunately in the redrawing of the boundaries, 50,000 Palestinians found it almost impossible to get to their jobs in Israel.

The peace with Jordan was celebrated at what was perhaps the high point in Israeli-Arab relations at Casablanca on late October 1995. The Casablanca Economic Conference was convened by King Hassan of Morocco to consider cooperative endeavors in economic development for the nations of North Africa and the Middle East. Both Shimon Peres and Yitzak Rabin spoke urging that the 700 million dollars annually spent on arms in the region be cut in half. This could support the development of water resources for the area, which was 90% desert, and also to aid the economy of the new autonomous Gaza Strip in Palestine. A theme was "Let's fight the desert instead of each other." Israel, Egypt, Jordan and Morocco were in agreement. Other Arab nations like Iraq, Iran and Saudi Arabia held back fearing the openness of the Casablanca Conference. Did they fear that Israel was getting too much recognition? These three nations were, after all, committed to Israel's destruction.

Casablanca was followed up by another economic conference in Jordan with King Hussein. Proceedings gave encouragement of future cooperation with Israel by Jordan and Egypt and also Qatar and some of the Persian Gulf states. Things really seemed to be "looking up" a little.

But in January 1996 twenty-nine soldiers and a civilian were blown up at a bus station in the city of Netanya in northern Israel. Every time Israel and the Palestinians collaborated for peace, the terrorist organizations, especially Hamas, literally "blew up" the cooperation. During this whole period of negotiation a total of 100 Israelis had been killed and 500 injured by the *shahid*—Arab suicide bombers.

Israel was working toward a plan to allow the Palestinians complete autonomy in the West Bank. Even Arafat tried to stop militants from sabotaging these plans by arresting many terrorists. It took meticulous preparation, but finally a four stage plan was worked out to give the Palestinian Authority most of the control over the West Bank. The 314 page agreement called Oslo II was signed in Washington D.C. by Arafat and Rabin on September 28, 1995. One has to ask how the Israelis could go ahead with more and more concessions when none of the original agreements had ever been kept by the Palestinians? The negotiators on Israel's side seemed to be possessed with a strange kind of blind insanity.

Conservative Jews hated the agreements and reviled Yitzhak Rabin calling him a traitor even likening him to a Nazi SS officer. Tens of thousands marched in Jerusalem in front of the Knesset protesting what they called "the ceding of Biblical land to murderers." Ariel Sharon called Rabin a traitor for collaborating with a terror organization.

It is seldom mentioned that there was a very active Communist party in Israel that was a prime supporter of making any sacrifice to appease the Palestinians and establish a Palestinian state. The Knesset just barely passed the bill giving autonomy to the Palestinians on the West Bank by a vote of 61 to 59. It would be accurate to say that the Communist party influence probably turned the tide in favor of this compromise. All aspects of civilian life there were now under the control of the Palestinian National Authority. According to the original Oslo plan, the PNA were to secure the territory with their own police force, which had been armed by the Israelis. Also more than 1000 Palestinian prisoners were granted amnesty and released from Israel's jails including some murderers. Israel's concessions were nothing less than outrageous. They received nothing but empty words and promises in return.

On November 4, 1995, Prime Minister Rabin and Shimon Peres were speaking to a rally in Tel Aviv celebrating the Oslo II agreement. As he left the meeting while walking to his car Rabin, as he had been warned, was assassinated by a young Israeli university student Yigal Amir who had been stalking him for several weeks. The extreme frustration of Jewish conservatives with these one-sided agreements with the Arabs had borne bitter fruit.

Rabin's funeral drew heads of state from all over the world including President Bill Clinton, King Hussein, and even President Hosni Mubarak of Egypt, who had never set foot in Israel before. Yasser Arafat was warned not to come, but he showed his concern by secretly visiting Rabin's wife Leah in Tel Aviv one evening to express his sincere sorrow. Perhaps he realized that it could have happened to him. It seems that Rabin had become a friend and had made a mark for compromise and at least a temporary truce with the Palestinians and some of the Arab states. At the least Arafat owed Rabin a great deal, because this king of all Arab terrorists had put on "sheeps' clothing" and had taken and taken and taken and had given nothing in return. With Rabin's death all real hope for any kind of success, if it had ever even been possible, was dashed to pieces.

The elections of 1996 sounded the death knell to a continuation of serious negotiations. Benjamin Netanyahu, head of the conservative Likud Party, won the election over the liberal Shimon Peres by a whisker. One-half of a percentage point separated the candidates. Netanyahu and the Likud took a hard line and initiated the continuation of the building of settlements near Jerusalem and on the West Bank. They cut the Palestinian share of the area from 80% to 40% and divided it into area blocs or cantons. They also expressed total opposition to a future Palestinian state and refused even to consider giving up any part of the Golan Heights. The Oslo Accord and Oslo II were in tatters. Arafat continued to support the terrorists. If there had been any chance for peace, as unlikely as it was before, now it had been shattered to the point of being snuffed out completely.

There was then another fruitless attempt to bring Israelis and Palestinians together again at Wye River, Maryland in October 1998 in order to restart the peace process. The new Israeli Prime Minister Benjamin Netanyahu had opposed the Oslo Accords and sought to withdraw from the peace negotiations because of Palestinian non-compliance. He was, however, virtually forced by President Bill Clinton and public opinion in Israel to sign an accord on October 23, 1998 with PNA President Yasser Arafat, which reiterated an agreement to implement the Oslo peace process. Both the meeting and the agreement, however, proved again to be a meaningless farce. The Palestinians continued to violate all previous commitments. They took and took from the Israelis, but never implemented a single promise. The only result was that these conferences kept the two parties talking with each other, and led eventually to the meeting of the Palestinians and Israelis with President Bill Clinton at Camp David in

July 2000, which finally unmasked Arafat for the total dissembler and fraud that he was.

The Camp David Meeting
President Clinton, Barak, and Arafat—July 2000

The former military hero Commander General Ehud Barak was elected Prime Minister of Israel, defeating Bibi Netanyahu on May 18, 1999. The economy may have been a major concern, but the stalled peace process with the Palestinians was also an issue. Barak promised to try to revive efforts for peace along the lines of the Oslo Accords.

Ehud Barak and Yasser Arafat met with President Bill Clinton at Camp David for two weeks in July of 2000. President Clinton was committed to hammering out an agreement between Israel and the Palestinians like the historic peace pact that President Jimmy Carter had mediated between Menachem Begin and Anwar Sadat of Egypt in 1979. Clinton may have had visions of a Nobel Peace prize, as he was always very concerned for his legacy and his place in history. That he failed to get a response or even an attempt at negotiations from Arafat, who rejected every offer, was a bitter pill to swallow. He felt that Arafat was not really serious, and Clinton had wasted his time.

To the world the terms offered by Barak and Clinton to Arafat seemed the most generous ever. If Arafat had been truly serious about reaching an agreement, he could have responded with at least something in return, but he rejected the offer out of hand and suggested no alternative. Clinton was furious. Here is his account of the meeting:

> *The true story of Camp David was that for the first time in the history of the conflict the American president put on the table a proposal, based on UN Security Council resolutions 242 and 338, very close to the Palestinian demands, and Arafat refused even to accept it as a basis for negotiations, walked out of the room, and deliberately turned to terrorism. That's the real story—all the rest is gossip.*

What had been offered? What did Arafat reject? It was a comprehensive proposal:

1. The establishment of a demilitarized Palestinian state on 92% of the West Bank and 100% of the Gaza Strip.

2. Some territorial compensation for the Palestinians from Israeli territory for the 8% of the West Bank kept under Israel's control.

3. The dismantling of most of the settlements and the concentration of Jewish settlers on this 8% of the West Bank.

4. A capital for the Palestinian state in East Jerusalem with Palestinian sovereignty established over half the Old City of Jerusalem, which included the Muslim and Christian quarters, and the administration of the Temple Mount.

5. A return of refugees from Syria, Lebanon or Jordan to the Palestinian state, but with no "right of return" to Israel proper.

The international community also would provide a massive billion dollar aid program for the resettlement of refugees in a Palestinian state. These were more generous terms than the Palestinians had ever been offered, but Arafat refused even to consider them. Clinton was enraged and banged his fist on the table shouting, "You are leading your people and the region to a catastrophe." Two months later that same year the bloody Second Intifada had overtaken Palestine. It went on for 4 years and forced Israel to build a fence to stop the invasion of suicide bombers. (See Benny Morris, "Camp David and After," *The New York Review of Books*, Vol. 49, No. 10, June 13, 2002. Reprinted on the Internet under material on Ehud Barak.)

Arafat had wanted complete sovereignty, not just

supervisory control, over East Jerusalem including Haram al-Sharif, the Noble Sanctuary and even the Western Wall. For Israel to give up all sovereignty over the site of its ancient worship and sacrificial center, however, was unthinkable. Barak and Clinton offered Arafat control of the top of the Mount with its two famous mosques. Israel would retain sovereignty only over the Western Wall as a place of prayer plus what was beneath the surface of the Mount because some remains from Solomon's Temple must be there. Arafat refused, denying that Solomon's Temple had ever existed, which has become Arab dogma. Another outrageous lie!

Today excavations are being made on the Mount by the Arabs for the building of another mosque. Trenches have been dug across half the extent of the Mount. Debris from the excavations is being destroyed, especially any evidence of previous structures. The reason that excavators have been commanded to utterly destroy any artifacts that have inscriptions or writings on them is because Arabs are trying to protect their claim that Solomon's Temple never existed. Archeologists are aghast. It has been reported very recently, however, that artifacts from the time of David and Solomon and the First Temple have been found in debris dumps in the Kidron Valley from these excavations. This may have far reaching implications for future negotiations concerning the Temple Mount. One has to ask the question, how can the Israelis who have the ultimate sovereign control over all of the area permit this kind of destruction and desecration? It makes no sense at all except when you find that the Israeli antiquities official that gave permission for this desecration was not an archeologist at all, but only a politician. Someday Israel will be judged by history as thoughtless, negligent, and irresponsible. It seems that some pagan Jews will sacrifice anything for an ephemeral promise of peace and recognition.

At a follow-up meeting at the Egyptian resort Taba in the Sinai where Arafat and Peres had concluded Oslo II in

1995, Clinton, with Barak's consent, sweetened the pot for Arafat. (1) 95%, not 92%, of the West Bank would be Palestinian; (2) A more generous portion of Israel's territory would be swapped for the remaining 5% of the West Bank; (3) Palestinians could have sovereignty over all the Arab sections of Jerusalem; (4) Israel was giving up the Jordan Valley settlements and an international peacekeeping force would replace the Israeli Defense Force along the Jordan River. No concession, however, could be made for any Palestinian refugees to be resettled in Israel proper.

Arafat was not interested in even the new more generous offer. He would be satisfied with nothing less than all of East Jerusalem, sovereignty over the entire Temple Mount, and a home in Israel for Palestinian refugees. Arafat refused to compromise, which is the typical Muslim response. Further negotiations were impossible. It was obvious Arafat did not want peace, and he had to have excuses to reject it. What Arafat wanted and the only thing Palestinian leaders will accept to this day is the ultimate possession of all the land of Israel for themselves and the abandonment of all thought of a Jewish State in Palestine. This being the case, any reasonable person must ask, "Of what use is the pursuit of any further negotiations unless there is a genuine change in the hearts and minds of the Palestinian Arabs?"

Arab citizens already constituted 20% of Israel. They had taken the side of the Palestinian Authority and therefore had become hostile aliens in their own nation. It would be comparable to 45 million Hispanics living in the United States who had sworn allegiance to Fidel Castro and Cuba. This is an intolerable and monstrous dilemma!

What bothered Prime Minister Ehud Barak most was all the lying, the deceit, the prevarication, and the outright, blatant duplicity displayed by Yasser Arafat. He described it in this straightforward fashion referring to Arafat and his associates:

They are products of a culture in which to tell a lie creates no dissonance. They don't suffer from the problem of telling lies that exists in Judeo-Christian culture. Truth is seen as an irrelevant category. There is only that which serves your purpose and that which doesn't. They see themselves as emissaries of a national movement for whom everything is permissible. There is no such thing as 'the truth.'

In this area of the compromise of truth, Islam is identical to Marxist-Leninism and Nazism. They all practiced "the big lie" as a matter of state policy. Truth was relative to only what worked for them or what they wanted it to be. Leftist-liberals in the West also have little respect for the concept of truth. Leftists in America and Europe nor only have no concern for truth but also at the same time consistently accuse their opponents of lying when they are invariably the ones who are guilty. Where does it originate? Jesus said that Satan was "a liar from the beginning and the Father of lies." Jesus would likely have also characterized all of these miscreants as "children of the devil" as he did certain leaders in His own society (John 8:44). The Apostle Paul would have said that the "ruler of the kingdom of the air" or Satan was the "spirit who is at work in these children of disobedience" (Ephesians 2:2).

There are too many examples of this dissembling in the words and actions of Arafat to list them all. Some examples are as follows:

1. Arafat made an unabashed profession to his people that his agreement with Israel would be like the ten-year truce of Hudaybiyyah, which Muhammad unilaterally violated after seventeen months when he felt strong enough to attack Mecca in 629.

2. Arafat called Israel's attacks on Palestinians unprovoked and indiscriminate. All the Israeli attacks, however, had

been in retaliation for the horrendous Palestinian suicide bombings and murders of innocent Israeli civilians. It has been proved to the contrary that the Israeli military has been more discriminating than most defense forces in seeking military rather than civilian targets.

3. Arafat promised to recognize the Jewish state, but never put it into any of the PLO documents, all of which continued to deny Israel's right to exist.

4. Arafat always deceitfully claimed to have accepted what he actually had rejected.

5. Arafat accused Israel of carrying out suicide bombings against Palestinians, which never happened.

6. Arafat blamed an Israeli Defense Force soldier for the suicide bombing attack on the Dolphinarium Disco where 25 young Israelis were killed. Similarly Jews today are blamed for the attack on the Twin Towers and the Madrid railway bombing by Arab propagandists who have become notorious for their exaggerations and outright lies. It is so predictable that it is ridiculous!

7. Arafat routinely accused Israel of using poison gas and radioactive materials against Palestinian civilians. Palestinians took Arafat's word seriously and hated Israelis more than ever, but this was nothing but fabricated propaganda. Lying and fraud was incarnate in Arafat. Only one word describes this; namely, "This is an unmitigated evil."

Clinton finally recognized recognized Arafat as the cunning con man and fraud that he was. When Israeli Intelligence, the Mossad, and the CIA discovered strong evidence that Arafat had planned the Second Intifada, the United States refused anymore to deal with him as a representative of the

Palestinian people. He was regarded as an untrustworthy rogue in the same category as Saddam Hussein. Both of them had similar roots in the Muslim Brotherhood, Egypt's original Islamist terrorist organization. Arafat also was related to the grand nephew of the archenemy of Israel, the former Grand Mufti of Jerusalem, and Hitler's friend Hajj Amin al Husseini, whom we have seen was an implacable enemy of the Jews and a supporter of the Holocaust. Arafat called Hajj Amin "our hero" in 2002. For all his stubborn fakery Arafat is regarded as a hero in the Arab world today. He is right up there in the Arab pantheon of heroic figures with Der Fuhrer himself.

Why had it taken so long to unmask Arafat? Why did these mediators and negotiators refuse to recognize Arafat for the duplicitous, deceitful politician that he was? An old adage says, "Hope springs eternal in the human breast." The Jews and others in the West wanted peace and a settlement of the Palestinian conflict so much that they refused to give up and throw in the towel, no matter what. There is a time, however, when to pursue an unrequited hope becomes an utterly perverse, foolish, and irrational gesture.

Chapter 8

CONFLICTS WITH THE PALESTINIANS
THE SECOND INTIFADA
CONTINUING EFFORTS FOR PEACE—
2000 TO THE PRESENT

The Second Intifada: 2000

The peace process had endured for seven years. But hopes that had been raised by the Oslo Accords with the handshake between Arafat and Rabin on the White House lawn in 1993 were thoroughly dashed to pieces by a renewed eruption of violence between Palestinians and Israelis in September of 2000. This became known as the al-Aqsa Intifada because it was triggered by a fiery sermon by Sheikh Hayan al-Idrisi in the al-Aqsa mosque on Friday September 30, 2000. It was the day after Ariel Sharon had visited the Temple Mount named in Arabic, *al-Haram al-Sharif*—The Noble Sanctuary—to demonstrate that Jews still had sovereignty over the area. Israel's sovereignty over the Mount had been called into question by Arafat at the Camp David meeting with Clinton and Barak.

Sharon was the leader of the Likud, the conservative opposition party in the Israeli parliament, which had opposed Prime Minister Ehud Barak's attempts at peace with Yasser Arafat at the Camp David meetings with President Clinton. As a secular leftist Barak had indicated a willingness to sacrifice Israel's claim to the sacred site and to give up most of East Jerusalem. Sharon's visit to the Temple Mount was to publicize his opposition to this decision. It caused an immediate uproar among the Palestinians. But just this one provocative visit, which Sharon had every right to make as an Israeli citizen, would probably never have triggered the days and days of violence without the rabid attacks of Sheikh Idrisi at the very next day's prayer services at al-Aqsa mosque.

Sheikh Hayan al-Idrisi was an avowed anti-Semite who had fiercely opposed the Camp David negotiations from the beginning. He, in fact, was opposed to any peace with Israel. He warned with incendiary oratory that the Jews were going to tear down the Muslim sacred mosques and erect their own Temple and synagogues. This, of course, was another outright lie. If Israel had wanted to tear down these mosques, they would have done it 23 years earlier when they retrieved Jerusalem from the control of Jordan. Al-Idrisi urged his hearers to "eradicate the Jews from Palestine." The response of the crowd to his words was the final blow destroying the peace process. The Second Intifada had begun.

Arabs emerged from the mosque with passions inflamed and immediately attacked a nearby Israeli police station. They also threw down stones and bottles from the top of the Temple Mount onto the heads of Jewish worshippers at the Western Wall. One Israeli policeman was murdered in cold blood defending himself. Israeli police then tried to break up the riot, and four Palestinians were killed. It was the beginning of months of disorder, turmoil, and violence.

On October 4th Palestinian television stirred up the people by showing tapes of the violence during the first Intifada dating from 1988 to 1990, played martial songs, and urged Palestinians to take to the streets. A general strike was called, and many Palestinians refused to show up for work. Schools were let out so that students could join in the "shaking."

Israel has always been blamed for provoking the attacks, but any objective evaluation of the events must show the culpability of a Palestinian leadership, which, no matter what Israel did or didn't do, was utterly opposed to any kind of peace. Their goal was the obliteration of the State of Israel and all the Jews they could possibly kill. They were simply obeying with a religious fervor the vision of their own prophet Muhammad.

This is still the unabashed aim of the terrorist organizations, such as Hamas, to this very day. With them there is no compromise at all—no middle ground, not even any possibility for negotiations. An Hamas spokesman Dr. Ismail Radwan in an interview with the newspaper Al-Risalah said:

> We will liberate Palestine, all of Palestine. Palestine will not be liberated by negotiations, committees and decisions. It will only be liberated by the rifle and the al-Kassam rocket. Therefore prepare yourselves.

The Western press, including the media in the United States, almost universally blamed Israel for provoking the riots and the violence. But they never ever told the whole story. The fact was that Israel had held sovereignty over the Temple Mount since the 1967 war. They had permitted Muslim clerics to be in charge of the Mount because the Muslim holy places were there. This was very different from the policy of the Muslims when they had controlled Jerusalem. We have seen that the Arab Legions of Jordan destroyed the Jewish quarter including the ancient synagogues in 1948 and would not allow any Jew to live in the area or come anywhere near the Temple Mount, which included their prayer center at the Western Wall. The "tolerance" was obviously all one-sided. So why was the Western Press so deceived?

Arafat and his minions continued to claim that Israel was entirely to blame and was aggressively massacring the Palestinian people. This was the Palestinian mantra for the next three years. Israelis were accused of "premeditated murder." They said, *It's a massacre being committed against the Palestinian people, a complete massacre."* The Palestinian cause was driven again by a monstrous lie, and very few news sources were willing to point this out.

I remember hearing Palestinian spokeswoman Hanan Ashrawi claim on CNN television that it was a *"unilateral war*

by Israel against the civilian population." This was an outright
fabrication, a complete falsehood, and clearly fraudulent.
The Palestinians initiated the original violence. The Israelis
were defending themselves and seeking to reestablish order,
which was their responsibility as governors in the land. In
light of the unprovoked Palestinian aggression, what was
Israel supposed to do, "lie down and play dead"?

The Palestinian security chief Muhammad Dahlan
added, *"Israel started this war, and everything Israel is doing is making Palestinian's anger stronger."* This again was a completely
false statement, but ABC News cited this quotation without
any recognition that Israel, of course, was definitely not
responsible for the renewed violence. (See Muravchik,
Covering the Intifada, p. 28.) It seemed that the liberal Press
just wanted another excuse to condemn the Jewish state.

Here is the true story as confessed by the Palestinians
themselves. In a bold, even arrogant, forthright statement,
the Palestinian Authority's Minister of Communication
Emmad El Faluji boasted in Arabic to the Palestinians, *"The
Intifada was already planned from the time Arafat returned from
Camp David where Arafat stood up to President Clinton."* He spoke
proudly of the fact that Arafat had rejected the American
proposal right in the heart of the land of America itself. With
this admission the *coup de grace* was given to any accusation
that Ariel Sharon's visit to the Temple Mount was what had
triggered the Second Intifada, or that Israel was the initiator
of the renewed conflict.

The Palestinians used the Intifada to seek sympathy
from the entire world; and much of the media in the United
States and Western Europe assisted them. Their lying propaganda effort was largely successful. Throughout the conflict
Israel had the upper hand in armaments and did have to
resort to "deadly force" when soldiers were in danger for
their lives. Now, however, Palestinians were also fighting not
just with stones but also with guns and explosives.

The Israeli Defense Force had to be called in to retaliate

and protect the population when terrorists among the Palestinians began to employ suicide bombers, purposely targeting women, children, tourists, shoppers, and every variety of civilian. The IDF responded by destroying the homes of the bombers and whole sections of towns like Jenin on the West Bank where many of the suicide bombers originated and the bombs were made. They even took out many buildings in Ramallah including the headquarters of Yasser Arafat's government. Arafat remained in the midst of the rubble staunchly defying the Israeli army, continuing to sit in his office, as if daring the Israelis to make him a martyr.

I have examined scores of reports on the Internet, which list the brutal attacks of the Israeli Defense Force. They are almost always exaggerated and never described as retaliation for Palestinian aggression. Page after page describes the fighting without a single recognition that there was ever a Palestinian suicide bomber or any kind of unprovoked attack on Israeli civilians. This slanted information is not only produced by Arab news sources but is common fare put out by the Western liberal media including CNN. One would think that the Palestinians are all angelic victims and the Israelis are monsters. It is a flagrant injustice, and again, a monstrous lie. I can think of no objective excuse for media complicity in these falsehoods except for the presence of an ingrained anti-Semitism or some kind of demonic control of the media. Otherwise there is no explanation for journalists, who are supposed to be trained to present an accurate account of the facts, totally ignoring the truth.

Suicide Bombers

Eight months into the conflict on June 1, 2001 the first of the now famous suicide bombings took place outside a Tel Aviv Disco called the Dolphinarium. Twenty-seven Israelis were killed mostly teenage girls. Four months earlier the Likud Party leader Ariel Sharon had amassed a landslide victory over Labor Party leader Prime Minister Ehud Barak whose attempt at appeasement had borne bitter fruit. The Palestinians reacted to Israel's choice of the old warrior with a proclamation calling for another "day of rage." Palestinians hated Ariel Sharon. They called him a "war criminal" because of the disaster in the Palestinian refugee camps Sabra and Shatila in Lebanon almost twenty years earlier. (See Chapter 6 under the "War in Lebanon—1982.")

Two weeks before this first suicide bombing Sharon had announced a "policy of restraint." He was hoping that the George J. Mitchell Commission report of the American fact-finding committee published April 30, 2001 would result in a cessation of hostilities and kick-start a new chance for peace. Both Israel and the Palestinians accepted the report, which recommended (1) a cease-fire, (2) sincere Palestinian efforts to restrain terrorism and Israel's freezing of settlements, and (3) the resumption of negotiations. Like most other well-meaning efforts before and since, the Commission's Report was given lip service but never implemented.

Dozens of the suicide bombings had been documented by the world press and need no further description except to say that a large number of the Palestinians who are being used in this form of terror are very young people from 11 to 17 years of age. These teenagers are emotionally driven and hardly have the life experience to make a responsible decision. They are brainwashed from the time they are children to hate Jews and glorify death by martyrdom. It is an unspeakable tragedy rooted in misinformation, false teaching, deceit, and hatred.

In April 2001 two months after Sharon's election, the Palestinians for the first time fired mortars from Gaza into Israel escalating the stakes. As a part of the Oslo Accords, Israel had granted the Palestinians autonomy or self-rule in the Gaza Strip. These kinds of arms, however, had been forbidden to them as a part of the agreement. So in retaliation Sharon commanded that the Palestinian attackers in Gaza be bombed. The Israeli military invaded Gaza for one day.

They were restrained from remaining any longer because of a word of warning from the United States.

Two days earlier the terrorist faction Hizballah in Lebanon had attacked northern Israel with rockets. Israel retaliated by taking out a radar installation, which was manned by Syrians who supported Hizballah. Either the correlation of these separate attacks was planned, or the Palestinians in Gaza simply copied what Hizballah was doing. In both cases the Western media blamed Israel for the escalation. But it was Arabs that had initiated both attacks. Didn't the Israelis have a right to defend themselves? The United Nations, the European Union and the Western press have always condemned Israel for aggressions for which the Palestinians have virtually always been responsible. Is not this demonic?

After an extensive study of the Second Intifada and its coverage in the media, Joshua Muravchik of the Washington Institute for Near East Policy made the following evaluation in 2003. *"The Arabs have behaved more violently toward Israel than vice versa; most Israeli violence has been retaliatory, and Israel has relentlessly sued for peace. It may be true that the Arabs feel that it is they who have been the victims of violence, but this is a highly distorted, self-exculpating image"* (*Covering the Intifada*, p. 61). By and large the western media has not been evenhanded in its reporting but has taken the side of the Palestinians, even believing and supporting their obvious dishonesty, deceitfulness, and outright lies.

The terrorist organization Hamas was rising in popularity among the Palestinians. It had gained favor by supplying food and building schools with funds from supporters all over the Arab world including sympathetic Muslims in America. In fact, this support group became its most important source of income, as we shall see in Book III. Hamas was in favor of violence, and they were the major instigators of the suicide bombers, although Islamic Jihad and the al-Aqsa brigade also participated. Hamas launched 113 suicide bomber attacks against Israelis from 1993 to 2005. We have seen that this was inspired by the Shia example in Lebanon in the previous decade. The Shiites really were the ones to invent suicide warfare.

Hamas constantly cried for a withdrawal of Israel to the pre-1967 boundaries, but they neither promised to recognize a Jewish state in return nor to cease their Jihad. It was always intolerably one-sided. The principle of the Palestinians was to get as many concessions as they could get by negotiations and then take the rest by force. A true peace was never an option for the Islamic radicals. Truces or cease-fires, as we have seen, simply gave the militants a chance to regroup and rearm. This is basic Islamic teaching and strategy taught by the example of the prophet Muhammad.

Yasser Arafat promised to resume the peace talks if Israel would only call a halt to the "massacre of Palestinians," but it was obvious that he could not control the terrorists. Finally it became crystal clear that he never really had any intention of doing so. He even encouraged them. Arafat's word was worthless. Arafat doubtless feared being labeled a collaborator with the Israelis by the terrorists, making himself a candidate for assassination. Arafat's own terror arm, the al-Aqsa brigade led by Marwan Barghouti, participated with Hamas in the suicide bombings. Barghouti, who was rumored to be a possible successor to Arafat, was arrested, tried, and given five separate life sentences for his part in the murder of Israelis. He is still in prison in spite of many efforts to release him for the purpose of leading al-Fatah against Hamas.

Sometimes Arafat would be persuaded to disavow the terrorist acts when confronted by something like the cancellation of a meeting with the visiting American Secretary of State Colin Powell in April of 2002. But no enlightened person could see this as anything but false pretense. Often he would say one thing in English to the Western media, and then the exact opposite, in Arabic, to his supporters. Finally both Israel and the United States refused to negotiate with Arafat at all. One cannot negotiate for peace with a man who has no desire or intention for peace. It is ironic that Arafat had fooled the world so thoroughly that after the Oslo Accords, as we have seen, he was awarded a Nobel Peace Prize. This is unbelievable when you think of it. It seems that in Israel's deep yearning for security they wanted to believe that somehow, someday Arafat's heart would be changed. Time and events have shown that this was nothing but a gullible dream.

One of the best examples of Arafat's duplicity and dishonesty was the event of the arms freighter the Karine-A. The vessel was apprehended by the Israelis on the high seas early in January 2002 after leaving an Iranian port. It was found to be carrying 50 tons of arms for the Palestinians in Gaza. Its destination was confirmed by the testimony of the ship's Palestinian Captain Omar Akawi who himself was a member of Arafat's military arm Al Fatah. For a week Arafat vehemently denied knowing anything about it. Israel was accused of fabricating the story and of using propaganda to subvert the peace process. It was finally proved, however, that Arafat had authorized and arranged for the shipment. It became obvious who the real liars were. The policy of the Muslim terrorists seemed to be, "When you don't know what else to say, tell a lie!" This was in direct contradiction to the terms of the Oslo Accords and a good example of Arafat's true intentions.

The incontrovertible facts shown to officials in Washington concerning Arafat's chicanery and double dealing was what finally resulted in the United States' rejection of Arafat as a partner in any further peace negotiations. How could one negotiate with an inveterate, unrepentant and uncompromising liar, bluffer, fake, and dissembler? The question one must ask is "What took the Washington bureaucrats so long to catch on?"

Because of continuing Palestinian aggression with suicide

bombers, Israel launched its Operation Defensive Shield on March 29, 2002. It was Israel's largest military action during the Intifada and included the invasion of Palestinian territory to root out the bomb making and the suicide bombers. This was when much of the refugee camp of Jenin was leveled. Jenin had been a suicide bomber and bomb-making center.

Before the Israelis attacked Jenin, Arabs had booby-trapped the houses, which was the cause of much of the destruction. Palestinians wailed that thousands, or at least 500 of their people had been brutally killed. The Israelis found only 37 bodies, many of them killed by their own booby traps. A United Nations' commission examined the site and arrived at approximately the same figure. Again the Western press went wild in its condemnation of Israel, believing all the accusations of the Palestinians, which as usual proved to be false.

What was Israel to do when the goal of the militants was the utter destruction of the entire Jewish nation, and the means for accomplishing this goal was a constant, unremitting "armed struggle" or Holy Jihad? As early as the second week of the Second Intifada, Ehud Barak himself had warned that if the rioting and violence continued Israel would respond harshly.

The Palestinians didn't seem to care. It is a technique of Holy Jihad that you wear your enemies down with unremitting, random attacks. In retaliating, the Israeli military was accused by Palestinians and the world media for using a disproportionate show of force. It should be noted, however, that Israel was simply using the weapons it had at its disposal. When stone and bottle throwing escalate into using guns and real ammunition, rubber bullets and tear gas are not very viable. At any time the Israelis could have utterly and ruthlessly destroyed all Palestinian opposition if they had desired to do so. Historians may conclude in retrospect that given the circumstances of the Palestinian assaults against them, Israel really used an uncommon amount of restraint.

Considering the repetition of all this unending murderous rebellion on the part of the Arabs continuing for months with no let up, one could have expected the Israelis to have used even stronger and more lethal measures to once and for all stop the riots and all the suicide bombings. Since this kind of Islam is a cult of death, the only response that they will really understand is deadly force.

During this serious conflict there were many efforts by the United States to encourage a cease-fire and peace between the combatants. There was the Mitchell Commission led by former Senator George Mitchell. Secretary of State Colin Powell made an official visit to both Sharon and Arafat. Special envoy Anthony Zinni was sent to establish new ground for negotiations. There was finally, however, a general acceptance of the fact that the Oslo Accords were dead. Again a good question to ask is, what took the West so long to discover the obvious?

The World Trade Center Bombings
What America Learned On September 11, 2001

The suicide bombings were continuing as before. In defense against the indefensible, Israel began to build a wall to keep out the Palestinian bombers, and Sharon considered plans to unilaterally withdraw from the Gaza Strip, which was headquarters for Hamas. Then came the destruction of the Twin Towers in New York City on September 11, 2001.

Since this al-Qaeda attack on America, Americans became more sympathetic to Israel's fight with terrorists. It was no secret that we wanted the terrorist leader Osama bin Laden dead or alive. In fact, now there was a huge price on his head just like any vicious criminal whose face adorns a Most Wanted poster. President Clinton had belatedly tried to take out Bin Laden with a cruise missile strike against one of his camps in Afghanistan in 1998. The United States had had many earlier chances to eliminate Bin Laden, but liberal leadership was squeamish and hesitant.

The Palestinians had many such terrorist leaders, including one we have already met, Sheikh Ahmed Yassin. He was crippled from his youth and in a wheel chair, but he had founded the Hamas movement in 1987 and was its inspiration, motivating scores of suicide bombings, which killed hundreds of Israeli civilians. Yassin was to Hamas what Osama bin Laden is to al-Qaeda. He had been jailed twice—1983 and again in 1989—but always was released in hostage exchanges. His 1989 imprisonment was for life, but in 1997 he was exchanged for two Mossad agents who had botched an assassination attempt of a leading terrorist in Jordan and had been captured.

Israel tried several times to assassinate or execute Yassin, the one they called "the mastermind of evil." They finally succeeded on March 22, 2004. The Sheikh was exiting a mosque in his wheelchair when an Israeli missile strike from a helicopter ended his life, leaving nothing but his head intact. The hundreds of thousands of Palestinians that participated in Yassin's funeral may have marked the final Hamas' upstaging of the Palestinian Authority.

Only one month after Yassin's assassination Israel also "executed" his successor Abdel-Aziz Al Rantissi, who had pledged to continue Hamas' commitment to suicide bombers and the annihilation of all the Jews. Rantissi, who was a Palestinian pediatrician and a staunch advocate of suicide bombing, had voiced the orthodox principle that, according to Islamic law, Israel could not remain as a nation on land that had formerly been controlled by Islam. He had vowed to continue Hamas' terrorist attacks on Israelis.

Almost 1000 Israelis were killed during the three and one-half years of the Second Intifada. This furious uproar will never end, and peace may never come to the Promised Land until the Prince of Peace, Israel's Messiah, who is Jesus the Christ, returns to bring judgment, to set things right, and to rule the world in righteousness "with a rod of iron" (Psalm 2:9).

The Death of Arafat, the Road Map For Peace, and Israel's Withdrawal from the Gaza Strip

Yasser Arafat died in a Paris hospital on November 11, 2004. The cause of death was not revealed which aroused some suspicion, but French doctors denied that he was poisoned. Most recently it was revealed that he died of AIDS, which appears to have been verified. The Israeli intelligence did have evidence that Arafat was both a homosexual and a pedophile. Whatever the mystery of his death, it temporarily has changed the equation in the Middle East conflict. Arafat had control of the billions of dollars which had been collected in taxes or given to the PLO primarily by western nations to support the Palestinians in nation building and a hoped for quest for peace. How many billions of dollars exist in banks and investments around the world is not known, but estimates run as high as $50 billion, which is probably an exaggerated figure.

Yasser Arafat himself had put billions of dollars in personal bank accounts and investments to assure his own political future. All of this money, much of which was provided by America and European governments, has not yet been recovered. Arafat certainly had proved to be one of the most corrupt men on Earth, although for the time being he is still held in high esteem by most Palestinians. His grave in the West Bank is a shrine, and many want to see him permanently interred on the Temple Mount.

Mahmoud Abbas, whom Arafat had named as his first prime minister in April 2003, was elected chief of the Palestinian Liberation Organization on the day of Arafat's death. Abbas' appointment by Arafat had been made under pressure from the United States and others pushing for a peaceful solution to the Palestinian/Israeli conflict. Abbas, also called Abu Mazen, had been active behind the scenes during the framing of the Oslo Accords and had called for a halt to the attacks on Israel during the 2nd Intifada. He was regarded even by Israelis as the best hope to urge Palestinians to the peace table.

In the conflict with Hamas in the Gaza Strip, Abbas' offices were destroyed, and he fled with some al-Fatah leaders to the West Bank. He has dissolved the Palestinian government. It seems that if new elections were held today, Hamas might receive as little as 15% of the vote because of the uprising. Hamas showed its true colors as a fierce terrorist organization. Israel and the United States have chosen to support Abbas and al-Fatah in this fight. Since Hamas stole all the weapons and armaments, which had been supplied to the Gaza Strip, the United States is having to rearm Abbas and his supporters in the West Bank. The problem is that Mahmoud Abbas is at heart just as against Israel as Hamas, but only wants to move more slowly in implementing a takeover of Palestine. No matter how you look at the continuing conflict, it is an impasse, a "no-win" for the West and Israel.

Before Mahmoud's appointment as prime minister, the United States had set forth a Road Map For Peace. This was a new initiative of what became known as the Quartet or the Big Four—the United States, the United Nations, the European Union, and Russia. It was a plan supported by these four powerful political entities to solve once and for all the Israeli-Palestinian conflict. President George W. Bush outlined its principles in a speech on June 24, 2002. He said, *"The Roadmap represents a starting point toward achieving the vision of two states, a secure State of Israel and a viable, peaceful, democratic Palestine. It is the framework for progress towards lasting peace and security in the Middle East."* However, it was the same old story with the same unhappy ending. Palestinians were supposed to make democratic reforms, which would include elections and abandon terrorism. Israel was to accept the existence of a Palestinian state and withdraw from the Gaza Strip and the West Bank as the terrorism ceased.

In spite of much opposition from Islamic militants, Abbas was also later elected as President of the Palestinian National Authority on January 9 and sworn into office on

January 15, 2005. This gave some encouragement to those who backed the peace process, but it was unlikely that Abbas in either of his new positions would be able to stem the tide of Palestinian hostility and attacks on Israel. An indication of the true spirit of the Palestinians was the elevation of hard-liner Farouk Kaddoumi as Arafat's successor as leader of the Fatah party.

The Oslo Accords had promised an eventual evacuation of the Gaza Strip by Israel. There were 9,500 Israeli settlers who had established very lucrative farms in land next to the Mediterranean Sea. Under pressure from the United States, Prime Minister Ariel Sharon finally did lead Israel in a dramatic, unilateral evacuation in August/September 2005. It was a very traumatic undertaking with much resistance from orthodox and conservative Jews who see all of Palestine as God's "Promised Land" given to Abraham, Isaac, and Jacob and their descendants. Jewish settlements in the Gaza Strip were abandoned altogether. The 9,500 Israelis were literally forced by Israeli soldiers to leave their villages and farms.

I have a theory that President Bush and Sharon had made a secret agreement that if the United States would get rid of Sadaam Hussein, who was regarded as the principal immediate danger to Israel, Sharon would initiate a withdrawal from Gaza to help to move along the new peace initiative The Road Map For Peace. This seems the only way to explain Sharon's complete about face from his previous position that resisted both a withdrawal from the territories and the establishment of a Palestinian state. It was made, nevertheless, as a first step—a gesture for peace and a demonstration of Israel's good will and determination to break the impasse in negotiations with the Palestinians.

After the withdrawal from Gaza was accomplished, there was not a single word of appreciation or thanks from the Palestinians. In fact Hamas and Islamic Jihad claimed victory. Terrorism had triumphed! The militants took credit for "kicking out" the Jews with Allah's help. Gaza is now being used as

The Gaza Strip, 2000

Map : © Jan de Jong

a staging area for attacks against Israel. This action of appeasement therefore which was suggested by the Road Map For Peace and encouraged by President George W. Bush himself totally failed in its purpose, as had every other effort for settling the Palestinian problem. When will the appeasers learn that the only offering that radical Muslims respect is a firm hand or even deadly force? If any who supported the Road Map For Peace thought that this would mollify the militants among the Palestinians, which include Hamas, Islamic Jihad, the Popular Resistance Committee, and Fatah's al-Aqsa Martyr's Brigades, they were to be very disappointed. Any neutral observer would have to say, "What did you expect?"

The withdrawal from Gaza instead of being received as a "peace offering" was declared by the Palestinians to be a victory, a reward, and a justification for suicide bombings and other militant actions against Israel. For example, Iran's leader the Ayatollah Ali Khamenei said, "Although the retreat of the Zionist regime from Gaza is short of Palestinian rights and demands, it is however a big victory that shows the inability of the occupier regime of al Quds (Jerusalem)." Israel's withdrawal from the Gaza Strip was interpreted as a sign of weakness by Muslims, and will just encourage more aggression. This will also be true when the United States withdraws its troops from Iraq. The principle and the response on the part of the terrorists will be the same; namely, the belief that "Allah has conquered."

There was absolutely no acknowledgment by any Islamist that Israel was showing good faith that could lead to a peaceful political engagement. They continue to believe that their Holy Jihad is what had made Israel back down. Their resistance had won them the territory of Gaza. The same would apply to any other settlements that would be ceded to the Palestinians from the West Bank. Instead of stimulating a desire for peace, Israel's withdrawal from Gaza only hardened the radicals in their determination to obliterate Israel and acquire all of Palestine. They chanted to Israeli soldiers, "We will continue with the rest of Judea, Samaria, Jerusalem, until we control all of Israel." The Hamas leader Mahmoud al-Zahar's response was, "Let Israel die." From any reasonable point of view, the withdrawal made little sense, and must be judged a failure. How long will it take the West to learn that the appeasement of radicals will never succeed? Jan Markel, a well-known radio talk show host, has called these continuing fruitless efforts on the part of the diplomats "the appease disease."

After Israel's withdrawal. the Palestinians in a demonstration of infamous stupidity demolished all remnants of what they called "the occupation." They wanted to erase all memory of an Israeli presence in their land. They were especially eager to deface and destroy all the synagogues. They foolishly even wiped out Israel's successful agricultural industry, which if managed well could have helped feed all the Palestinians as it had the Israelis.

In spite of protestations by the feckless Mahmoud Abbas, both the border to Egypt and the Mediterranean Sea are open to the importing of as many arms and terrorists as the Palestinians want to admit and maybe even more than they want to contend with. Every hater of Israel perceives this as a golden opportunity. Already we are seeing an unending barrage of homemade Kassam rockets falling on the town of Sderot in the Negev and other Israeli targets. Israel is retaliating by bombing rocket sites in the Gaza Strip. This is largely the work of Hamas that has dedicated itself to Israel's destruction. Gaza is now becoming an armed camp, a haven for terrorists of every stripe including al-Qaeda, and a future base of continuing rocket attacks against Israeli farms, villages, and towns. It will be a training center for those committed to Israel's destruction. Israel also has decided that the assassination attempts on terrorist leaders, called terrorists-in-suits, will continue. When one considers that the Israelis could obliterate the Palestinians in one day, their forbearance is quite amazing.

Sharon proposed that strategic West Bank settlements would be secured, but others would be given up. The conservative Likud party rejected Sharon's proposals, and Benjamin Netanyahu made another effort to replace Sharon but without success. Israel, however, has almost completed erecting a security fence to protect itself from the infiltration of suicide bombers and other terrorists. The fence has succeeded in cutting these attacks to a trickle.

The Victory of Hamas over Al-Fatah in Gaza

Elections were held by the Palestinians in January 2006. The ruthless, intractable terrorist group Hamas won a majority of the seats in the Palestinian legislature. Hamas has since taken complete control of the Gaza Strip defeating al Fatah in a brief civil war. Remnants of al Fatah have fled to Egypt and the West Bank, and Hamas has continued rocket attacks on Israel. The Road Map For Peace like every other initiative seems dead.

Hamas is trying to replace the Palestinian National Authority with new leadership for Palestinians. If they were to succeed, any further negotiations between Palestinians and Israelis will be very unlikely. Hamas and al-Fatah, the terrorist group representing the old PLO and the Palestinian National Authority, finally came to bitter blows. A full-blown civil war between rival terrorists groups erupted in the Gaza Strip. Hamas has won. This Resistance Movement has murdered most of the Fatah leaders and has taken complete control of the territory. Other Fatah leadership fled to Egypt. This conflict is spilling over into the West Bank, and Syria, backed by Iran, may enter the fray. Hamas and Hizballah have become the arm of Syria and Iran in the Palestinian conflict with Israel. In fact, we are close to another all out war between Muslims and Jews. The new PA leader Mahmoud Abbas and his counterpart in Hamas, Prime Minister Ismail Haniyeh, sought a cease-fire, but were unable to stop the fighting in the Gaza Strip. With the Hamas win, al-Fatah was forced to establish a new headquarters in the West Bank.

In light of this new civil war, American diplomats were wondering which side they should support or which side will they deal with to extend to them new terms of peace in Palestine. We have put our hope in Mahmoud Abbas and al-Fatah. We are resupplying them with arms that they lost in the defeat to Hamas, who confiscated all the American arms in Gaza. It has just been reported that a lot of the money was embezzled—only $7 million was left in a $52 million account in the West Bank. Not being able to take over the West Bank, Hamas has been extending gestures of reconciliation with al-Fatah and Abbas. I do not believe, however, that anything that America or any other nations in the world may try to do will succeed. Hope, if it ever really existed, in my opinion is certainly lost for any peaceful solution to the Palestinian conflict between Jews and Muslims.

There are some who believe, furthermore, that America's insistence on "dividing the land" of Israel and pushing for the establishment of a Palestinian state has not been in our nation's best interest. The prediction of the Old Testament prophet Joel is clear that God will judge the nations severely who have "divided up my land" (Joel 3:2). Also the promise of God to Abraham has existed for centuries and applies here:

> *I will make you into a great nation and I will bless you; I will make your name great, and you will be a blessing. I will bless those who bless you, and whoever curses you I will curse; and all peoples on earth will be blessed through you* (Genesis 12:2-3).

There are those who point to reversals in America's fortunes including the last hurricanes in the South and a persistent national drought in many areas as retaliation for America forcing this curse on Israel. How many more disasters will it take to get our attention? (Note the extensive article by Aaron Klein of World Net Daily's Jerusalem Bureau, "Did God send Katrina as Revenge over Gaza?" posted on September 7, 2005; and also a new book by White House Correspondent Bill Koenig, *Eye to Eye: Facing the Consequences of Dividing Israel*.)

The New Iraqi War and the Capture and Execution of Saddam Hussein: Striving for Democracy in the Middle East

A new foreign policy for the Bush Administration was born in the aftermath of 9/11. The aggressive hijacking of four passenger jetliners by 19 al-Qaeda terrorist pirates and the ensuing national tragedy, which saw airplane bombs destroy the Twin Towers of the World Trade Center and part of the Pentagon, changed everything. It awakened President

George Bush and his administration to the fact that we were being forced into a new world-encompassing war. It is being called a War on Terror, but in reality it is a war against a reawakened, resurgent, militant, radical Islam, called Islamism or Islamofascism, which has displayed its ugliness in its renewed goal to dominate all civilizations. It is truly a conflict that threatens to invade the whole world. We endured World War I and World War II. The Cold War with Marxist/Communism could certainly be considered World War III. The worldwide conflict with Islamofascism, therefore, should be called World War IV.

Many reject the idea that this could honestly be the true face of Islam. Being reassured by moderates and friends in the Islamic world, President Bush has publicly stated that he believes Islam is at heart a peaceful and tolerant religion. We have seen, however, that the orthodox teachings of Muhammad, the Qur'an and the Hadith are anything but peaceful and tolerant. As President Bush has become more thoroughly informed in the history and teachings of Islam, we hope that he has changed his mind.

Islam has never been a "noble religion" as President Bush once declared. It has proved itself in its orthodox form over and over again to be ruthless, blood thirsty, aggressively militant, uncompromising and downright evil. As we learned in Book I, it is Satan's counterfeit substitute for Judeo/Christianity, and as such reflects the character of Satan himself. Just two contrasting phrases from the New Testament and the Qur'an tell the story. Jesus said, "Love your enemies." Muhammad said, "Assassinate your enemies."

The aggressions of militant Islamists are part of the long Muslim tradition of Holy War or Holy Jihad, which has as its goal the conquest and control of all the nations of the earth by Islam. This is orthodox Islam. It is an essential part of the teaching and commands of Muhammad himself. In the collection of his teachings called the Hadith is found this statement by the prophet:

The sword is the key of heaven and hell; a drop of blood shed in the cause of Allah, a night spent in arms, is of more avail than two months of fasting or prayer: whosoever falls in battle, his sins are forgiven, and at the day of judgment his limbs shall be supplied by the wings of angels and cherubim.

For Muslims who are the most serious in their commitment to their Islamic religion, their personal convictions will usually come out on the side of the Islamists. A poll taken in Saudi Arabia, for example, concluded that 95% of the men in the society, which really is the only half of the population that counts in that country, were on the side of Osama bin Laden. Many who publicly decry and even condemn the bombing of "innocent infidels" wear a smile of triumph in their hearts. A recent poll of Muslims in America has concluded that as many as 5% of them support al-Qaeda. This is a substantial number of enemies in our midst numbering at least as many as 150,000 to 250,000 individuals who may wish to do us harm. A recent poll of Muslim young people under 30 years of age, who were brought up in the mosques and madrassahs of America, concluded that 26% support suicide bombing as a method of defending Islam. And with Islam it is a short step from defense to offense. The world is in deep trouble especially America, because we are along with Israel the principal target that the Islamists want to hit and defeat.

President Bush has told us that he is convinced that all people have an innate desire for freedom. This should be no surprise to a nation that began by declaring to the world, "All men are created equal, and have been endowed with rights including liberty by their Creator. Former British Prime Minister Tony Blair agreed. In addressing Congress in 2003, Blair reminded our lawmakers that it is a myth that our values and principles are only Western values and principles. They are universal, and given the opportunity all "ordinary people" will embrace them. Consequently the expressed goal of our preemptive military strikes in both Afghanistan and Iraq has been the liberating of the common people and the establishment of democracies in the Middle East.

Both of these ideas no matter how noble, however, are utterly foreign and in direct contradiction to orthodox Islamic teaching. The American values of liberty and government of, by, and for the people are an anathema to Islamic teachers and leaders who are committed to the "rule of Allah" as expressed in shari'ah law. With orthodox Muslims, theocracy trumps democracy every time. Democracy means the "rule of the people." Devout Muslims at heart will only accept the "rule of Allah."

Time alone will tell us if President Bush has had a stroke of courageous inspiration or if he has been foolishly idealistic. Russian society has found the adoption of capitalism and democracy difficult, because after 70 years of atheistic communism the people's worldview is so different from the West. This is even more true in the Islamic countries of the Middle East where the Muslim religious mindset finds it almost impossible to adapt to the values of capitalism and democracy.

It was really a reaction to western ways and western values that provoked the resurgence of radical orthodox Islam in the first place. This was true in Egypt in the rise of the Muslim Brotherhood, which objected to the encroachment of western civilization. The revolution in Iran was also a reaction by the clerics and the conservatives against efforts of the Shah to westernize their country. The rise of the Taliban in Afghanistan happened for the same reasons. Osama bin Laden agrees with them all. Hatred for the west, including Israel's intrusion into the Middle East carrying western culture and values, is the number one motivation for terrorism and the resurgency of ultra orthodox Islam. This is Islam's Reformation—a return to the original values of the Qur'an and the teachings of the Prophet.

Shortly after his reelection victory in 2004, Bush invited Natan (Anatoly) Sharansky, a Ukrainian and much celebrated

Soviet dissident, who had become housing minister in the Israeli cabinet, to the Oval office. Sharansky is the author of *The Case for Democracy,* a book whose thesis echoes Bush's own convictions that people desire to be free, and that if all the nations of the world were democratic, the world would be a safer place. He believes with Bush that "democracies do not make war against democracies."

Sharansky is convinced that only a democratic Palestinian state can work side by side with Israel. On the other hand, he opposed the pullout from Gaza and believes that only a hard line similar to what Ronald Reagan took with the Soviets will work with the Palestinians. He agrees with Bush that we must confront evil and not appease it. However, unlike other Israeli hawks, he is willing to negotiate with the Palestinians and even give them some land. He praised Bush for turning his back on the duplicitous Arafat's dictatorship before the latter's death, and is enthusiastic about Bush's drive to democratize the Middle East.

So far Bush has seen some superficial success. Victories even without the complete subduing of insurgents in Afghanistan and Iraq have been followed with more or less successful elections. This seemed to stimulate hope in the hearts of some citizens in the Middle East and fear or contempt in the hearts of others. Elections followed in Lebanon, in the Palestinian National Authority and in Egypt. Without an educated, free, and honorable electorate, however, elections by themselves are unlikely to yield positive results. Elections may put tyrants and terrorists in power, such as Hamas in Gaza, and maybe even the Muslim Brotherhood in Egypt, and Hizballah in Lebanon. Bush and his supporters in this policy are fooling themselves if they think that this is the answer.

It is unlikely that these latter gestures toward democracy will produce the changes that the West is hoping for. Where efforts for democracy have been backed up by the U.S. military, however, there has been some superficial progress. The belief that the average citizen desires freedom and will exercise this freedom by participating with his vote appears to be true. It will not be encouraged by any Islamic clerical or teaching authority, however, and therefore has little hope for a lasting success. There is a militant Muslim saying about adapting to the democratic process. They will support "one man, one vote, one time." We are already facing the grave danger of popular terrorist groups winning many seats in the legislatures of Lebanon, Egypt, and the Palestinian Authority. In our hope for democracy in the Middle East, we should be careful what we wish for.

Democracy, however, is much more than having elections. A viable constitution and government must be established to reflect these values. It seems unrealistic to believe that this can be accomplished in nations who have no "idea" or "value" basis for such kinds of principles or institutions. We should remember that our principles of liberty and democracy and our democratic institutions were developed at least over a period of 500 years from the time of the Magna Carta to the Declaration of Independence. Also they had a Biblical and evangelical Christian base, which taught liberty and individual responsibility to the Creator God of the Bible who has much different principles and a far different character from Allah of the Qur'an. (See chapter on "Allah, the God of Islam" in *Book I, Islam Rising: The Never Ending Jihad Against Christianity*.) It is not surprising that the Iraqi government elected by the people is showing signs of resulting in a complete failure.

Are there any traditions or institutions or leadership in any of these nations upon which to build or foster democratic principles? Joshua Muravchik, resident scholar at the American Enterprise Institute, a Jewish neoconservative, recently went to the Middle East to find out. He attended a number of conferences with Arab intellectuals and politicos. He described his findings in an article in *Commentary Magazine* called "Among Arab Reformers" (Sept. 2005, pp. 45-52).

Among them he found some Muslims who wanted to see an Islamic Reformation, which would reinterpret religious texts to show that Islamic values are in harmony with the principles of human rights and freedoms. Muravchik said that he *"heard the voices of people who genuinely yearn for freedom—Saudis, Kuwaitis, Tunisians, Lebanese, Iraqis and Egyptians."* He concluded, *"Their voices are stronger today than ever before. What happens next in Iraq will, obviously, have a powerful effect on their prospects at home. They deserve whatever support we can give them. . . for, from what I also saw and heard, a considerable journey lies ahead before their countries are likely to hearken to what they have to say"* (p. 52).

A major obstacle to democracy in the Middle East is the Arab obsession with Israel and their deep hatred for both Israel and the United States. Until the hatred of our two democracies can be quelled, how can the system and political philosophy that we represent be welcomed by a majority of the Arab peoples? Some Arabs have given President Bush credit for stimulating the political ferment for reform and democracy especially in Egypt. Perhaps the future is not hopeless for political democracy at least in this nation. It is feared, however, that even if Egypt were to have more elections, the Muslim Brotherhood, the mother of all terrorist groups, might win, just like Hamas won the majority in the Gaza Strip.

In both Afghanistan and Iraq it appears that the Islamic form of authority will take over. Democracy will certainly have a different face, because even if there is an executive branch and a legislature elected by the people, the third branch of government, the judiciary, will doubtless prove to be the real authority. The judges will determine the law, and it will be Islamic. Presidents will be figureheads and the legislatures elected by the people will simply rubber stamp decisions of the judges, which will be according to their understanding of the will of Allah or shari'ah law as interpreted by Islamic religious leaders and teachers. It is my firm belief that a western style democracy, which assures freedom and human rights to its people, has no possibility of surviving in any Muslim nation that exists today.

The new Iraqi constitution not only states bluntly that no laws can be created that are not in harmony with Islam, but also that the Central or Supreme Court is the sole interpreter of the Constitution. It also has the responsibility to veto any legislation that is inconsistent with Islamic principles and teachings before it is even passed. We will doubtless find that we have only liberated Iraq from Saddam and his secular rule to "free" Iraq to become an Islamic Republic.

President Bush did not begin a preemptive war against Iraq motivated only by a Wilsonian ideal to spread democracy. Saddam Hussein had to be removed from power. He was a threat not only to his own people and his neighbors but also potentially to the whole world. He considered himself a man of destiny like another Hitler. He invaded Kuwait just like Hitler went into the Sudetenland or Austria. If Saddam had been successful in his Kuwait venture, he would have continued his march through the Middle East. Saudi Arabia would probably have been his next victim. He wanted to control the oil of the Middle East and become a world player as the head of a conglomerate of Muslim nations, perhaps even the Caliph of a revived Islamic caliphate.

Weapons of Mass Destruction, Iraqi Oil, and Prospects for Peace

Another major motivation for the second Iraq war was the conviction that Saddam Hussein had created weapons of mass destruction. The whole world believed that he had chemical, biological and even nuclear weapons. It was obvious that he had used at least chemical weapons against the Kurds in Northern Iraq in the mid-1990's. That Saddam had some WMD's was universally believed by all the intelligence services and the United Nations who had sent inspectors into Iraq. The fact that Saddam stonewalled the inspectors and violated several United Nations resolutions seemed enough evidence to justify an invasion of his country to force a regime change.

Bush is being blamed for not being truthful about the WMDs and being accused of devious motives relating to Iraq's oil. Any knowledgeable person can see plainly that this is political mudslinging. Just because we did not find WMDs in Iraq doesn't mean that they were not there or that anybody told lies about them. There is incontrovertible evidence provided by Saddam's own military advisors that chemical and maybe biological weapons were transferred to Syria. President Clinton's own security advisor Sandy Berger had said about Saddam, "He will use those weapons of mass destruction again, as he has ten times since 1983." (Georges Sada, *Saddam's Secrets*, p. 253.)

Few in the media have paid any attention to the testimony of Iraqi General Georges Sada in his book *Saddam's Secrets*. Sada was head of the Iraqi air force and a close advisor to Saddam. He writes, *"It is difficult to understand why so many people in the West have been unwilling to acknowledge the fact that WMDs were not only a fact of life in Iraq for more than thirty years but they were Saddam's obsession"* (p. 255). Sada goes into detail on the progress that was made and how Saddam allowed most of his WMDs to be destroyed because he had forced all of his top scientists, researchers, and technicians, with a threat of death or dismemberment, to memorize all their plans and records so that everything could all be recreated when the United Nations Inspectors had left (pp. 254-55). Those few WMDs that remained were primarily spirited into Syria. Sada claims to be familiar with all the details including the names of the personnel, the trucks, and the aircraft that were involved (pp. 258-59). Then he concludes:

> Since none of this information has been made public, there's been a feeding frenzy in the media for years now, coming particularly from opponents of the Bush administration, claiming that there never were or could have been WMDs in Iraq. This is not true, but I've often wondered

*why this information hasn't appeared in the media. Why
has it been withheld? The Israelis have not hesitated to talk
about it. Israel's intelligence service, the Mossad, is notoriously well informed about military and paramilitary operations in the Middle East, and they've said repeatedly that
Saddam had weapons of mass destruction. They have also
said that some of those weapons were transferred to countries
in the region (Saddam's Secrets, p. 252).*

Finally General Sada examines Saddam's ambitions to
produce atomic weaponry. Saddam had made progress in
the direction of creating nuclear material, but it was inter-
rupted first by Israel's bombing of the Osiraq nuclear reactor
on June 7, 1981. There were many facilities in Iraq involved
in trying to create nuclear weapons, but Saddam knew that
he would not be able to complete the task in secret. Sada
reveals for the first time that Saddam had contracted with
Chinese scientists to pay them as much as $100 million to
manufacture a nuclear weapon for him (pp. 257-58). The
Chinese were given a down payment of $5 million dollars,
but never produced a single bomb for Saddam.

If Bush had any ulterior motive for the invasion of Iraq it
probably concerned Israel and Palestine. As I already shared,
I believe that Bush made a deal with Israel's Prime Minister
Ariel Sharon in 2003. This was the gist: If America removed
the threat of Saddam, who was supporting the Palestinian
intifada by giving $25,000 to each family of a suicide
bomber, Sharon would be obligated to unilaterally withdraw
Jewish settlements from Gaza and parts of the West Bank.
This would show Israel's good faith to the Palestinians and
would jump-start the new initiative called the Road Map For
Peace. Experience shows that this did not work because radical Islamists will not be satisfied with anything short of the
whole enchilada.

Bush also met with the Saudi King Abdullah and assured
him that the United States would do everything possible to

pressure Israel to allow the establishment of a Palestinian state and bring peace to that area. In turn the Saudis would continue to support us in the critical matter of an adequate oil supply and in seeking to defund terrorism. The Saudis, however, can only help so much because their oil supply is not without limits, and India and China are putting a greater and greater demand upon energy products driving up prices. Also there are 6,000 Saudi princes and some are willing to support the Wahhabi terrorists from their own ample allotment of oil receipts. I personally think that the Saudi royal family has an arrangement with the Wahhabi clerics and leadership that the royal family gets so much of the oil revenue and the Wahhabists get their substantial percentage in order to support ultra orthodox Islam around the world, e.g., in building mosques and madrassahs and in all the nations, providing Wahhabi literature, and staffing the institutions with Wahhabi imams and mullahs.

The Saudis have offered their own plan for peace. The terms are as follows: If Israel will withdraw to their borders before the Six Day War, giving up Jerusalem and all other lands acquired; and if Israel will allow all Arabs that were displaced by the wars to return to Palestine, then negotiations for peace can begin. Notice only negotiations are mentioned; there are no guarantees. Israel would be foolish even to consider such an offer, which would leave them open to ultimately being exterminated from the land of Palestine. This is, of course, what all orthodox Islamists want to take place, including the Saudis. This plan is nothing but a deceitful ruse.

Finally the Bush administration gambled on Iraqi oil eventually being made available to cover any shortfall in the future. Iraqi oil reserves are second in volume only to Saudi Arabia. The Saudi's, being ultra orthodox Wahhabi Muslims, are not really our friends, and we may not always be able to depend upon their oil supply. If Iraq became a democracy and an ally of the United States, Iraqi oil might someday replace at least some of our oil needs. It was also hoped that revenues from the Iraqi oil could even help to defray the cost of our liberating Iraq from Saddam. How this will all work out remains to be seen. It is unlikely that we will receive any repayment for our effort in liberating that nation, and our hopes to create a democracy there and retain Iraq as a friendly ally are slim indeed. Muslims, because of their fatalistic theology, tend to be notoriously ungrateful.

Iraq is conflicted in having three disparate constituencies, which resulted from the arbitrary division of the Ottoman Empire following WWI. There are 5 million Kurds in the north numbering 20% of the population. Another 5 million Iraqis, or 20% of the population, are Sunnis in the central region, mainly the Anbar province. Shias to the south number 15 million or 60% of the total. Only the north and south have oil. The Sunnis, who ruled Iraq for years, have no oil and fear being dominated by the Shia majority. These sects have been enemies for centuries. Another dangerous dynamic that even endangers Iraq's future independence is the fact that the Iraqi Shiite population borders on Iran, a belligerent Islamist nation of 75 million people, 60 million of whom are also Shia.

Saddam ruled the Kurds and Shia with an iron hand, and Iraqi Sunnis, who make up the insurgents joined by other Sunni Arabs from Syria, Saudi Arabia, and Jordan, fear retaliation. There is, in fact, a low-key civil war going on right now, which has been stimulated by al-Qaeda and other terrorists who have infiltrated the country over the Syrian, Saudi, and Iranian borders. This insurgency may keep American military forces in Iraq for many years. There is hope that we can reduce our forces there from 150,000 troops to about 50,000 next year (2008) as Iraqi police and military take over, but most analysts believe that we will have as many as 30,000 military personnel based in Iraq for another 6 to 8 years just as we have forces in Korea, Europe, and many other places. One would have to be naïve not to know that the reason for this is to protect an important part of the world's supply of oil from the radical Islamists who wish to cripple the West. The faster we can find relief from dependence on petrochemicals, the more secure we will be, and our world may be cleaner and safer too. It could dry up the finances of these nations and their ability to spread Islam around the world. They have no appreciable economy outside oil production. Without it they would be third world nations.

The majority of Americans are questioning the wisdom of our going into Iraq in the first place, which may be a valid position. Once we are there, however, getting out is another matter. Whenever we withdraw, it will be declared a win for Allah and his handful of Holy Jihadists against the other major superpower in the world. It will become the greatest piece of propaganda possible, encouraging other "believers" to join the Holy Jihad against the West. With literally hundreds of millions of possible candidates to enlist, the world could find itself covered by Muslim aggressors and suicide bombers like a plague of locusts on the face of the Earth. Without a doubt this is the most dangerous problem that has ever confronted the human race and the free nations of the world. I hope that people are beginning to realize that this is the frank truth of the matter.

In the meantime, the Shia in Iran will find common cause with their Shia brothers in Iraq. This is what the Saudis feared would happen if Saddam had been removed from power after the first Gulf war. Saddam was a Sunni like the Saudis. The Shia, however, have been enemies of the Saudis for many years. A combined Iran with 60% of Iraq could be a future threat for the Saudi Kingdom. The Iraqi Shiite clerics like Moqtada al-Sadr are surely anxious for this to happen. It is the reason they are so insistent on America withdrawing our military forces from their nation. President Maliki said just recently that American troops could leave because the Iraqis had trained their own police force and army. I believe that this is a transparent effort in a Shiite move to get rid of the Americans so that they can eventually take over eventually take over Iraq and form a partnership with Iran, who is our sworn enemy.

It was Saddam's intention to join with Iran and Syria and perhaps others to invade Israel and retake Jerusalem. According to the British Intelligence Digest in 1973 the Soviet Union had pledged to help them. All this has now been slowed down, and the leadership has changed, but the pieces are still in place and someday the attempt will be made. Ezekiel's prophecy in chapters 38 and 39, which predicts that these nations will invade a reconstituted nation of Israel in order to take Jerusalem and obliterate the Jews, is on the verge of being fulfilled. In this Biblical prophecy, Persia or Iran leads the nations, whom we now know are mostly Islamic, with Russia's assistance. With the removal of Saddam Hussein, Iran has become the natural leader of an alliance of Muslim nations arrayed against Israel. President Mahmoud Ahmadinejad of Iran has had no inhibitions in declaring that Israel must be "wiped off the face of the earth" and that it is Islam's destiny to "rule the world."

A 6000-word letter of 13 pages from Ayman Al Zawahiri, Osama's second in command, to Abu Musab Al Zarqawi, al-Qaeda's late leader in Iraq, was intercepted in Iraq before Zarqawi's death. Its exhortation is an uncanny echo of what Ezekiel prophesied would happen in years to come. First Al Zawahiri rebuked Al Zarqawi for killing Muslims and beheading prisoners on television. He said that such actions would offend the "Muslim masses" and were counterproductive. The main goal, which must be remembered, he added, was to make Iraq an Islamic state that would be the basis of an attack on Israel. He calls victory in Iraq "the greatest battle of Islam in this era" because it could be followed by the establishment of the ancient Caliphate in Baghdad. Then the war to create Islamic states could be taken to Syria, Lebanon, Egypt, and other Muslim nations. When

Islamic governments were established in all the Muslim nations surrounding Palestine, they could then join together under the Caliphate in a final victorious thrust to obliterate the Jews and take Jerusalem. Sounds like the fulfillment of prophecy in the making! (See Chapter 10: "Islam in Biblical Prophecy.")

Chapter 9

CURRENT HAPPENINGS

Five names are appearing in the headlines about the Middle East these days: Iraq, Iran, President Ahmadinejad, Hizballah and Hamas.

The Rise of Hamas and Hizballah

Since Hamas has forcibly taken over the Gaza Strip from Fatah and Palestinian Authority President Mahmoud Abbas, Iran is supporting this Sunni group because of their common enemy Israel. Hamas next goal is to also take over the West Bank. Iran wants Hizballah and Hamas to shake up Israel to interfere with Israel's plans to attack Iran's nuclear facilities.

Hamas has said that it wants to establish an Islamic state from the Mediterranean Sea to the Jordan River. Of course, this has been the desire of every ultra-orthodox Islamic group from before the time of Yasser Arafat. Hamas' constitution reads, *"The day of judgment will not come about until Muslims fight Jews and kill them. Then Jew will hide under rocks and the rocks will cry out. 'Oh, Muslim, a Jew is hidden behind me; come and kill him.'"* None of this is new; Hamas is simply quoting Muhammad. Hamas also created a TV cartoon show called "Tomorrow Pioneers," which has featured a Mickey Mouse style character who with songs and poems urges the killing of Jews because they are only unclean animals—monkeys and pigs. Dr. Mike Evans in a recent report on his website warns, *"An unrestrained Islamic revolution is spreading through Iraq, Lebanon, and the Palestinian Authority while the world sleeps. This revolution is fueled and fed by Iran; its final move is to take it to the streets of America"* Jerusalem Prayer Team, June 21, 2007.

A new terrorist force was motivated by the 1982 Israeli-Lebanese War. Hizballah, which means "Party of Allah," was

ISLAM RISING BOOK TWO

made up primarily of Lebanese Shias who were trained and supported by Iran. Hizballah could be called the "terrorist arm" of the Iranian revolution and the Ayatollah Khomeini. Three of its goals have been (1) Liberating Jerusalem; (2) Eliminating Israel; and (3) Achieving Islamic rule in Lebanon. Hizballah has been very active in Lebanese politics and holds seats in the nation's parliament. Its present leader is the charismatic Secretary General Hassan Nasrallah, who has said that it would be a great idea if all the Jews in the world immigrated to Israel where they could all be killed at the same time. He has also said that the group's slogan will always be "Death to America."

Hizballah or Iranian trained terrorists have been active in attacking American targets including the Beirut Marine barracks, the Khobar Towers, the Embassy Annex in Beirut, hijacking TWA flight 847, and the kidnapping of many American personnel in Lebanon in the 1980's. This terrorist group has established bases in Latin America including one at Foz da Iguassu (Iguassu Falls) on the border of Brazil, Paraguay, and Argentina. In Brazil they were not regarded as terrorists but as revolutionary freedom fighters and a political party in Lebanon, and they were welcomed to the country. They were, however, instrumental in the bombings of the Israeli Embassy and Culture Center in Buenos Aires. They have founded other bases in Latin America in cooperation with al-Qaeda. We may find al-Qaeda and Hizballah working together to infiltrate the United States from the South and attack America on her own soil. It is frightening how many Latin nations have elected left wing leadership, which has shown an enthusiastic willingness to cooperate with America's enemies. These are truly "dangerous times."

Europeans have been slow to identify Hizballah as a terrorist group, preferring to label them as freedom fighters or a legitimate resistance movement and now a political party in Lebanon. The European community is still looking for a political solution as they did with Hitler. I predict that just as this approach did not work with someone with Hitler's mindset, it will not work with militant Muslims. They are ideologues possessed with a mystical sense of their own destiny and will not be deterred by anything but deadly force.

Besides holding 14 seats in the Lebanese parliament, Hizballah runs a radio and satellite TV station in Lebanon and is involved in charitable and educational enterprises, running hospitals, a news service, and reconstruction projects. This has also been true of Hamas in the Gaza Strip, which also explains their popularity with the people and the fact that they took the majority of seats in the Palestinian legislature. Hizballah, and now Hamas, are receiving support and training from both Iran and Syria. It is believed that Iran supplies Hizballah with as much as $100 million a year to carry out their plans.

Just 21 years after the IDF withdrew from Lebanon and the Shia took control of the south, Israel and Hizballah were locked in a conflict in southern Lebanon from July 12, 2006 until the United States and others forced a cease-fire on August 14. The fight began when Hizballah terrorists crossed the border and kidnapped 2 Israeli soldiers. Israel reacted immediately with force crossing the border with tanks, which hit land mines and 8 more Israeli soldiers were killed. In retaliation Israel pounded Lebanon, including southern Beirut, with bombs. All told 300 enemy fighters and 900 Lebanese civilians were killed. Israel's attacks had partially crippled Lebanon's infrastructure, but didn't stop Hizballah.

Hizballah's response was to fire almost 4000 Katyusha rockets on targets in northern Israel destroying 6000 homes, displacing 300,000 people, and wounding over 4200 Israelis. In the 33 day war that followed 43 civilians in Israel and 119 Israeli soldiers were killed. The IDF invaded Lebanon and struggled vainly to control Hizballah. After the cease-fire, Iran, Syria, and the rest of the Arab world rejoiced in what they considered a Muslim victory over Israel. As usual Hizballah used civilians to shield their bases and activities, and Israel found that isolating the terrorists from the rest of the population was difficult and a great hindrance to their counterattacks. Heavy casualties among the civilians was largely due to Hizballah's military tactics.

Hizballah used a new strategy. Well-armed by Iran they tried not to openly attack the Israeli army but just sat back in their "bunkers" and launched rockets and inflicted significant casualties on the Israelis when they came to try to root them out. Just like so many Muslim fighters they hid in the midst of unarmed civilians. It was a new and successful tactic of warfare against what had always been an unbeatable Israeli Defense Force. A cease-fire was called and the United States pressured Israel to stop the fighting before any estimate as to which side might have prevailed could be made. Whatever the outcome, this little war did give the Arabs hope that a battle against Israel could be won.

If the cease-fire had not been instituted and the IDF had been given a free hand to fight without interference, however, it is unlikely that the Arabs could have claimed any kind of victory. Since most of Hizballah are Lebanese Shias and have been trained and supported by Iran, the President of Iran Ahmadinejad has viewed this "victory" of Hizballah as a herald of Israel's eventual defeat. It has also brought about a new cooperative spirit between the Sunni Muslims and the Shia state of Iran, who have been traditional enemies for years.

Iran is now taking the lead and has been involved in training and equipping Sunni terrorists, such as Hamas in Palestine. Hamas ousted al-Fatah from Gaza because they did not think that they were aggressive enough. It was a vicious, one-sided fight and Fatah headquarters was destroyed. So Hamas has complete control of Gaza now, and al-Fatah with Arafat's successor Mahmoud Abbas are in charge of the West Bank. In spite of all the changes, America and the western nations are still trying to find a formula to bring peace to Palestine.

Someday Iran may consider a kind of pincers movement

in a future combined attack on Israel from the Gaza Strip in the South and Lebanon and Syria in the North all under their inspiration and leadership. What happened in Lebanon in 2006 has certainly encouraged the nations surrounding Israel to look forward in a "count down" to the day when they will eliminate all the Jews and obliterate Israel with Sunnis and Shias working together in the final attack. This incidentally is exactly what is predicted in Ezekiel's prophecy concerning the final war against Israel—the Muslim nations being led against a restored nation of Israel and Jerusalem by Persia, which is Iran (Ezekiel 38-39).

In the meantime, Hizballah and its supporters have been clamoring in the streets for the resignation of the Lebanese Sunni Premier Fouad Sirioni. This Shiite "Party of Allah" wants to take over the Lebanese government and make Lebanon an independent Islamic state. Hassan Nasrallah, the Secretary General of Hizballah since 1992 has given indications that he wants to become accepted in the international world of politics. He has organized Hizballah as a national political party in Lebanon and has won 2 cabinet positions as well as the seats in Parliament. There is no doubt that he would like to become the political leader or Premier of Lebanon himself.

Nasrallah is a Shiite cleric trained in Najaf and Qom. He does not want to be a guerrilla leader like a Che Guevara or an Osama bin Laden hiding in a cave in the backwoods of some Muslim country. He took the initiative even to meet with Kofi Annan, Secretary General of the United Nations, in 2006 and was welcomed almost as a partner by one of the Christian leaders of Lebanon. Nasrallah has condemned the al-Qaeda attack on the Twin Towers. He opposes the tactics of Osama bin Laden and said that the Taliban was a hideous example of Islam. He is against the Palestinians and al-Fatah and will not support any effort to make them a part of Lebanon. The 400,000 Palestinians in refugee camps are a major problem as they provide a haven for Palestinian terrorists in Lebanon.

Nasrallah is still unequivocally opposed to Israel's

existence, but said that he was sorry he had ordered the kidnapping of the two Israeli soldiers because it led to such disastrous consequences in the bombing of Lebanon. The Arab world, however, is accepting Nasrallah as a hero because Hizballah had been successful in expelling Israel from southern Lebanon and then was able to turn back the attacks of the Israeli Defense Force in the July/August 2006 encounter. He is very close to Iran and has spent much time there.

A lot of the Iranian money has been spread around the population of Lebanon, which has made Hizballah very popular in the country. Now it is likely that, having expelled the Israelis and devastated northern Israel with their rockets as a punishment for Israel's invasion, there may be a rest from military action or even a kind of unspoken truce until Iran feels that everyone in the area is strong enough to take on Israel together. This might bring us down to the final Muslim attack portrayed in Ezekiel's prophecy. (See the next chapter.)

The Rise of Iran and President Ahmadinejad

Iraq was the cradle of civilization going back to Sumer and Akkad in the fourth millennium B.C. The famed ancient cities of Ur of the Chaldees, Abraham's home, Susa, the capital of the Elamites, Nineveh of the Assyrians, Babylon of Hammurabi, the law codifier, about 1800 B.C., and then of Nebuchadnezzar, the conqueror of Judah, 606 to 562 B.C. were all located in Iraq. A few years later the Persians controlled the territory of Iraq and Iran and an empire that extended to Egypt, Syria, Asia Minor, and points east. Then there were Alexander the Great and the Hellenists, the Seleucids, the Parthians, and the Sassanids. Finally what is now Iraq and Iran were conquered by the Arab Muslims in 637 and have been in the Islamic culture sphere for 1370 years.

Iraqis are Semitic Arabs and speak Arabic; Iranians are IndoEuropean Aryans and speak Farsi. Najaf and Karbala in Iraq are sacred cities to the Shia who are the spiritual descendants of Caliph Ali, Muhammad's son-in-law and his son

Husayn, Muhammad's grandson. Both were martyred by what are now called Sunni Arabs. Ali is buried in Najaf and Husayn in Karbala. The Shia believe that the Caliph, or representative of Muhammad, should be in the Prophet's bloodline and regard these cities as very sacred in addition to Mecca, Medina, and Jerusalem.

The Shiites or Shia comprise only 15% of Muslims worldwide today and have their largest populations in Iran (60 million) and Iraq (15 million). Sunnis, who are the majority of Muslims, are only 23% of Iraq's population or about 5 million. Conflict between Sunnis and Shias has erupted around the Muslim world from time to time, because Shias are less secular, more mystical, have spiritual leaders almost like priests called Ayatollahs meaning "the shadow of Allah", and use rituals and pictures which are an anathema to the purist Sunnis. A civil war provoked by terrorist insurgents in destroying the Samarra Mosque is going on right now between Shias and Sunnis in Iraq.

Because "the enemy of my enemy is my friend" Shiites in Iran and Lebanon have inspired some Sunnis to join them in plans to obliterate Israel. Iran's #1 foreign policy is to recover Jerusalem from the Jews. Key to this is the charismatic, hard line, conservative leadership of President Mahmoud Ahmadinejad of Iran who was a senior commander of the Revolutionary Guards Jerusalem Force. As Mayor of Tehran he was catapulted to the Presidency of Iran on June 24, 2005. He is a civil engineer by training with a Ph.D. and has been a university professor as well as an activist in the military and in the Iranian revolution.

Ahmadinejad feels that he is on a divine mission, inspired by a religious messianism. He believes that he has a divine appointment to herald the imminent return of the "Ruler of All Time", who is the Mahdi, the 12th or Hidden Imam who will rule the world in peace and justice for seven years before the end of the age. Muhammad called the Mahdi, or "the Guided One," the 7th Prophet. President

Ahmadinejad is a member of an organization called the World Islamic Order, which he says will be the vehicle for the Mahdi who may reveal himself in the next two or three years. Some have dubbed the President a new Hitler because he has a totalitarian ideology combined with a mystical belief in his own mission. He believes that he is to be the forerunner for this long awaited Islamic Messiah and must take responsibility to see that this supernatural leader reveals himself.

President Ahmadinejad is also a member of a radical Shia sect called the Hojjatieh who believe that they can hasten the coming of the Mahdi by creating chaos, disorder, and bloodshed in the world. If you couple this conviction with Iran's serious and determined effort to achieve nuclear weaponry, the possible scenario gets very scary. There is no doubt that if Ahmadinejad gets the nuclear bomb, he will use it. This will be hard to predict, because estimates as to when Iran will have a nuclear arsenal range from two to ten years.

With the defeat and removal of Iraq's Saddam Hussein, Iran has been set free to assert aggressive leadership in the Muslim world. President Ahmadinejad has said publicly that Israel must be "wiped off the face of the Earth", that America must be compromised or converted, and that Islam must rule the world. Iran without doubt is trying to develop an arsenal of nuclear weapons to help accomplish these goals.

Suggestions have been made that precision bombing should be used to stop Iran's nuclear program. If Iran's nuclear reactors are to be taken out and their other nuclear sites bombed, it will be Israel who will have to do it as they did in 1981 when they knocked out Saddam Hussein's Osiraq reactor. The United States and Britain are tied up in Iraq and dare not open a new war with Iran. Israel has been told privately that if it is to be done, she will have to do it. It is unlikely that anyone could stop Iran's entire program, however, because much of it is being carried out underground.

Iran has been taking the lead by sponsoring terrorists, such as the Shia Hizballah in Lebanon, whom they keep well supplied with weapons and armaments. The same courtesy is also being extended to the Sunni Hamas, which has taken over control of the Gaza Strip. Both have their guns trained on Israel that Ahmadinejad says heads up the "world of arrogance" in the Middle East. This is his description of the western world. Therefore Israel must be destroyed. Iran is also quietly sneaking in arms and insurgents to the war in Iraq to disrupt the presence of American troops. Since their taking of 52 hostages from the America's embassy in Tehran in 1979, Iran has been committing one small act of war after another against the United States. They are currently our most dangerous enemy.

The question has been asked many times: How much success has Iran had in building "the bomb" or how soon might Ahmadinejad have the weapon he wants to destroy Israel.

Reports by the International Atomic Energy Agency are suggesting that Iran will have the 3,000 centrifuges it needs to make one bomb by the end of July 2007. By the end of the year Iran will have 8,000 centrifuges. The great catastrophe the militants in Iran want to create is getting closer. Since Ahmadinejad is convinced that the Mahdi should come within two years, and he also believes that he will come at a time of great global catastrophe, he wants to use a nuclear weapon soon. I think that we should see Israel try to preempt this happening with aerial attacks in the very near future.

A final prophetic note: In the examination of Islam in Biblical prophecy we will find in chapter 9 that Persia is listed in Ezekiel's prophecy as the leader of the forces which come to destroy Israel in the "last days." Shah Muhammad Reza Pahlavi changed the name of his country from Persia to Iran in 1935. The nations listed, who join Iran or Persia in this military venture against Israel, are Islamic. So everything is pointing to another more serious, disastrous conflict coming to the Middle East. There does not seem to be any certain reference to the United States in Biblical prophecy. Is it possible that our nation will be neutralized so that we are unable to come to

Israel's defense? In Biblical prophecy it is God Himself who comes to Israel's defense against these nations, which is the time He reveals Himself to the world. (See Chapter 10.)

When we look honestly and realistically at events in the world today, there does not seem to be much hope. When men lose hope, they can lose the will to live or to fight for their survival. The message of Islam in the Qur'an and the teachings of Muhammad is that their only hope is the coming of "the Guided One," a representative of Allah who will bring peace and just judgment to the world. The thing for Muslims to do therefore is to create as much chaos on Earth as possible, because this will cause their charismatic leader or Islamic Messiah to appear. Muhammad said he would come at the time of a great earthquake.

The message of the Judeo/Christian revelation in the Scriptures teaches that the only hope for the world is in the second coming of Jesus the Messiah, who will come first to rescue from off the Earth all those who have trusted in Him called believers, the elect, or the children of God. In fact, in the Bible this is called the "Blessed Hope." Then Christ or Messiah, who is God incarnate, will bring a severe judgment on the Earth punishing unbelievers and the disobedient. The Earth will then be cleansed and Christ will set up a kingdom to "rule the nations with a rod of iron" (Psalm 2). Thus the Judeo/Christian Messiah, not the Mahdi or the Islamic Messiah, will establish peace and justice on the Earth.

Arnold J. Toynbee's *A Study of History*, 1934-61, was comprised of 12 volumes of philosophical analysis of the rise and fall of 26 civilizations worldwide. He concluded his historical study with a very similar idea. He believed that a superman, one he calls a Transfigured Savior, must appear to bring a peaceful solution to the problems on the Earth. Who will it be? He doesn't answer the question.

All of these teachings mentioned above have prepared the world's thinking for what, according to many prophecies, will actually take place in the future; namely, Christ vs. Antichrist.

Chapter 10

ISLAM IN BIBLICAL PROPHECY
THE LAST DAYS

I believe that we are on the threshold of the end of the age. This, in fact, is a belief shared by Orthodox Jews, conservative Christians, and literalist Muslims today especially among the Shia, who are trying to hasten the coming of the Twelfth Imam, who is the Islamic Messiah. A major cosmic conflict in today's world exists between Judeo/Christianity, the revelation of the Bible, and the LORD God Almighty (Yahweh), on the one hand, and Islam, the Qur'an, and Allah, on the other. What do Jesus and the prophets in the Bible say about this future? How will it affect us in the United States of America as we face those in the world who consider us to be the Great Satan, and believe that all Christians and Jews are infidels, and that Israel especially must be destroyed?

The content of this chapter is a brief introduction to Book IV in this series, which may be titled *Islam Rising: Islam in Biblical Prophecy and the End of the Age.* This is a distinctly Christian portrayal drawn from the teachings in the Bible. It is a viewpoint of the author who has arrived at these ideas after over 50 years of study. I do not claim any divine inspiration for my interpretation. It may be different from what the reader has understood, and, if so, it is my hope that it will challenge more investigation and consideration of the meanings of the texts of the Scriptures.

It should be emphasized again that orthodox Christianity, Judaism and Islam all share the belief that the times that we live in are what the prophets called "the last days." Other religions including the Mayans believed that we have entered the season of the beginning of a new cycle in human history. In fact, the Mayan astronomers and priests in studying the heavens and the cycling of their calendars concluded that the end of the present era would take place on December 21, 2012. It is even more fascinating and astonishing that a Chinese system called I Ching when pushed to its limit on the computer comes up with the same date. I frankly have no suggestion right now as to its meaning, if any.

A new mystical-scientific examination of supposed messages underlying the text of the Torah and the Old Testament called the Bible Code suggests five alternative dates for the end of the age, the last of which is 2010. Three events are juxtaposed in the text that may take place in that year: (1) A world war; (2) An atomic holocaust; and (3) A global earthquake. There are many even outside of the Biblical tradition, who are impressed that we may be approaching the time of the end.

The Hebrew prophets, Jesus, and the Apostles all give information concerning what is supposed to happen in the future called the "last hour," "the last days," or "the end of the age." It is only recently that we could fit the new resurgence of Islam into these predictions, which include (1) the reconstitution of the nation of Israel in the land now called Palestine and the great conflicts with neighboring nations surrounding this event; (2) tremendous catastrophes on the Earth causing the death of millions, even billions, of human beings; (3) the second coming of Jesus, the Judeo/Christian Messiah, whom Muhammad called the 5th Prophet; (4) the coming of a counterfeit Savior of mankind called the Antichrist, or a pseudo-Messiah. Muslims are looking for the Mahdi or "Guided One," called the 7th Prophet, or the Twelfth or Hidden Imam who is the Islamic Messiah; and (5) extensive cataclysmic warfare between God and His people vs. Satan and his hordes of which a battle called Armageddon has received the most publicity.

The Old Testament Prophets called this end time "The Day of the Lord" or the *Yom Yahweh* in Hebrew. It was the long-awaited Day when the true Creator God of Israel would reveal Himself to the world in (1) blessing for his children, called believers, the children of God or the elect or chosen ones, or (2) judgment on those who followed the ways of the god of this world called that old devil or Satan, and who were possessed by his spirit. In the New Testament they are called "children of the Devil" by both Jesus and the Apostle John.

A Preview—The Great Antichrist System

Islam is the greatest organized "Antichrist" system ever to exist in history. We have shown in Book I that Muslims vehemently reject the specific claims of Jesus that He was the Son of God and the incarnation of Jehovah (Yahweh)—"I am who I am"—the name that God gave Himself in Exodus 3. It was the name, in fact, that Jesus called Himself in John 8:58-59. Islam teaches, however, that Jesus was sent by Allah as the 5th major prophet to "confirm the Torah and the Gospel." He was born of a virgin, performed miracles, and lived a sinless life. He was not the Savior of all mankind, however, but was sent only to the "lost sheep of the House of Israel." He was not crucified on the cross and was not resurrected, although He was received into heaven alive and will return to the Earth with the Mahdi of Islam. Muhammad was the 6th Prophet and was sent to the whole world. The Mahdi will be the 7th Prophet.

Jesus' disciples, who knew him intimately and from whom they learned everything, claimed that He was revealed to them as the Son of God or as God incarnate. The beloved Apostle John, in fact, wrote his entire biography of Christ, which is known as "The Gospel According to St. John," to show that Jesus was surely the Son of God and the one sent by God to be the Savior of all mankind.

But these are written that you may believe that Jesus is the Christ, the Son of God, and that by believing you may have life in his name (John 20:31).

John then devoted a significant part of his first letter to the Church (The Epistle of I John) to Jesus' Sonship and deity, and he firmly stated that all who reject this revelation concerning Jesus as Son of God are "antichrists."

The Apostle John, exercising his gift as a prophet, I believe, warns that the proliferation of many antichrists would be a sign of the "last hour" of man's sojourn on the earth. Note he does not just say the "last days," but the "last hour," which is an indication to me that the Spirit of God wants us to understand this as the closing hour of the last day.

Dear children, this is the last hour; and as you have heard that the antichrist is coming, even now many antichrists have come. This is how we know it is the last hour (I John 2:18).

It is also significant that there are many others in the liberal, secular world of atheism that believe many of the same things about Jesus Christ that Muslims profess. This is true also of the Da Vinci Code. There are many that have concluded that Jesus is neither the Son of God nor the Savior of the world. Truly, "Many antichrists have come."

Muhammad taught that at the time of the end there would be one final or 7th prophet who would come to teach and lead the people. He was named the Mahdi meaning "The Guided One." He is called the 12th or "Hidden Imam" by the Shiites and is the Islamic Messiah. This is similar to the teaching in the Bible that a religio-political leader would be revealed on Earth during the end time. However, he is called the Antichrist and "the man of sin." Antichrist means "in the place of" the true Christ or the Judeo/Christian Messiah. For those who believe that the Antichrist must come out of Europe, it might be well to note that Muhammad said that the 7th Prophet would conquer the Romans, or southern Europe, and rule part of the time from Rome.

The following parallel makes sense: Just as the true

Messiah, Jesus Christ—the Anointed One of God—was physically descended from Isaac, the Antimessiah, or Antichrist, may be a descendant of the older brother Ishmael. That would make the Antichrist an Ishmaelite Arab, who very likely will be received by the world of Islam as their Messiah. If this analysis is true, he is probably alive today. Both Christ and Antichrist therefore are in the line of Abraham. There are some who believe that Antichrist must be a Jew. This suggestion that Antichrist will be an Ishmaelite and therefore still be a descendant of Abraham is akin to that idea.

The Antichrist is Satan's counterfeit Christ. Just as Jesus, the Christ, was the incarnate Son of God, the Antichrist will become an incarnation of Allah who represents Satan himself. Satan will empower the Antichrist to perform miracles just as Jesus Christ did. The mighty conflict of the last days is going to be Satan revealed as the imposter god Allah who is incarnated in the Antichrist versus the true Creator God revealed as Jehovah or Yahweh who is incarnate in Jesus Christ. Allah, the god of Islam, versus Jehovah, the God of Christians and Jews—they are the antithesis to each other and utterly irreconcilable. In the words of Ahmadinejad, the President of Iran, *"The skirmishes in the occupied land* (i.e., Palestine) *are part of a war of destiny . . . a historic war between the oppressor* (Christian Crusaders, America in particular) *and the world of Islam."*

The Rebirth of the State of Israel
A Sign of the "Last Hour"

Another sign that we have already entered this "last hour" is the rebirth of the nation of Israel, which is predicted in the Bible. (See Appendix 1.) The existence of this new Jewish state is an anathema to devout Muslims. They claim that God rejected the Jews who are the descendants of Isaac; and now they, the Muslim Arabs, descended from Abraham's first-born son Ishmael, are children of the promise or God's chosen people. Palestine, or the Promised Land, therefore belongs to Ishmael and the Arabs.

Israel's revival as a nation on May 14, 1948 and its defeat of five Arab armies in 1948-1949 humiliated Islam and awakened thousands of militant Muslims who deny the legitimacy of the Jewish State. Muslims were even more greatly humiliated and enraged by Israel's reoccupation of Jerusalem in 1967. From that time on, retaking their third most sacred city Jerusalem became the focus of the foreign policies of many Muslim states. Saddam called his army the Jerusalem Army. Iran had a "Revolutionary Guard Jerusalem (Quds) Force" and the most important goal of Iran has been to wrest Jerusalem away from the Jews. Incidentally President Ahmadinejad of Iran is a founder and former military commander of this group.

This new militant Islam revives without apology the uncensored teachings of Muhammad and the Qur'an. Islamists are simply returning to their origins and to their original goal of imposing the "will of Allah" on the entire world. The rise to a new level of wealth, power and influence of this great antichrist system of Islam in our day is another major sign from the Lord that we indeed have entered "the last hour" (I John 2:18).

A final cosmic battle on earth is between Jehovah God and the forces of Allah whose identity has been usurped by Satan. Israel's prophets predicted that in the end times, when Israel was resettled in the land of Promise, all the nations surrounding them would be their enemies who would wish to destroy them. The nations that surround and want to destroy Israel today, of course, are all Islamic.

The prophet Ezekiel predicts in detail the names of these nations that will attack the new state of Israel. This military confederacy includes Iran, Iraq, Syria, Lebanon, Egypt and the Sudan and many other Muslim nations. Most are listed by their ancient names in Ezekiel 32, 38-39. Most of these today have expressed their eagerness to destroy Israel and reclaim the city of Jerusalem. The prophet Isaiah predicts that at this time, when these nations join their armies together in an attempt to retake Jerusalem, the God of Abraham, Isaac, and Jacob will Himself fight against them. Isaiah's prophecy says that Yahweh, the Almighty God, will *"roar from Zion"* to *"uphold Zion's cause"* (Isaiah 34:8).

There are four parts and purposes to these prophecies:

1. That the nations might know that He, Yahweh, alone is the Most High God and there is no other god (Psalm. 83:18). (One of these "other" gods is Nanna-sin the Moon god who was the head of the pantheon of the gods of the western Semites called the "chief god," which is the original meaning of Allah.);

2. That the nations might know that in spite of their sins Israel has not been permanently rejected for their rebellion, as Muslims claim, but that God for His own name's sake still has a plan of salvation for them (Note Ezekiel 37:28, 38:23, and 39:21-23);

3. God is revealed as Jehovah—in the person of Jesus the Messiah—who has come to rescue his elect, the children of God, to protect them from "the outpouring of His wrath" on the world (I Thessalonians 5:9, Matthew 24:30-31, Revelation 7:14-17); and finally

4. He also pours out His awful judgment on all unbelieving and rebellious men throughout the rest of the world, which is called "the terrible outpouring of the wrath of God" (Joel 2:10-11). This includes the disastrous judgments predicted in Revelation.

Isaiah predicts this same thing in 61:1-2. *"The Spirit of the Sovereign LORD is on me because the LORD has anointed me . . . to proclaim the year of the LORD's favor and the day of vengeance of our God."* The first part of this passage was quoted by Jesus in his home synagogue in Nazareth as a prophecy portraying the beginning of His ministry or His first coming, which was to preach God's grace (Luke 4:16-21). Jesus, however, did not quote the final portion of this passage, *"and the day of vengeance of our God,"* because it will be fulfilled in the future by Jesus at His second coming. This is the "Day of the LORD" when His vengeance will be poured out on the wicked who hate and oppose Him, and who have hated and persecuted His people.

The true Christ or Messiah, Jesus the Son of God, called "the pierced one" by the prophet Zechariah (Zech. 12:10), is going to return in the air in power and great glory and will destroy the work of the Devil, which includes Islam and all its predatory armies. This return of Jesus in the clouds of heaven was predicted at His ascension. When Jesus rose up off the surface of the Earth into the sky, as was witnessed by his disciples and recorded in Acts 1:9-11, the disciples were told by God's messengers, *"Men of Galilee, why do you stand here looking into the sky? This same Jesus, who has been taken from you into heaven, will come back in the same way you have seen him go into heaven."*

The stage seems almost set for this all to happen. The enemies of Israel mentioned in the Old Testament prophets are in place and ready to go. This great conflict during "the last hour" is in reality Satan versus God, Islam versus Jews and Christians, Allah versus Yahweh, and Antichrist versus Jesus the Christ (Messiah).

This situation that exists today is portrayed in Psalm 83. As we noted in the "Introductory Chapter," this Psalm was called to the world's attention recently by the fantastic discovery of a 1200-year-old Irish Psalter in a bog in Ireland that was opened to this part of the Psalms. It is an ancient prayer asking Jehovah God to protect Israel from the enemies that surround them. Everything is in place in the Middle East as depicted in this prophetic Psalm. Orthodox Jews, in fact, are well aware of its significance and are praying these very words:

O God, do not keep silent; be not quiet, O God, be not still
See how your enemies are astir; how your foes rear their heads.
With cunning they conspire against your people;
They plot against those you cherish.
Come, they say, "Let us destroy them as a nation,
That the name of Israel be remembered no more."
With one mind they plot together; they form an alliance against you—
The tents of Edom and the Ishmaelites, of Moab and the Hagrites, Gebal,
Ammon and Amalek, Philistia, with the people of Tyre. Even Assyria
Has joined them to lend strength to the descendants of Lot.
Do to them as you did to Midian, as you did to Sisera and Jabin
At the river Kishon, who perished at Endor
And became like refuse on the ground (Judges 4).
Make their nobles like Oreb and Zeeb,
All their princes like Zebah and Zalmunna (Jud. 7-8),
Who said, "Let us take possession of the pasturelands of God."
Cover their faces with shame so that men will seek your name, O Lord.
May they ever be ashamed and dismayed; may they perish in disgrace.
Let them know that you, whose name is Jehovah—
That you alone are the Most High over all the earth.

The nations mentioned include Iraq (Assyria) which supports the Palestinians ("descendants of Lot") and also the Arabs (Edomites, Ishmaelites, Hagrites), modern Gaza (Philistia), and Lebanon/Syria (the people of Tyre). I believe that this Psalm also foresees (1) the final conflict between Jehovah and Allah when all of the Muslim armies unite to try to bring a final destruction upon Israel, and (2) "the Day of the LORD" when the God of Israel, who is also the God of all Christian believers, will reveal Himself to all men that He alone is God and "the Most High over all the earth." All other gods including Allah are false usurpers. It is a prayer asking that the famous *Yom Yahweh* of the prophets be fulfilled.

That Islam is involved as the enemy here was foreseen by a Patriarch of Jerusalem Sophronius. At the time when it was conquered by Muslim armies in A.D. 638 Jerusalem was a

Christian city. There was a church on the Temple Mount, whose pastor and leader was the patriarch Sophronius. As the Muslim Caliph Omar took charge of the city, and he and his guards strode up on the Temple Mount, Sophronius was heard to say, "Behold the Abomination of Desolation spoken of by Daniel the Prophet." This phrase was used by Jesus to define a happening in the last days (Matthew 24:15). The word "abomination" in Hebrew and Greek always refers to a false religion and its representation as either an idol or a false religious leader or both. Many students of prophecy today identify it with the Antichrist. He is the leader of and personifies this false religion and this great antichrist system—an abomination to the true Creator God. I believe that this "abomination" is Satan's counterfeit religio/political creed, Islam.

A Cosmic Struggle For the Control of the Earth

There is a significant spiritual dimension to all that has happened in the world in the last 100 years. It is a cosmic conflict originating, produced, and directed from the spirit world. From the time of the Garden of Eden, Satan has sought to control both man and the Earth. He has been especially active in these last days because he knows that his time is short. His effort to do this politically through Hitler's Nazism and then Marxist/Communism failed because of the intervention of the United States. Satan therefore hates this country and will do everything in his power to destroy us.

The spirit of Nazism, embodied in Arab terrorism, and the philosophy of Marxist/Communism are still with us. Marxism is alive among elite leftists around the world including in the academy, the media, and liberal politicians in Europe and the United States. Many leftist liberals in our own Democratic Party are Marxist in their philosophy. It may be a surprise to many that Marxist concepts are also duplicated in the social and economic philosophy of Islam, such as the teachings in favor of a radical egalitarianism and against capitalism.

Nazism and Communism failed to take over the Earth with their political systems. Islam is also a political system as well as a religion, and now Satan is trying to dominate the Earth by manipulating a victory for Islam. Not only is he empowering Islamists to fulfill this goal, but also he will use the intense Muslim hatred of Israel to try to destroy the Jews. Again the United States, as with Nazism and Communism, is the main bulwark standing against the Islamist revival and the ambition of militant Muslims to obliterate Israel and rule the world. Therefore we are becoming their primary target. Their slogan is "Death to America."

Let me make this further observation; namely, that Satan's opposition to God in the world primarily focuses on His people—Jews and Christians. The only real friend and Protector that Israel has in the world today is the United States. The United States is not a Christian nation, as such, but it comes closer than any other. According to recent polls, 82% of Americans claim to believe that Jesus is God or the Son of God, and almost 50% claim to have been "born again." We have an evangelical Christian President in George W. Bush, who is leading the war against Islamism, and it was another Christian President Ronald Reagan whose bold persistence and leadership finally won the Cold War against Marxist/Communism.

Osama bin Laden and other Muslims call Americans "the Crusaders" looking upon us as representatives of a past warfare of Christianity against Islam. The implication of this conclusion puts Christianity in a very bad light when Muslims around the world view America's libertinism and moral turpitude. To them Christianity is represented by what they see in our salacious exports in movies, TV, and pornographic media. They do not understand the separation of the religion of Christianity from an American nation or a paganized European society, because Islam and the nation, the religion and the government, are ideally in union, cut out of the same cloth. Each reflects the other. Christianity is not supposed to reflect the society or the state, it is supposed to reflect Christ and influence the society with His power and righteousness. Christians are commanded as were the Jews of old to "'*Come out from them and be separate,*' *says the Lord*" (2 Corinthians 6:17).

The Bible prophets have much to say about this final attack of Islam on Israel. Islam is not mentioned by name, of course, but the nations of the confederacy, which attack Israel in the last days, include the names of the ancient nations that follow the Muslim faith today.

Jerusalem: The Focal Point of the Conflict

To recapture Jerusalem and to obliterate all the Jews are goals of the Islamic nations opposing Israel. This purpose has at one time or another occupied the number one spot in the foreign policies of Egypt, Jordan, Syria, Libya, Arab Lebanon, Iraq and Iran. As a result Israel and Jerusalem have become a concern and a focal point for many other nations in the world.

Zechariah prophesied that Jerusalem would be a millstone (or immovable rock) hung around the necks of the nations at the end of the age (Zech. 12:3). It is a problem, which neither the United States, nor Russia, nor the European Community, nor even the United Nations can solve. Jerusalem is a sacred city to Jews, Christians and Muslims. The Jews called it the City of David. It was the original capital of the kingdom of Israel for over 400 years. (Approximately 1000 B.C. to 586 B.C.) As such it was the site of Solomon's magnificent Temple, which was the home of the Shekinah Glory—God's presence among men on the Earth.

In subsequent years, Jerusalem changed hands many times, but the Jews have never given up their claim to the City of David. During the time of Jesus, it was Jewish head-quarters under the Romans. King Herod, with the permission of Emperor Augustus, had greatly enlarged the Temple Mount and built a second magnificent Temple. This was the worship center of the Jews in Jesus' day and is mentioned many times in the Gospels. The Western Wall is regarded as sacred by contemporary Jews because it is an actual physical remnant, a retaining wall of the Mount, which was close to the site of this Second Temple.

This was the Temple that Jesus said would be destroyed with all the stones being thrown down (Matthew 24:2; Luke 21:6). The Jews were incredulous and condemned Jesus for this prediction. Within 40 years of the Crucifixion, however, the Roman wars with the Jews erupted. Jerusalem was captured in A.D. 70, and Herod's magnificent Temple was burned. Josephus tells the story in his *History of the Jewish Wars* in which he participated on both sides. We have already noted that the gold coverings and artifacts of the building melted, and the Roman soldiers and others tore the building apart to retrieve the treasure. This is why "not one stone was left upon another" just as Jesus had prophesied (Matthew 24:2). Eventually all the stones of the Second Temple disappeared being recycled into other construction.

We have noted that in A.D. 131, the Emperor Hadrian visited what was left of Jerusalem, which had been totally destroyed. He built a Roman city on the site where Jerusalem had stood and called it Aelia Capitolina. The name Aelia was part of Hadrian's full name and Capitolina referred to the god Jupiter. A temple to Jupiter was then erected on the Temple Mount. A garrison of Roman soldiers was housed nearby to prevent any Jews from returning to Jerusalem.

It was this Roman act of desecration of the Jews' holy site, which triggered the final Jewish rebellion under the false messiah Bar Kokhba in 132-135. After the Jews' final defeat and deportation by the Romans, not only did Jerusalem continue to be called by its new Roman name but also idols to Roman gods were set up all around the area. This lasted until the time of Constantine when Jerusalem was reclaimed as a Christian city.

Since its destruction in A.D. 70, Jerusalem, as Jesus predicted, has been "trodden down by the Gentiles." It would not be a Jewish city again for a long time (Luke 21:24). Jesus said that this would be the status quo until the time of Gentile domination was over, or until history ceased to focus only on the Gentile or non-Jewish world. This seems to have been fulfilled in 1967 when the Jews recaptured the Old City of Jerusalem after almost 2,000 years. They will never give it up.

Israel has now withdrawn unilaterally from the Gaza Strip. Many Israelis today may also find it possible to give up the West Bank, or even part of the Golan Heights, as was offered by Israeli premiers Ehud Barak and Ehud Olmert, but 86% of Israelis recently said that they would never consider giving up Jerusalem. Since its capture in 1967, Jerusalem has been declared by the Jews to be the capital of their nation. On the other hand, Muslims will never give up on efforts to reclaim Jerusalem solely for themselves.

Recently President George W. Bush braved the wrath of the Islamic world by recognizing Jerusalem as Israel's capital. On the 40th anniversary of the capture of Jerusalem in the Six Day War, the United States House of Representatives also passed a resolution calling for moving the American Embassy from Tel Aviv to Jerusalem. This was a resolution and not legislation. It may take some time before this change takes place.

The Palestinians declared an "intifada for Jerusalem" immediately following the failure of peace efforts at Camp David in the fall of 2000. This was the beginning of the Second Intifada, which has continued more or less until now. The Palestinian rebellion has continued unabated from the Gaza Strip and in attacks from Lebanon on northern Israel. The war with Hizballah in Lebanon in 2006 was a part of this. Syria has recently purchased thousands of missiles from Russia with money from Iran. Both Syria and Iran are making threats as if in preparation for attacking Israel. Ahmadinejad even indicated that since the war between

Hizballah and Israel, a countdown has begun for Israel's destruction. This may be the catalyst for the beginning of the end when all the Arab nations, possibly with Russia's support, will attack the Jewish nation (Ezekiel 38-39). This whole situation is an utter impasse, a totally insoluble problem, with no political solution—truly an "immovable rock."

Jerusalem of the Last Days:
More on "The Immovable Rock"

Zechariah, a Jewish priest and prophet, born in Babylonia and contemporary with Zerubbabel who led the return to Judea after the Babylonian captivity (ca 538 B.C.), has much to say about Jerusalem in the last days. Here is his oracle:

> *This is the word of the Lord concerning Israel. The Lord. . declares 'I am going to make Jerusalem a cup that sends all the surrounding people reeling. Judah will be besieged as well as Jerusalem. On that day, when all the nations of the earth are gathered against her, I will make Jerusalem an immovable rock for all the nations. All who try to move it will injure themselves. On that day I will strike every horse with panic and its rider with madness,' declares the Lord, 'I will keep a watchful eye over the house of Judah, but I will blind all the horses of the nations . . Jerusalem will remain intact in her place. . On that day I will set out to destroy all the nations that attack Jerusalem'* (Zechariah 12:1-9).

Some interpretations of this prophecy place it at the end of the so-called Tribulation. Whatever the timetable, an amazing fulfillment of this prophecy is that Jerusalem at this very moment is the announced, principal objective of the next attack of the Muslim nations on Israel—Iraq, Iran, Syria, Libya, and others. It has been the centerpiece in all negotiations relating to Palestine and continues to present an insoluble problem. It will continue from now to the end of the age to be an "immovable rock."

Since its beginnings in 1948, Israel has fought various combinations of Arab nations, which included Iraq, Syria, Egypt, Jordan, and Lebanon, five separate times—1948, 1956, 1967, 1973, and 1982. (See Chapter 6 "The Five Arab Israeli Wars.") The Old Testament prophets predicted just such a situation in these final days. Yet there is another Muslim attack scheduled to come sometime in the foreseeable future. This war will be led by Iran or Persia, its name in the Scripture. The next major Islamic-Israeli war could very likely be the fulfillment of Ezekiel's prophecy in chapters 38-39.

Some leading students of prophecy in America today have been teaching that Ezekiel 38-39 should be identified as the same event as the final battle of Armageddon. Our strong objection to this is as follows:

1. In Ezekiel there are a specific group of nations that are named; at Armageddon all the nations of the world are included.

2. In Ezekiel the western nations are still identified, whereas preceding Armageddon there has been a reorganization of the Earth and world government. The organization of national powers appears different.

3. This attack of the nations on Israel in the last days, as we shall see, marks the beginning of the famed "Day of the LORD." (Ezekiel 39:8) Armageddon, on the other hand, is part of the concluding events of that Day.

4. Israel is identified in Ezekiel 38-39 as a nation living in a state of security, not peace. This is the word *batak* in Hebrew, not *shalom*, which means peace. This is the situation that exists today. After the defeat of the Muslim nations, Israel is granted a peace treaty by the Antichrist, which presumably is the situation at the time of Armageddon.

5. Although both events involve Jerusalem, the battles of Ezekiel's prophecy take place in "the mountains of Israel," whereas the battle of Armageddon is presumably centered on the plain of Megiddo, which has been the site of many historical battles in the past (Revelation 16:14-16). (These include the battle of Pharaoh Thutmose III with the Canaanites in 1468 B.C., Deborah and Barak's defeat of the Canaanites several hundred years later, King Josiah's defeat and death by Pharaoh Neco II in 609 B.C., and General Allenby's defeat of the Turks in 1917.)

6. The war in Ezekiel results in a victory for Israel who then has the responsibility to bury the hundreds of thousands of dead bodies. It specifically states that it will take seven months to bury the dead. But the battle of Armageddon, on the other hand, is a final battle, which results in such a shattering of the Earth and human life that few from any nation will be left to perform this kind of task. (See Revelation 16:16-21 and Isaiah 24.)

7. God's purpose for the judgment on the nations in Ezekiel is so that they may know that Israel was dispersed because of her sin but is being reclaimed for the glory of God's name, and that the nations might know that He is the Most High God. This implies that the Jews have recently been returned to the "Promised Land" as is the case today. Armageddon is the final battle when God is judging the nations for their rebellion against Him and their refusal to recognize His authority and preeminence. It precedes by just a short time the setting up of Christ's kingdom on Earth.

The Final Muslim Attack Against Israel—
The Nations of the Anti-Israel Confederacy of Ezekiel 38-39

Ezekiel's prophecy is the most significant prediction detailing the participating nations and the event of what is very likely the next Muslim invasion of Israel. Ezekiel probably recorded his prophecy just after 597 B.C. Judah and Jerusalem had been invaded by Babylon and many captives had been taken to Babylon including King Jehoiakim and later his son Jehoiachin (II Chronicles 36:5-10). Judah continued to rebel under the newly appointed King Zedekiah, so Nebuchadnezzar returned to wipe out the rebellion and destroyed the walls around Jerusalem and Solomon's Temple in 586-85 B.C. (II Chronicles 36:11-21).

Then beginning with the proclamation of King Cyrus of Persia, who conquered Babylon in 539 B.C., Jews under Sheshbazzar and Zerubbabel returned to Israel (Ezra 1-2). More Jews returned under Ezra the priest (458 B.C.) and Nehemiah (445 B.C.) to rebuild the temple and the walls of the city of Jerusalem. A Jewish presence then continued in Israel through the times of Hellenistic domination and Alexander the Great (330-328 B.C.). After Alexander's death in 323 B.C., his kingdom was divided. First the Ptolemies of Egypt ruled Israel and then the Seleucids from Syria and Babylon. The rebellion of the Maccabees against the Seleucid monarch Antiochus Epiphanes (167 B.C.) produced an independent Jewish state for just about 100 years. In 63 B.C., the land of Israel was incorporated into the Roman Empire by the Roman General Pompey.

The Romans were the next to destroy Jerusalem 130 years later during the Jewish Wars in A.D. 66-70. Even after their loss of Jerusalem and the Second Temple, Jews continued to rebel for decades and prepared for more war against the Romans. The Emperor Hadrian finally sent huge forces of at least 12 battle-hardened Roman legions to Palestine where they wiped out 50 Jewish strongholds and 985 villages. At the last battle of Behar on the 9th of Av in A.D. 135 all Jewish fighters were killed. The remaining civilians were expelled from Judea and Jerusalem, which was plowed under with yokes of oxen, and Hadrian renamed the province Syria-Palestina. The latter name probably refers to the ancient Philistines.

Jews were enslaved and permanently scattered among all the nations (The Jewish Diaspora). From Roman times until May 14, 1948 no nation of Israel has existed. This prophecy of Ezekiel almost 750 years earlier concerning a future major attack on Israel by the surrounding nations therefore could have no meaning or be fulfilled until after 1948.

None of the above five wars of Israel with the Arabs, furthermore, could be a fulfillment of Ezekiel 38-39. Iran, or Persia, mentioned first in Ezekiel's list of nations, has never been a combatant in any of the previous Arab-Israeli wars. Since the fall of the Shah of Iran, the revolution of the Ayatollahs, and the control of Iran by rabid fundamentalist Shiite Muslims in 1979, however, the retaking of Jerusalem has become a primary focus of Iranian foreign policy. Iran, an Indo-European nation of over 60 million Shias, will surely be a part of any new conflict. Ahmadinejad, the President of Iran or modern Persia, has been threatening Israel with obliteration for some time now and has recently released what he says is a count down to doomsday for the Jews. So you see, what is happening today all fits Ezekiel's historical prophecy.

Some of the invading nations listed in Ezekiel's prophecy are easily identified. Persia, of course, is modern Iran and possibly also includes Iraq because ancient Persia conquered most of Mesopotamia and King Cyrus ruled from Babylon. (Since there are so many Shias in Iraq who are now in charge of that nation, a close relationship will exist between Iraq and Iran.) Libya, or the land west of Egypt, is called Put in the Bible. Cush historically has been identified with the Upper Nile region, which includes the Sudan another avowed enemy of Israel.

Another "sleeper" identification of Cush, however, is based on the ancient Biblical tradition that Nimrod, the son of Cush, founded eight cities in Mesopotamia, including Babylon, Erech, Akkad, Nineveh and Calah (Genesis 10:8-12).

Cush, therefore, could be linked to modern Iraq, which occupies the famed Mesopotamia of ancient history, the "land between two rivers," the "cradle of civilization." This territory was the site of both the Assyrian and Babylonian Empires who conquered the Jews. It was later absorbed by the Persian Empire. The land that is now Iraq is mentioned more times in the Bible than any area outside of Israel.

Iraq's leader Saddam Hussein was an implacable enemy of Israel. He was preparing for an invasion in league with other nations, specifically Syria and Iran. In the recent past these nations had been his natural enemies. But according to the *British Intelligence Digest*, in 1998, Saddam urged them both to join in a common cause to fight their archenemy Israel. He had given permission for Iran's military to cross his land, which is amazing considering their previous conflict. Saddam believed that he was a modern reincarnation of Nebuchadnezzar and had named his army the "Jerusalem Army." Saddam's saber rattling against Israel was more reason than any will admit for Bush and his advisors to commit to removing his regime. It would appear now that one more "antichrist" has been removed from circulation. Bush, however, may find that we have put out a small fire only to be faced with a fiery holocaust. Shias dominate in the new Iraq as they do in Iran. They surely will join together in the future in a common goal to eliminate Israel.

The nations enumerated in Ezekiel—Iraq, Iran, Libya, and the Sudan—are leading adversaries of Israel today and are all totally committed to retake Jerusalem and obliterate the Jewish nation. The leader of this confederacy in Ezekiel 38-39, however, is called Gog who comes out of the far north. The name Gog may come from a Hebrew word, which means "roof" indicating perhaps the "roof of the world," which would be the North Country with respect to Israel.

Gog has no certain national identity. He is probably not even a human leader at all but the presiding demonic prince who has control under Satan over these nations.

This would be like the "prince of Persia" in Daniel's prophecy (Daniel 10:12-13), who for twenty-one days held up the angelic emissary who was bringing a message from the LORD to Daniel. Gog is the ruler of the "land of Magog," which is identified in ancient traditions with territory to the north that includes Russia. In most translations the "prince of Rosh" is included in this roster of nations. Gesenius in his standard, authoritative Hebrew Lexicon identifies Rosh with the Rus peoples north of the Caucasus Mountains or with Russia. It seems plausible because Russia has been a supporter of both Iraq and Iran, and the USSR supported all of these Muslim nations with arms in their wars to subdue Israel. In fact, the British Intelligence Digest revealed that the USSR promised these Muslim nations in 1973 to help them recover Jerusalem. That promise continues to be a precedent for the future.

Many other nations attach themselves to this alliance described in Ezekiel 38. These probably include Turkey, Egypt, Arab Lebanon, Syria, Jordan, Saudi Arabia and some other Muslim nations, such as those former Soviet states in southern Russia and the Caucasus—Kazakhstan, Uzbekistan, Turkmenistan, Tajikistan, Kyrgistan, Azerbaijan, Dragostan, Chechnya, and maybe even Afghanistan to the east.

Egypt is not mentioned specifically in Ezekiel 38, but according to a similar description of the events in Ezekiel 32, Egypt, in spite of its "peace" with Israel, seems surely to be a part of this final Islamic war against Israel. Other ancient names mentioned as a part of this army are Togarmah, Gomer, Meshech and Tubal. All can be historically or linguistically identified with ancient ethnic groups, such as the Cimmerians, the Sarmations, and the Scythians in Asia Minor, the Caucasus, and north of the Black Sea in the area, which is generally under the cultural and political influence of both Russia and/or Islam.

In 1973, the *British Intelligence Digest*, as we have already mentioned, unearthed a secret pact made by the USSR with some of the Islamic nations, notably Iraq whom the KGB was supplying with money and arms. The Soviet Union in this agreement promised to help the Arabs retake Jerusalem. We noted that the Soviets gave a tremendous amount of aid to the Arabs in their attempt to conquer Israel in the Yom Kippur war of 1973, even sending a ballistic missile laden ship to an Egyptian port. Only the action of Richard Nixon in mobilizing the American military at that time stopped the USSR from continuing the effort to fulfill her promise to the Arab states.

Russia refused to side with the United States in the 2nd Iraq War. The President of Russia Vladimir Putin regarded the invasion of Saddam's sovereign nation a mistake. According to the latest intelligence, Russia has not given up on its earlier promise to help the Muslims against Israel. Russia has had close relations in the past with both Iraq and Iran. In fact, Russia has continued to supply Iran to this day with material and expertise, specifically for the construction of nuclear reactors. It is believed that Iran's purpose is to use the enriched uranium or plutonium to create nuclear weapons. These weapons President Ahmadinejad wants to use someday soon against Israel. Because of international pressure, Russia's support of Iran has been a little ambiguous but still leans very much toward the positive.

This unholy alliance against Israel recorded in this prophecy is not fanciful conjecture. Virtually all the nations of the world except the United States stand more or less in antagonism to the state of Israel today. That the specific nations of Ezekiel's prophecy of 2500 years ago should exist at this time in history is nothing less than amazing. It supports the belief in both the gift and the truth of predictive prophecy and the inspiration of Scriptures by the Spirit of God, which are assumptions contained in the Biblical record itself. It is obvious to any student of the Bible that we are "on the brink."

A Final Review

It would be well for the reader to review in detail this prophetic passage of Ezekiel 38-39. Here is a summary:

> The nations: PERSIA (Iran), CUSH (Iraq, Ethiopia or the Sudan), PUT (Libya), GOMER (North of Black Sea and the Caucasus Mts.), BETH TOGARMAH (Part of Turkey), ROSH (Possibly Russia), MESHECH and TUBAL (Possibly Asia Minor or north of the Black and Caspian Seas). GOG is the leader—the demonic Angel in charge of these armies. 30% of the old Soviet Union is Islamic—Turkestan, Uzbekistan, Tadjikistan, Kirghizstan, Kazakstan. Afghanistan, Azerbaijan, and Chechnya are also Islamic. "Many nations with them." Egypt is a part of this group and Saudi Arabia may join—Ezekiel 32:7. Some believe that even a few European nations may be included.

According to Ezekiel's prophecy, it is the Most High God of Israel Himself who intervenes in the support of His people. This leads me to believe that Israel's only major ally and defender, the United States of America, has somehow been compromised or neutralized otherwise we would come to Israel's defense. Ezekiel tells us exactly the means God uses to defeat these Arab armies and why.

1. A great earthquake, which makes all the people of the world tremble.

2. All the attackers fight each other. These armies, e.g., are made up of both Sunnis and Shias who have been traditional enemies for hundreds of years.

3. Plague, torrents of rain, hailstones, and burning sulfur. This is probably the result of the earthquake and volcanic action.

4. The result is a host of dead bodies on the ground, which provide a great sacrifice for the animals and birds, which eat their fill of the bodies of Gog's army. It takes 7 months to bury the dead.

5. God sends fire on Magog and the coastlands—Russia and the USA. Magog historically includes the land area we now call Russia, and "coastlands" in Scripture is a euphemism for "colonies," which were established by ancient peoples along the seacoasts. The United States began as perhaps the most famous "colonies" in the history of the world, a ribbon of land along the Atlantic coast of North America. Both these nations still have thousands of missiles and nuclear warheads. Could this "fire" be a nuclear exchange allowed by God?

Note Ezekiel's description:

In my zeal and fiery wrath I declare that at that time there shall be a great earthquake in the land of Israel. The fish of the sea, the birds of the air, the beasts of the field, every creature that moves along the ground, and all the people on the face of the earth will tremble at my presence. The mountains will be overturned, the cliffs will crumble and every wall will fall to the ground (Ezekiel 38:19-20).

Then God executes judgment specifically on these nations:

I will summon a sword against Gog on all my mountains, declares the Sovereign Lord. Every man's sword will be against his   brother. I will execute judgment upon him with plague and bloodshed I will pour down torrents of rain, hailstones and burning sulfur on him (Gog) and his troops and on the many nations with him. And so I will show my greatness and my holiness, and I will make myself known in the sight of many nations. Then they will know that I am the Lord (Ezekiel 38:21-23).

It is God's purpose at this time to vindicate His name and reveal Himself to the nations. Ezekiel 38:16 reads, *"In days to come, O God, I will bring you against my land, so that the nations may know me when I show myself holy through you before their eyes."* (Note the same kind of declaration is found in Psalm 83:18 already cited.)

Finally, God revealed through Ezekiel's prophecy how this event fit into God's plan and purpose for the future of the world. Ezekiel quotes God as saying, *"This is the day of which I have spoken"* (39:8). What could this mean? To what *day* is God referring? Most of the Jewish prophets over a period of several hundred years had received the same message; namely, that there would be an extraordinary day in the future when God would reveal Himself to His people and to the world. It was one of the major themes of Old Testament prophetic teaching. It was called the *Yom Yahweh* in Hebrew. This means "The Day of the LORD" or the "Day of Yahweh" or "Jehovah."

The prophets warned that this would be a terrible day of judgment featuring "thick darkness" (Amos 8:18-20). But judgment is not its only characteristic. Its first and most important meaning is that it is the time that God had promised through His prophets that He would reveal Himself to the world. This means blessing for God's people and a continuing judgment on those who are on the side of Satan, who is called in Scripture "the god of this world." This special day begins at the time of God's judgment on the confederation of Muslim nations that attack Israel as portrayed in Ezekiel's prophecy (39:8). Considering everything happening in the Middle East at this very hour, it seems likely that we are coming very close to the fulfillment of this prophecy and the beginning of a new era in human history.

Following the great event of God's defeat of the Muslim

armies, there will only be a few years remaining of the final history of the world, as we know it. This eschatological study, much broader and with much greater detail, will be the subject for Book IV in this series.

Appendix 1

God's Promises That There Will Always Be An Israel

The early Christians were all Jews, and for years they were looked upon as a sect of Judaism. After the Roman conquest of Palestine and the destruction of the Temple, the Jews that remained who had not become Christians developed what was called Rabbinic Judaism led by teachers or rabbis who used the Babylonian and Jerusalem Talmuds that became the basis of the synagogue-centered Judaism throughout the Diaspora.

These two offshoots of Judaism were very much at odds. Some Jews who did not become Christians and who were active in the Roman Empire even encouraged the Imperial persecutions. A deep suspicion and mutual hatred developed, which can be seen in the anti-Judaizing sermons of John Chrysostom, the golden-tongued orator/preacher of Antioch (ca 385), later a Patriarch of Constantinople. A doctrine developed in the Roman Catholic Church that the Jews had been totally forsaken by God, and that Christians were the only true spiritual descendants of Abraham. All the prophecies and promises of the Old Testament were now considered to be the inheritance of the Roman Catholic Church. This is called Replacement Theology meaning that the Church has replaced the Jew in all God's plans for the ages. This is the theological position of the Catholic Church today, and the Vatican has refused to recognize the State of Israel as legitimate. Pope John Paul II, in fact, befriended Yasser Arafat and was a long time supporter of the Palestinians and a Palestinian state.

269

This interpretation of Scripture is also alive and well among some Protestants who trace their historical roots to the Reformation, in particular Reformed theologians. There is a small, but well-trained teaching community of professors and pastors among Protestants in America who also adhere to Replacement Theology. They do not believe that the restoration of Israel as a nation has any biblical or theological significance. Some may even believe that the Jews are usurpers and occupiers of Arab land and will someday all be destroyed. As such they may also sympathize with the Palestinians in their struggle against Israel.

We have noted in Chapter 3 that when the Scriptures were translated into English and distributed in England, the 17th century Puritans and many other Christians began to see in the Scriptures that God's plan for Israel was an "everlasting covenant," and they came to believe that God intended someday to restore the Jews to their Promised Land. This belief became known as the Restoration and prevailed among many Christians in England for over 200 years, resulting in the Balfour Declaration in 1917. The British therefore legitimized the restoration of Jews to their "homeland" in the land of Palestine. Supporters of this position have been called Christian Zionists.

Following are some of the passages from the Scripture that influenced this Restoration movement, which holds to a literal interpretation. Replacement theologians interpret these passages allegorically or give them a symbolic, spiritualized meaning in order to apply many of the promises and prophecies only to the Church. Let the reader make up his own mind after studying these passages from the Scriptures.

1.   God's promises to Abraham, Isaac, and Jacob:

The LORD said to Abram after Lot had parted from him, 'Lift up your eyes from where you are and look north and south, east and west. All the land that you see I will give to you and your offspring forever . . . Go walk through the length and breadth of the land, for I am giving it to you' (Genesis 13:14-17).

Question: What does God mean by "forever"?

When Abraham was ninety-nine years old, the LORD appeared to him and said, 'I am God Almighty, walk before me and be blameless. I will confirm my covenant between me and you and will greatly increase your numbers . . . I will establish my covenant as an everlasting covenant between me and you and your descendants after you . . . The whole land of Canaan, where you are now an alien, I will give as an everlasting possession to you and your descendants after you and I will be their God' (Genesis 17:1-2, 7-8).

Question: What did God mean by "I will establish my covenant as an everlasting covenant between me and you and your descendants . . The whole land of Canaan . . . I will give as an everlasting possession to you and your descendants . ."?

The LORD appeared to Isaac and said, 'Do not go down to Egypt; live in the land where I tell you to live. Stay in this land for a while, and I will be with you and will bless you. For to you and your descendants I will give all these lands and will confirm the oath I swore to your father Abraham. I will make your descendants as numerous as the stars in the sky and will give them all these lands, and through your off-spring all nations on earth will be blessed, because Abraham obeyed me . . .' (Genesis 26:2-4).

Question: What was the "oath" that God swore to Abraham that he is confirming with Isaac?

After Jacob returned from Paddan Aram, God appeared to him again and blessed him. God said to him, 'Your name is

Jacob, but you will no longer be called Jacob; your name will be Israel.' So he named him Israel. And God said to him, 'I am God Almighty; be fruitful and increase in number. A nation and a community of nations will come from you, and kings will come from your body. The land I gave to Abraham and Isaac I also give to you, and I will give this land to your descendants after you' (Genesis 35:9-12).

Question: What was the land God had promised to Abraham and Isaac and in this passage promised to Jacob and his descendants?

O descendants of Abraham his servant, O sons of Jacob, his chosen ones. He is the LORD our God; his judgments are in all the earth. He remembers his covenant forever, the word he commanded, for a thousand generations, the covenant he made with Abraham, the oath he swore to Isaac. He confirmed it to Jacob as a decree, to Israel as an everlasting covenant; to you I will give the land of Canaan as the portion you will inherit (Psalm 105:6-11).

Question: Again what do "covenant forever" and "everlasting covenant" mean? Does God keep His word? His oath? How can "Replacement Theology" which says that God has completely discarded the Jews and that therefore the above passages, must refer to Christians, who are grafted into the stock of Israel, stand up to these promises? The following is the explanation of what has happened and is happening today with the restoration of the nation of Israel.

After you have had children and grandchildren and have lived in the land a long time—if you then become corrupt and make any kind of idol, doing evil in the eyes of the LORD your God and provoking him to anger, I call heaven and earth as witnesses against you this day that you will quickly perish from the land that you are crossing the Jordan to possess. You will not live there long but will certainly be destroyed. The LORD will scatter you among the peoples, and **only a few of you will survive among the nations** *to which the LORD will drive you. There you will worship the man-made gods of wood and stone, which cannot see or hear or eat or smell. But if from there you seek the LORD your God, you will find him if you look for him with all your heart and with all your soul. When you are in distress and all these things have happened to you, then* **in later days you will return to the Lord your God and obey him. For the LORD your God is a merciful God; he will not abandon or destroy you or forget the covenant with your forefathers, which he confirmed to them by oath** (Deuteronomy 3:25-31).

Question: Were the children of Israel scattered among the nations? Over a period of about 850 years from 722 B.C. to A.D. 135 the Diaspora, or scattering of the Jews, took place until they were finally banished entirely from the land by the Romans. Now almost 1,900 years later they are coming back, many of them in unbelief like the dead bones in Ezekiel 37, but many sincerely seeking the God of their fathers. A small remnant, as this passage predicts, will have survived to be saved in the last day, fulfilling the "everlasting covenant" that God made with Abraham, Isaac, and Jacob to last "forever." As the Apostle Paul predicted, "Israel will be saved." God said, *"Only a few of you will survive among the nations."* Jews around the world today only number about 15 million people, whereas, the descendants of Ishmael and other relatives of Abraham that make up the Arab nations number over 250 million.

2. God's command to the descendants of the Patriarchs to possess the land—describing the extent of the territory promised to Abraham, Isaac, and Jacob:

> *The LORD our God said to us at Horeb, 'You have stayed long enough at this mountain (Sinai). Break camp and advance into the hill country of the Amorites; go to all the neighboring peoples in the Arabah, in the mountains, in the western foothills, in the Negev and along the coast, to the land of the Canaanites and to Lebanon, as far as the great river, the Euphrates. See, I have given you this land. Go in and take possession of the land that the LORD swore he would give to your fathers—to Abraham, Isaac and Jacob— and to their descendants after them* (Deuteronomy 1:6-8). (See also Genesis 15:18-21, Numbers 34-3-12, Deuteronomy 11:24, and Joshua 1:2-4.)

3. Prophecy of Amos—750 B.C. (About 30 years before the ten northern tribes are defeated and taken into captivity by Assyria)

> *'In that day I will restore David's fallen tent. I will repair its broken places, restore its ruins and build it as it used to be . . . The days are coming . . . when I will bring back my exiled people Israel; they will rebuild the ruined cities and live in them. They will plant vineyards and drink their wine; they will make gardens and eat their fruit. I will plant Israel in their own land, never again to be uprooted from the land I have given them,' says the LORD your God* (Amos 9:11-15 selected portions).

Because this promise in Amos says that God would restore Israel to their land after their captivity, and that they would "never again" be uprooted from the land He had given to them, this has to be a promise for today or the future. They were "uprooted from the land" under the Romans after an earlier return from Babylon. Israel has not been in the land since that time until its restoration in these last days. So God still has a plan for Israel, which is more than a spiritual fulfillment. The promised heritage of Christians is nowhere in Scripture declared to be restoration to "a land."

4. Prophecy of Isaiah—700 to 686 B.C. (25 to 40 years after the Assyrian captivity.)

> *In that day the LORD will reach out his hand a second time* (The exodus from Egypt is reckoned as the first time.) *to reclaim the remnant that is left of his people from Assyria, from Lower Egypt, from Upper Egypt, from Cush, from Elam* (Iran), *from Babylonia* (Iraq), *from Hamath* (Lebanon), *and from the islands of the sea* (This may refer to the continents.) *He will raise a banner for the nations and gather the exiles of Israel; he will assemble the scattered people of Judah from the four quarters of the earth . . .* (Isaiah 11:11-16 selected portion).

> *Do not be afraid, for I am with you; I will bring your children from the east and gather you from the west. I will say to the north, 'Give them up!' And to the south, 'Do not hold them back.' Bring my sons from afar and my daughters from the ends of the earth—everyone who is called by my name whom I created for my glory, whom I formed and made* (Isaiah 43:5-7).

Neither of the above passages can refer to the return of the exiles from only the land of Mesopotamia—Assyria and Babylon. It must refer to a future return after the final Diaspora, which resulted from the Roman conquest from A.D. 70 to 135, because all the far-flung parts of the earth are referred to as points of origin for their return. It is a picture of what has been happening to the Jews in the last 100 years, which will continue into the future until the climax of the "last days."

Though in anger I struck you, in favor I will show you compassion (Isaiah 60:10). (Over and over again the Word of God tells us that He will not ultimately forsake His people, *"the sheep of His pasture."* See Jeremiah 51:5.)

5. Prophecy of Jeremiah—626 B.C. to about 586 B.C.
    (Jeremiah is the prophet of the time of the Babylonian conquest of Judah, the captivity, and the destruction of Jerusalem and the Temple. His predictions include the return within 70 years of the exiles from Babylon, but are expanded to include the final regathering of Israel from all the nations in the world to the Promised Land in the last days.)

    The Lord said to me, 'Go, proclaim this message toward the north: Return, faithless Israel,' declares the Lord, 'I will frown on you no longer, for I am merciful,' declares the LORD, 'I will not be angry forever . . . Return faithless people,' declares the LORD, 'for I am your husband. I will choose you—one from a town and two from a clan—and bring you to Zion . . . No longer will they follow the stubbornness of their evil hearts. In those days the house of Judah will join the house of Israel, and together they will come from a northern land to the land I gave your forefathers as an inheritance (Jeremiah 3:14-18 selected portions).

The piecemeal return of Jews from Germany, Poland, Eastern Europe and Russia after the holocaust had shattered families during WWII is accurately predicted in the text as *"one from a town and two from a clan (a family)."*

However, the days are coming,' declares the LORD, 'when men will no longer say, 'As surely as the LORD lives, who brought the Israelites up out of Egypt, but they will say, 'As surely as the LORD lives who brought the Israelites up out of the land of the north and out of all the countries where he had banished them.' 'For I will restore them to the land I gave their forefathers. But now I will send for many fishermen.' declares the LORD, 'and they will catch them. After that I will send for many hunters, and they will hunt them down on every mountain and hill and from the crevices of the rocks' (Jeremiah 16:14-16). (See duplicate passage in Jeremiah 23:7-8.)

One interpretation of the above might be that those of the Restoration movement and the Zionists "fished" for prospects and persuaded them to return to Palestine. Others who were enemies in hunting Jews down in every nation during WWII forced them to flee to the land. God used any and every means to bring these descendants of Abraham back to the Promised Land even in unbelief. Remnants of Jewish tribes were found in Yemen, Ethiopia, and most recently a part of the tribe of Manasseh was found in India, who were invited to return to Israel.

See I will bring them from the land of the north and gather them from the ends of the earth. Among them will be the blind and the lame, expectant mothers and women in labor; a great throng will return. They will come with weeping; they will pray as I bring them back. I will lead them beside streams of water on a level path where they will not stumble, because I am Israel's father, and Ephraim is my firstborn son. Hear the word of the LORD, O nations; proclaim it in distant coast-lands: 'He who scattered Israel will gather them and will watch over his flock like a shepherd' (Jeremiah 31:8-9).

Other passages in Jeremiah speak only of the "return from captivity," such as Jeremiah 24:6,7 and 30:1-3, 23-34 and 33:7-9 whereas the above prophecy and others say that the returnees come from the "ends of the earth." The return from the Babylonian captivity, however, does seem to be viewed also as mirroring an event to come in the future when

Israel and Judah are united in a renewed, "born again" style commitment to their Shepherd God, who has made a "new covenant" with them.

> *For Israel and Judah have not been forsaken by their God, the LORD Almighty, though their land is full of guilt before the Holy One of Israel* (Jeremiah 51:5). (See also Isaiah 60:10.)

6. Prophecy of Ezekiel—593 to 571 B.C. (Ezekiel was taken to Babylon in the 597 B.C. captivity and like Jeremiah, who was left in Jerusalem, went through the later destruction of Jerusalem and the Temple by the Babylonians and the major displacement of the Jewish population that followed. Ezekiel echoes all the predictions of previous prophets; namely, that Judah and Israel would be returned together to the land God had promised their forefathers. Here they would be spiritually converted and receive a new covenant relationship with their God.

Ezekiel goes one step further and tells us the procedure by which God engineers this transformation. What we now recognize as the armies of a new implacable enemy, Islam, God Almighty will use to bring Israel to the end of itself in dependence upon Him who *"roars from Zion"* (Joel 3:16) against Israel's enemies as he comes to *"defend Zion's cause"* (Isaiah 34:8). This is the time of the Yom Yahweh, the Day of the LORD, when God reveals himself to the world that they may know that He alone, Yahweh not Allah or any usurping god, is the Most High God. Note especially Ezekiel 39:8— *"This is the Day of which I have spoken."*—namely, the Day of the Lord.

> *Therefore say: This what the Sovereign LORD says: Although I sent them far away among the nations and scattered them among the countries, yet for a little while I have been a sanctuary for them in the countries where they have gone.*

> *Therefore say: This is what the Sovereign LORD says: I will gather you from the nations and bring you back from the countries where you have been scattered and I will give you back the land of Israel again.*
>
> *They will return to it and remove all its vile images and detestable idols. I will give them an undivided heart and put a new spirit in them; I will remove from them their heart of stone and give them a heart of flesh. Then they will follow my decrees and be careful to keep my laws. They will be my people, and I will be their God* (Ezekiel 11:16-20).

This is a summary of what Ezekiel describes in detail in chapters 35-39—the return of Judah and Israel from many nations in unbelief and their conversion when God Himself comes to reveal Himself and defend them against invading armies whose purpose is to capture Jerusalem and totally obliterate the renewed state of Israel. This has been partially fulfilled already with the return of many Jews to part of the land promised to Abraham, Isaac, and Jacob. We are on the verge of the events of Ezekiel 38-39 being fulfilled—the Most High God revealing Himself to Israel and the world, and the beginning of His day of vengeance on the nations, the restoration of a converted Israel, followed by the continuing pouring out of the wrath of God on a rebellious world.

> *As a shepherd looks after his scattered flock when he is with them, so will I look after my sheep. I will rescue them from all the places where they were scattered on a day of clouds and darkness. I will bring them out from the nations and gather them from the countries, and I will bring them into their own land. . . They will know that I am the LORD, when I break the bars of their yoke and rescue them from the hands of those who enslaved them. They will no longer be plundered by the nations . . . They will live in safety and no one will make them afraid. I will provide for them a land renowned for its crops, and they will no longer be victims of*

famine in the land or bear the scorn of the nations. Then they will know that I, the LORD their God, am with them and that they, the house of Israel, are my people, declares the Sovereign LORD. You my sheep, the sheep of my pasture, are people, and I am your God, declares the Sovereign LORD (Ezekiel 34:12-13, 27-31).

The Apostle Paul in his letter to the Romans quotes a similar passage from Isaiah 59:20: *"The deliverer will come from Zion; he will turn godlessness away from Jacob. And this is my covenant with them when I take away their sins."* Note that the founding of the church and Pentecost has already taken place. So this must be in the future. He prefaces this quote by predicting, *"And so all Israel will be saved."* He then said that the Jews were loved because of the patriarchs *"for God's gifts and his call are irrevocable. Just as you who were at one time disobedient to God have now received mercy as a result of their disobedience, so they too have now become disobedient in order that they too may now receive mercy as a result of God's mercy to you* (Romans 11:26-31).

I will show the holiness of my great name, which has been profaned among the nations, the name you have profaned among them. Then the nations will know that I am the LORD, declares the Sovereign LORD, when I show myself holy through you before their eyes.

For I will take you out of the nations; I will gather you from all the countries and bring you back into your own land. I will sprinkle clean water on you, and you will be clean; I will cleanse you from all your impurities and from all your idols. I will give you a new heart and put a new spirit in you; I will remove from you your heart of stone and give you a heart of flesh. And I will put my Spirit in you and move you to follow my decrees and be careful to keep my laws. You will live in the land I gave your forefathers; you will be my people, and I will be your God (Ezekiel 36:23-28).

Note that this cannot simply refer to the return from Babylon because the designations "the nations" and "all the countries" indicate that many areas are involved. Also God does not do this because the Jews have done anything to deserve it but simply to demonstrate that He was in charge from the beginning to scatter and to restore. God does this in order that His name might be exalted and glorified on the earth. This revelation of God will bring a great remnant of Jews to repentance, and God will save them when they turn to Him when He comes. Ezekiel tells us when and how this happens in chapters 38-39. Chapters 32 to 39 in Ezekiel are telling a continuous story giving different details leading up to the conversion of a remnant of Israel in the time of the end.

> *Then He said to me, 'Son of man, these bones are the whole house of Israel.* (God indicates that both Judah and Israel will return together from wherever they have been scattered to be one people.) *They say, 'Our bones are dried up and our hope is gone; we are cut off.' Therefore prophesy and say to them: This is what the Sovereign LORD says: O my people, I am going to open your graves and bring you up from them; I will bring you back to the land of Israel. Then you, my people, will know that am the LORD, when I open your graves and bring you up from them. I will put my Spirit in you and you will live, and I will settle you in your own land. Then you will know that I the LORD have spoken, and I have done it, declares the Lord* (Ezekiel 37:11-14).

This is the famous passage of the valley of the dry bones. The spiritual rebirth of the Jews is pictured by God uniting the bones together and putting flesh on the bones bringing the bodies to life. It is a graphic picture of the uniting of all the tribes of Israel and their being brought to live not only as a nation but also as children of God with the presence of the Holy Spirit in their lives. This is an extension or repetition of what happened at Pentecost in the book of Acts.

The Jews lost their land and lost their connection with God, which is symbolized in the destruction of their Temple. The Jews are today returning to their land, most of them in a state of unbelief. Now, however, God has promised also to bring about a transformation of His people for His own sake. Flesh will come on the bones of a dead nation of Israel and God's Spirit will be poured out on them in the last day. This prophesy in Joel 2:28-32 was only partially fulfilled in Acts 2. Paul says, *"And so all Israel will be saved."* The next two chapters of Ezekiel (38 and 39) tell us how it all happens.

Chapter 39 of Ezekiel tells us about the destruction of the armies of Gog and his forces that attack a restored Israeli nation. We know now that these nations are Islamic led by Iran. (See Chapter 10.) After the victory, which has been won by God Himself, the Jews in the land will use the material from the battlefield as fuel to burn for seven years. (39:9-10) "The house of Israel," which is in the land, will spend seven months burying the dead from the battle. There will even be special teams of men who go through the land looking for human remains to be buried so that the land may be cleansed. (39:12-16) This indicates that there are Jews present in the land of Israel; in fact, it says that they were a *"people gathered from many nations to the mountains of Israel, which had long been desolate. They had been brought from the nations and now all of them live in safety."* (38:8-9) There is no way that any theologian can spiritualize these passages.

Then God continues the regathering of all the remaining Jews on earth and returns them to the Promised Land. *"Therefore this is what the Sovereign LORD says: I will now bring Jacob back from captivity and will have compassion on all the people of Israel, and I will be zealous for my holy name. They will forget their shame and all the unfaithfulness they showed toward me when they lived in safety in their land, with no one to make them afraid. When I have brought them back from the nations and have gathered them from the countries of their enemies, I will show myself holy through them in the sight of many nations. Then they will know that*

I am the LORD their God, for though I sent them into exile among the nations, I will gather them to their own land, not leaving any behind. I will no longer hide my face from them, for I will pour out my Spirit on the house of Israel, declares the Sovereign LORD" (Ezekiel 39:25-29). Here is the further fulfillment of the pouring out of God's Spirit for the house of Israel, which happened to Jewish Christians at the beginning of the "last days" in Jerusalem recorded in the Book of Acts. (This will all be explained further in Book IV.)

7. Prophecy of Zechariah—520 to 480 B.C. Zechariah was a priest as well as a prophet who was born in Babylon. He returned to Judea with Zerubbabel in 538. His statement concerning Israel *"whoever touches you touches the apple of His eye"* is often quoted to show God's permanent commitment to His people, the physical descendants of Abraham (2:8).

Chapters 12 through 14 picture Israel as already restored to the land of Promise and being attacked by enemy nations with both Judea and Jerusalem being besieged. God gives His people almost supernatural power to defeat these nations. *"The people of Israel are strong because the LORD Almighty is their God"* (12:5). There is no doubt about these passages referring to events in the "last days" and Book IV will investigate many of these predictions. The significance for us is that the Jews are physically back in the land and in Jerusalem, which is being fulfilled in our day right in front of our eyes.

8. Some New Testament references about the Restoration of Israel:
    Jesus said, *"Jerusalem will be trampled on by the Gentiles until the times of the Gentiles are fulfilled"* (Luke 21:24).

    Jesus here indicates that there would be a time when

Gentiles would occupy Jerusalem, but that this occupation would come to an end when the time for Gentile domination had expired. The logical conclusion is that at the end of this Gentile occupation, Jerusalem would someday be back under Jewish control. This, of course, happened in June 1967. The events of history have confirmed Jesus' prophecy. The implications of Jesus words are obvious. He was trying to tell us that God still has plans for the Jews and Israel.

> He told them this parable, 'Look at the fig tree and all the trees. When they sprout leaves, you can see for yourselves and know that summer is near. Even so, when you see these things happening, you know that the kingdom of God is near' (Luke 21:29-31).

Since the fig tree was a type of Israel in the Old Testament, many have believed that this is an indirect allusion by Jesus' to the rebirth of the nation of Israel, which happened in May 1948—another sign that we are in the last days.

The Apostle Paul had a great love and concern for his people the Jews and had much to say about their condition in his letter to the Romans chapters 9 through 11. He concludes:

> I do not want you to be ignorant of this mystery, brothers, so that you may not be conceited; Israel has experienced a hardening in part until the full number of the Gentiles has come in. And so all Israel will be saved, as it is written: 'The deliverer will come from Zion; he will turn godlessness away from Jacob, and this is my covenant with them, when I take away their sins (Romans 11:25-27).

Here Paul seems to be alluding to Jesus statement about the times of the Gentiles coming to a conclusion, at which time the Jews would once again receive special attention from God. He also predicts the coming of the Deliverer through whom Israel will be saved from their sins. Now Jesus had already come for that purpose, so Paul must be speaking of a future time when a remnant of the Jews will no longer be blinded but will *"look unto Him whom they pierced"* (Zech. 12:10) and receive the fulfillment of God's covenant with them—the forgiveness of sins and the new life of God. (See Chapter 10 on Islam and Biblical Prophecy)

The Apostle Paul also says that Jesus came as *"a servant of the Jews on behalf of God's truth, to confirm the promises made to the patriarchs"* (Romans 15:8). These promises were very specific not only about Abraham having many descendants, whom we now know are in the spiritual realm of faith as well as the realm of the physical, but also concerning the land that God would give to Abraham's descendants through Isaac and Jacob. It was called a covenant "forever" or an "everlasting covenant." As a Son of David, whom God promised would have an heir forever to sit on the throne of Israel, Jesus is intricately connected to the visible Jewish nation as well as to his invisible body the Church.

The Apostle Peter's inspired message at Pentecost refers to the day when God will restore all things. He speaks of the time when God will *"send the Christ, who has been appointed for you—even Jesus. He must remain in heaven until the time comes for God to restore everything as he promised long ago through his holy prophets"* (Acts 3:21). To restore something means to bring back something that had previously existed. The invisible church did not have a previous existence so Peter must be speaking of the restoration of the nation of Israel as a physical presence on the earth in fulfillment of the everlasting covenant to Abraham, the father of the thousands of Jews to whom he was speaking on that Day of Pentecost. This was also the expectation in the words of the prophets of Israel who gave testimony to this "everlasting covenant" as noted in many Old Testament passages above.

Finally the book of Revelation mentions that there will be 144,000 Jews sealed in their foreheads that provides them with an ID and protection from the outpouring of God's wrath. It is believed that they become witnesses and preach-ers of the Gospel during this end time. The text reads, *"Do not harm the land or the sea or the trees until we put a seal on the fore-heads of the servants of our god. Then I heard the number of those who were sealed; 144,000 from all the tribes of Israel."* Then each of the tribes is mentioned from Judah to Benjamin noting that there are 12,000 Israelites from each tribe who are given this mission (Revelation 7:3-8).

Appendix 2

Special Tactics of the Left: Shared by the Marxist-Leninists, Nazis, Islamists and European and American Liberals

This is an article that I wrote about ten years ago after realizing that Communism, Nazism, Islamism, and Liberalism had many of the same motivations and used many of the same principles and tactics. Even though they were disparate in many ways, they shared what might be called a similar spiritual orientation. Although Nazis and Islamists have sometimes been categorized as conservative, they are just as liberal or even leftist as Communists and contemporary leftist/liberals in the West. The core characteristic of leftist/liberalism is its desire to change what exists in the socio-political and religious sphere into something new and different. By this definition this quartet of movements or philosophies are all leftist/liberal in their purpose. They all tend to be socialist or anti-capitalist in social philosophy and totalitarian politically. I found that they also shared an approach or a technique of operation that was similar; namely, hatred, lying, and a cult of death. These are all evil and I would label them all satanic.

THE ORIGIN OF CONTEMPORARY LIBERAL POLITICAL TACTICS

Most of the ideas, principles, and tactics of contemporary liberal political parties all over the world have grown out of Marxist/Socialism and its offshoot Leninist/Communism. This infected even America's elites from the 1920's to the

1960's. The American Communist Party during that time was under the direct control of Moscow. We know now from the Venona tapes and KGB files that during part of this period there were at least 300 Soviet agents and sympathizers within our Federal government bureaucracy, some in very strategic positions, reporting to Moscow.

With the weakening and demise of the Soviet Union in 1991, the leftists in America had few places to go except to embrace the left wing of the Democratic Party politically and to join the faculties of our major universities educationally. The latter fact has been documented in a recent book citing the invincible and stubborn arrogance of left wing educators who still whitewash the Soviet Union and support the ideals of communism to this very day. (John Earl Haynes and Harvey Klehr, *In Denial: Historians, Educators and Espionage.* San Francisco: Encounter Books, 2003)

Lenin taught that the Communist movement, or *International Socialism*, had really originated with the French Revolution, which eliminated the royalty and the aristocratic classes. The bourgeoisie or the middle class had arisen to take their place. Because of capitalism, however, this new "upper" business class became as much the oppressors as the aristocrats had been. They in turn had to be eliminated in favor of the proletariat or working class, which would ultimately lead to a classless society. The "workers" would own everything together under the umbrella of a centralized governmental bureaucracy. This "dictatorship of the proletariat" was the ultimate ideal of Marxist socialism.

A "new morality" was invented by Lenin to help in this transformation.

1. He taught that hatred was one of the prime motivating forces. It was directed at specific undesirables, especially the bourgeoisie.

2. He emphasized the use of strategic, intentional deception

or bold lying. This eventually became known by the relatively innocuous term *propaganda,* which involves a calculated deception.

3. Lenin's successor Stalin was guilty of genocide. In order to implement the communist ideal, he eliminated whole sections of the society, such as the Kulaks or independent farm families. Similar tactics of the murder of millions of undesirables was the policy of Mao Zedong in China and Pol Pot in Cambodia. No one knows for sure how many multimillions of people were officially purged in Communist countries. One suggested estimate is 135 million people killed, most of them by their own governments.

The Nazis were right in step with their Communist competitors in hatred, lying, and murder:

1. Adolf Hitler's hatred for the Jews was proverbial. He also used hatred as a motivator and as a technique for uniting the German people under his authority.

2. Hitler borrowed the idea of the "Big Lie" from Lenin. As Goebbels, who was wrongly given credit for its invention, said, "If you tell a lie big enough and long enough eventually people will believe it."

3. Hitler was the technological master of genocide. His death camps systematically wiped out perhaps as many as 12 million Jews, Christians, and political enemies. . In addition over 50 million people lost their lives in WWII.

Islam has been guilty of the identical practices of hatred, lying, and killing of millions.

1. The vitriolic hatred of Jews and even of America is well

known. Allah is portrayed as hating the sinner, the corrupt, and the infidel. Muslims follow this example. It is a major emotional drive motivating terrorists today.

2. Lying is the order of the day. Islam has no personal standard of truth, and Muhammad taught that a Muslim could lie to an infidel without sin. Muslim leaders like Nasser and Arafat have been notorious liars, and it is simply accepted or overlooked in the culture. I have never read or heard one condemnation of either hatred or lying. Even Allah can lie if he wants to; he can do whatever he wills. And then we all remember the ridiculous posturing of Baghdad Bob and his notorious lies about the Gulf War on Middle Eastern TV.

3. Finally Islam is the prime example of a cult of death. Osama bin Laden said, "We will win because you want to live, and we want to die." Palestinian children are being taught that death is better than life. Suicide bombers have become a favorite technique of warfare. Anyone killed in Holy Jihad is promised the reward of Paradise. Many therefore seek death. In the practice of Holy Jihad for the last almost 1400 years, Islam has been guilty of the deaths of well over 100 million people throughout the world, and there will be many more to come.

Both of these tactics—the cultivation of hatreds and purposeful lying as policy—seeped consciously or unconsciously into left wing liberal movements all over the world.

1. In the midst of claiming to promote tolerance and truth in America, for example, the left has really engaged in cultivating hatreds—class warfare—and often expresses deep hatreds for conservatives—radio talk show hosts, think tanks, Republicans, evangelical Christians, writers and academics, and sometimes even Jews like Senator Joe

Lieberman, Michael Medved and Dennis Prager. They also express deep hatreds for President George Bush and his administration and even for America itself.

2. They employ half-truths and lies as tools to achieve leftist goals. One can see this in action almost every day in the propaganda, now called "spin," of liberal activists, educators, and politicians. Liberals today very often play "fast and loose" with the truth and rationalize lying. A favorite technique of the liberal media is to deceive by not telling the whole story or ignoring completely what they do not want the public to know.

    Our leftist academic world goes one step further and denies that "truth" even exists. Values and morals are truth are all relative. Truth in values has been replaced with the safer principle of "political correctness," which is a translation from the Chinese words for "Party Line" dictated by the Communist autocrat Mao Zedong. In other words we can make up our own "truth." It is true if it is true for us.

3. Leftist/liberals in the West also have treated the value of human life either casually or with contempt. The Communists, Nazis and Muslims killed millions. Liberals also have supported institutionalized killing. They support on-demand abortion used even as birth control. In America alone they are ultimately responsible for sacrificing the lives of over 50 million babies. Partial birth abortion, which sacrifices the life of a baby almost fully expelled from the womb, or even the killing of new born babies out of the womb have been justified by many liberals. Euthanasia and the "science" of eugenics has been used in the killing of the defective, the old and the infirm, and other undesirables. For years in America the defective were sterilized and eugenics was supported by the so-called elite, even liberal or "modernist" Christians like

Harry Emerson Fosdick. Eugenics had much liberal support even before the days of Margaret Sanger, the founder of Planned Parenthood, which is in reality the largest abortion factory in America. They had been greatly influenced by the philosophy of evolution, which taught the "survival of the fittest." This philosophy and these evils were widely practiced also by the Nazis and the Communists.

Nazism was National Socialism. It taught many ideas which liberals champion today. Amazingly, liberals or leftists have often falsely used the terms *Nazi* and *Fascist* to describe conservatives. They have the mistaken notion that Hitler was conservative or right wing, whereas Stalin was liberal or left wing. Nothing could be further from the facts. Hitler championed *national socialism*, exalting the nation and the Aryan race in a very centralized, totalitarian government led by a dictatorial *fuehrer*. Lenin, on the other hand, championed *international socialism*, which was achieved also by a dictatorship of the working class, which he and later Stalin represented as autocratic leaders. Both Hitler's and Lenin's systems were socialist; both were totalitarian; both wanted to transform their respective societies into something entirely different from what they had been. This latter desire and goal is the principal objective, which defines leftism.

We labeled Italy and Germany *fascist* because they were also hyper-nationalistic. Those who have turned the slur *Nazi* against conservatives have walked in the steps of the master propagandist Joseph Goebbels, whose quotation on the Big Lie is mentioned above. Never is the pejorative *Nazi* used against the leftist socialists who are precisely the Americans doing most to advance a social agenda common to both the Nazis and the Communists. **One example of the left's totalitarian technique in America is their willingness to use an activist judiciary to bypass the Constitution and flout the will of the people and our entire democratic system.** Their concept of the "Living

Constitution" is a kind of extension of the "Big Lie." After all, "Big Brother knows best!" and "The Constitution is what the Judges say it is." Leftist liberals will tell any kind of lie, spread any kind of slander or sleaze, or smear anyone's reputation in order to get their way as is illustrated in the recent struggle over judicial appointees. It is called "the politics of personal destruction," and it was born in the bosom of Marxist Leninist Socialism.

The following contemporary assessment of the Democratic Party explains the monumental change in American politics. **"We're not up against honest, patriotic Democrats anymore. We're fighting nothing less than a hardened Leftist ideology that has managed to hijack the Democratic Party."** For the source of this quotation and a careful examination of this phenomenon see Democrat Georgia Senator Zell Miller's recent book *A National Party No More: The Conscience of a Conservative Democrat* (Atlanta: Stroud and Hall Publishers, 2003).

Today we are struggling with militant representatives of a new fascist movement that has been called Islamofascism. Their goal is similar to Communism and Nazism in that they want to take over the world and bend it to their will, or in the case of Islam, to the will of Allah. It is startling that they also are using these same tactics of hatred and lying and death in their psychological weapons arsenal. Islam is also a totalitarian movement, in that, liberty and democracy are considered evil because they compete with the will of Allah. All but one of the more than 55 nations where Islam is in the majority have a history of dictatorships, because their Perfect Model Muhammad became an absolute ruler—prophet, priest and king—when he rose to religio-poitical power in Medina.

There has been only one Muslim democracy. Turkey had democracy imposed upon it by the strong man Kemal Ataturk after WWI in 1924, but it has not been completely successful or universally accepted. Much persecution of minorities in Turkey, especially Christians and Kurds, has demonstrated the typical Muslim totalitarian intolerance. Of the leading nations in the world today persecuting Christians, seven out of the top ten are Islamic.

Where Muslim nations are organized as structural democracies, like the present Afghanistan under western influence, they are not true democracies. The judiciary is the supreme ruling body and the executive and legislative branches are only "window dressing." The judiciary determines what laws the legislature may pass and the executive enforce. A parallel exists here with leftist liberals in western democracies who try to control judicial appointments in order to influence the interpretations of laws and constitutions. In both instances the will of the people is subjected to an influential elite, and popular sovereignty is disdained and rebuffed. We see this also in some of the bills introduced by liberals in the Congress, which seek to run roughshod over the will of the majority of the people. Leftist/liberals are totalitarian at heart just as the teachers who preceded them. Because they use the same tactics is why there is an unholy alliance between radical Islam and the American left, which is the subject of David Horowitz' recent book. (See Bibliography.)

There are many parallels between all these totalitarian systems and the leftist mindset. All have been based in an arrogant faith that they know what is best or right for human society, and they use these similar immoral techniques to achieve their goals—hatred, lying, a totalitarian spirit and practice, and a cult of death. They can only be described as a Quartet of Evil.

BIBLIOGRAPHY

Babbin, Jed. *In the Words of Our Enemies*. Washington D.C.: Regnery Publishing Company, Inc., 2007.

Bard, Mitchell G. *Myths and Facts: A Guide to the Arab-Israel Conflict*. Chevy Chase, MD: American-Israel Cooperative Enterprise, 2001.

Bergen, Peter L. *Holy War, Inc: Inside the Secret World of Osama bin Laden*. New York: The Free Press, 2001.

Bostom, Andrew G. *The Legacy of Jihad: Islamic Holy War and the Fate of Non-Muslims*. Amherst, NY: Prometheus Press, 2005.

Burrows, Millar. The Dead Sea Scrolls. New York: The Viking Press, 1955 (One of the earliest books on the first discoveries of 1947).

Cahill, Thomas. *The Gifts of the Jews: How a Tribe of Desert Nomads Changed the Way Everyone Thinks and Feels*. New York: Nan A. Talese with Bantam Doubleday Dell, 1998.

Chapman, Colin. *Whose Promised Land?* Grand Rapids, MI: Baker Book House, 2002 (Originally a Lion International Paperback, Revised 1989. First Pub. 1983).

Darwish, Nonie. *Now They Call Me Infidel: Why I Rejected the Jihad for America, Israel, and the War on Terror*. New York: Sentinel, 2006.

DeHaan, M.R. *The Jew and Palestine in Prophecy*. Grand Rapids, MI: Zondervan Publishing House, 1950.

Dershowitz, Alan. *The Case For Peace: How the Arab-Israeli Conflict Can Be Resolved*. Hoboken, NJ: John Wiley and Sons, 2005.

Dolan, David. *Holy War for the Promised Land*. Nashville, TN: Thomas Nelson Publishers, 1991.

D'Souza, Dinesh. *The Enemy At Home: The Cultural Left and Its Responsibility for 9/11*. New York: Doubleday, 2007.

Dumont, Max I. *Jews, God, and History*. New York: New American Liberty (Penguin Books) (2nd Edition), 2003 (Copyright, 1962).

Fallaci, Oriana. *The Force of Reason*. New York: Rizzoli Books, 2006.

Friedman, Thomas L. *From Beirut to Jerusalem*. New York: Doubleday Anchor Books, 1989.

Gabriel, Mark A. *Islam and the Jews: The Unfinished Battle*. Lake Mary, FL: Charisma House, 2003.

Gilbert, Martin. *Israel: A History*. New York: William Morrow and Company, 1998.

Goiten, S. D. *Jews and Arabs: Their Contacts Through the Ages*. New York: Schocken Books, 1955.

Gold, Dore. *The Fight For Jerusalem: Radical Islam, The West, and the Future of the Holy City*. Washington, D.C.: Regnery Publishing Company Inc., 2007.

Gordon, Michael and General Bernard E.Trainor. *Cobra II: The Inside Story of the Invasion and Occupation of Iraq.* New York: Random House, Inc. A Vintage Book, 2007.

Gunaratna, Rowan. *Inside Al Qaeda: Global Network of Terror.* New York: Berkley Books (Penquin), 2002.

Hagee, John. *Allah and America.* San Antonio, TX: John Hagee Ministries Tape Series, 2002 (A set of three cassettes: *Allah and America, Islam and Israel, Israel and the Church*).

_____ *Jerusalem Countdown.* Lake Mary, FL: Frontline, A Strang Company, 2006.

Haynes, John Earl and Harvey Klehr. In Denial: Historians, Educators, and Espionage. San Francisco: Encounter Books, 2003.

Hunt, David. *Israel, Islam, and Armageddon—The Final Battle For Jerusalem* (1 hour video). Bend, OR: The Berean Call, n.d.

_____ *Judgment Day: Islam, Israel and the Nations.* 2nd Edition. Bend, OR: The Berean Call, 2006.

Hunting, Joseph H. *Israel: A Modern Miracle.* Murrumbeena, Australia: The David Press, 1969.

Jabbour, Nabeel. *The Rumbling Volcano: Islamic Fundamentalism in Egypt.* Pasadena, CA: Mandate Press, William Carey Library, 1993.

Johnson, Paul. *A History of the Jews.* New York: Harper and Row, 1987.

Kac, Arthur W. *The Rebirth of the State of Israel: Is it of God or of Men?* London: Marshall, Morgan and Scott, 1958.

Lamb, David. *The Arabs.* New York: Random House, A Vintage Book, 2002.

Levitt, Matthew. *Hamas: Politics, Charity, and Terrorism in the Service of the Jihad.* New Haven: Yale University Press, 2006.

Lewis, Bernard. *The Arabs in History.* New York: Oxford University Press, 1993.

_____ *The Middle East: A Brief History of the Last 2000 Years.* New York: Scribner, 1995.

_____ *Crisis in Islam: Holy War and Unholy Terror.* New York: Random House, The Modern Library, 2003.

Manji, Irshad. *The Trouble With Islam Today: A Muslim's Call For the Reform of Her Faith.* NewYork: St. Martins Griffin, 2005 (reprint).

Mansfield, Peter. *A History of the Middle East.* London and New York: Penguin Books, 1991.

Medved, Michael. *Why They Fight—The Story of the Arab/Israeli Conflict.* (2 tapes) Tree Farm Cassettes, 2001 (800-468-0464).

_____ *Five Middle Eastern Wars.* (2 tapes) Tree Farm Cassettes, 2002 (800-468-0464).

Mendels, Doron. *The Rise and Fall of Jewish Nationalism: Jewish and Christian Ethnicity in Ancient Palestine.* Grand Rapids, MI: William B. Eerdmans Publishing

Company, 1997.

Morey, Robert A. *Winning the War Against Radical Islam.* Las Vegas, NV: Christian Scholars Press, 2002.

Muravchik, Joshua. *Covering the Intifada: How the Media Reported the Palestinian Uprising.* Washington D.C.: The Washington Institute for Near East Policy, 2003.

_____ "Among Arab Reformers," *Commentary Magazine*, Vol. 120, No. 2, (Sept 2005), pp. 45-52.

Murk, James M. *Islam Rising: The Never Ending Jihad Against Christianity.* Springfield, MO: 21st Century Press, 2006.

Nasr, Vali. *The Shia Revival: How Conflicts Within Islam Will Shape the Future.* New York: W.W. Norton and Co., Inc., 2006.

Norton, Augustus Richard. *Hezbollah.* Princeton: Princeton University Press, 2007.

Oren, Michael B. *Six Days of War: June 1967 and the Making of the Modern Middle East.* New York: Random House Presidio Press, 2002.

Otis, George Jr. *The Last of the Giants: Lifting the Veil on Islam and the End Times.* Tarrytown, NY: Fleming H. Revell Company (Chosen Books), 1991.

Peters, Joan. *From Time Immemorial: The Origins of the Arab-Jewish Conflict over Palestine.* Chicago: JKAP Publications, 1984.

Rashid, Ahmed. *Taliban: Militant Islam, Oil and Fundamentalism in Central Asia.* New Haven: Yale University Press, 2000.

Rausch, David. *The Middle East Maze: Israel and Her Neighbors.* Chicago: Moody Press, 1991.

Robinson, Stuart. *Mosques and Miracles: Revealing Islam and God's Grace.* Queensland, Australia: City Harvest Publications, 1984.

Rydelnik, Michael. *Understanding the Arab-Israel Conflict: What the Headlines Haven't Told You.* Chicago: Moody Publishers, 2004.

Sada, Georges. *Saddam's Secrets: How an Iraqi General Defied and Survived Saddam Hussein.* Brentwood, TN: Integrity Publishers, 2006.

Schoeman, Roy H. *"Salvation is from the Jews."* San Francisco: Ignatius Press, 2003.

Shipler, David K. *Arab and Jew: Wounded Spirits in a Promised Land.* New York: Penguin Books, 1986.

Shoebat, Wally. *Why I Left Jihad.* Top Executive Media, 2005.

Shorrosh, Anis A. *Jesus, Prophecy and Middle East.* Dallas, TX: Acclaimed Books, 1979.

_____ *Islam Revealed: A Christian Arab's View of Islam.* Nashville, TN: Thomas Nelson, 1988 and 2001.

Smith, Wilbur M. *Israeli/Arab Conflict and the Bible.* Glendale, CA: Regal Books, 1967.

Spencer, Robert (ed.). *The Myth of Islamic Intolerance.* Amherst, NY: Prometheus. Books, 2005.

_____ *The Truth About Muhammad: Founder of the World's Most Intolerant Religion.* Washington D.C.: Regnery Publishing Company Inc., 2006.

Taha, Mahmoud Muhammad. *The Second Message of Islam: Contemporary Issues in the Middle East.* Syracuse, NY: Syracuse University Press, 1987.

Timmerman, Kenneth R. *Countdown to Crisis: The Coming Nuclear Showdown with Iran.* New York: Three Rivers Press, 2005.

Wright, Robin. *Sacred Rage: The Wrath of Militant Islam.* New York: Simon and Schuster, A Touchstone Book, 1985.

INDEX

ABOUT THE AUTHOR

D r. Jim Murk was trained as a Christian academician. He was a senior in high school at age 15, and by the age of 19 he entered graduate school at the University of Chicago by examination where he earned a Master's degree in the history of the Middle Ages, Renaissance, and Reformation. After two years in Bible College and Seminary, he earned another Master's degree from the University of Minnesota in Cultural Anthropology, specializing in the study of Japanese and Islamic cultures, and another Master's in Theology from Bob Jones University where he was also chairman of the history department. His Ph.D. from Louisiana Baptist University bridges all of his major fields of study.

He also taught linguistics for the Wycliffe Bible Translators' Summer Institute of Linguistics, served briefly in Mexico, and then joined the staff of the Navigators. He and his wife Donna opened the Navigator home and ministered with the Missionary Internship Training Program in the Chicago area. He was next invited on the faculty at Wheaton College where he taught for 8 years and was briefly the chairman of the Anthropology Department.

He received a Danforth Teachers Grant and was candidate for the Ph.D. at the University of Chicago.

While teaching Dr. Murk won the national championship of the Ted Mack Original Amateur Hour on CBSTV in 1963 as a lyric tenor, which opened a call to a national and international ministry in music evangelism, preaching and teaching. He felt called out of the academic world and has been pursuing this public ministry with his wife and family members for 40 years having over 6,000 meetings in all 50 states and 25 foreign mission fields.

Dr. Murk had studied Islam at the University of Minnesota Graduate School of Anthropology and developed a course called The Islamic Culture Sphere for the Summer Institute of Missions and anthropology majors at Wheaton College. Now since the recent resurgence of a militant Islam in the world, he has been conducting seminars around the country in churches, schools, and conferences on "What Christians Need to Know About Islam!" This book is Part Two of a four-part publication. Part One is called *Islam Rising: The Never Ending Jihad Against Christianity*. Part Three will be called *Islam Rising: The Never Ending Jihad Against the West and America.* and should be available in about six months.

Contact Information:

Jim Murk
Murk Family Ministries, Inc.
P.O. Box 341
Chippewa Falls, WI 54729.
E-mail: murkfam@citizens-tel.net